IMAGES
of America

OCEAN CITY BEACH PATROL

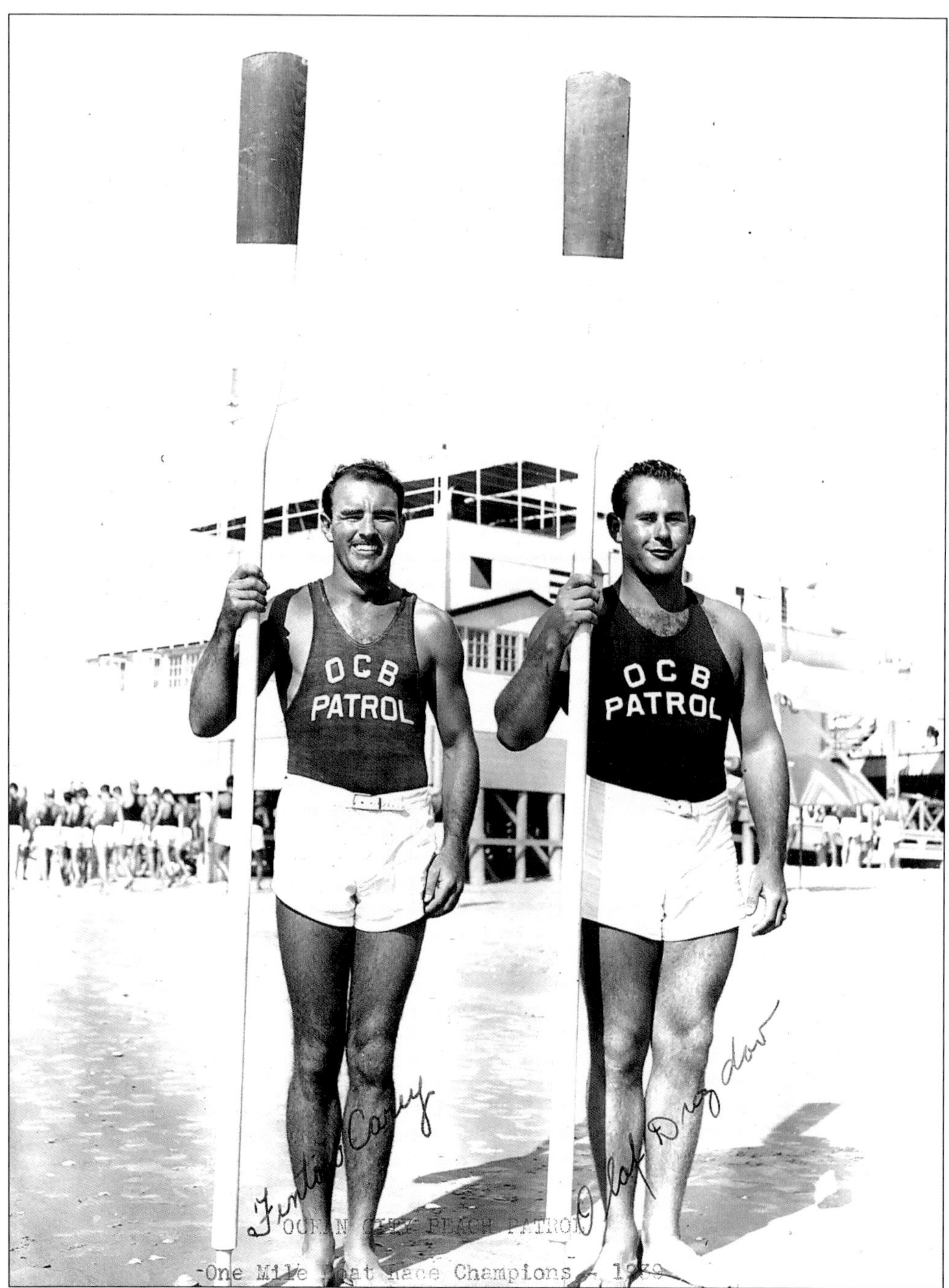

It was the summer of 1939, and Fenton Carey (left) and Olaf Drozdov won the doubles lifeboat championship. They won many rowing championships for the Ocean City Beach Patrol and are both in the patrol's Hall of Fame. Behind them is patrol headquarters at the 10th Street Beach.

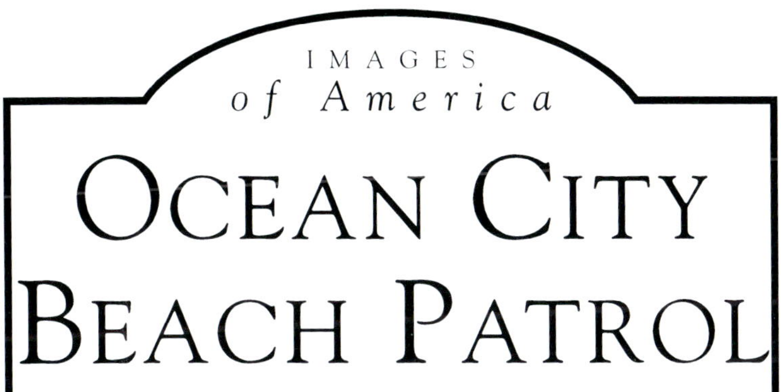
IMAGES
of America
OCEAN CITY
BEACH PATROL

Fred Miller

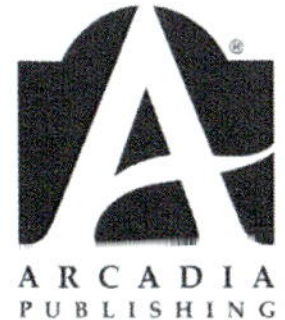
ARCADIA
PUBLISHING

ISBN 978-0-7385-3635-4

Published by Arcadia Publishing
Charleston SC, Chicago IL, Portsmouth NH, San Francisco CA

Printed in the United States of America

Library of Congress Catalog Card Number: 2004106380

For all general information contact Arcadia Publishing at:
Telephone 843-853-2070
Fax 843-853-0044
E-mail sales@arcadiapublishing.com
For customer service and orders:
Toll-Free 1-888-313-2665

Visit us on the Internet at www.arcadiapublishing.com

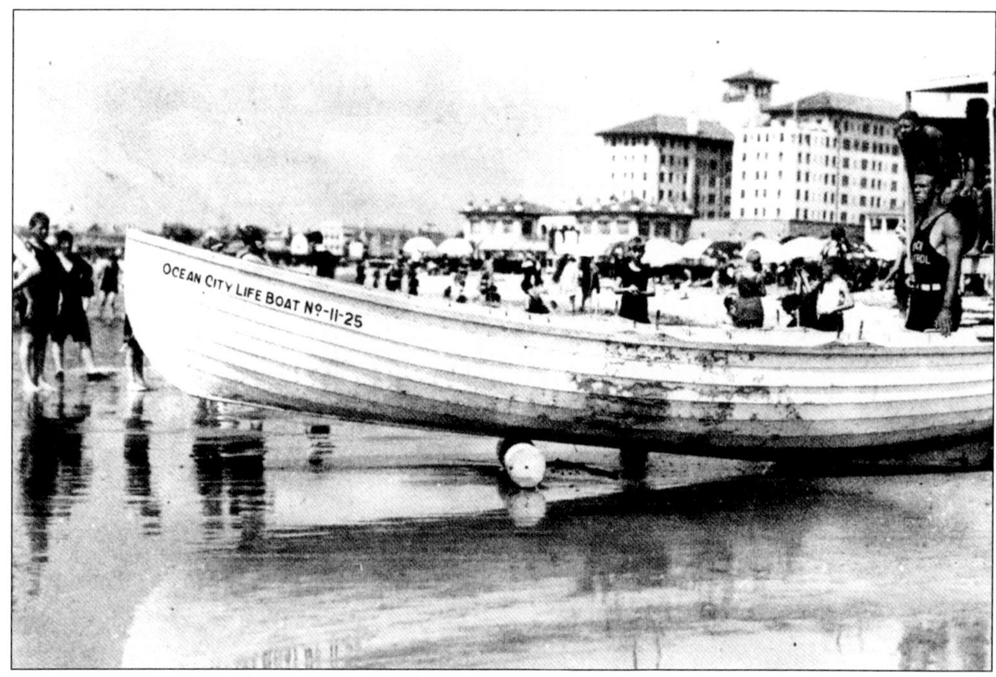

Pictured here is the 10th Street Beach during the summer of 1926. In 1926, Ocean City's motto was the same as it is today, "America's Greatest Family Resort." The Ocean City Beach Patrol has been a major factor in making this motto a reality.

CONTENTS

ACKNOWLEDGMENTS

I wish to thank my wife, Susan, for her patience and help, my sister and brother-in-law, Joan and Allan Okin, for their editing skills, and Stu Sirott for all of his technical help.

I also thank the following people for photographs: Bill Ashmead, Vesta J. Back, Chet Derr, Jack Devine, Jack Doerr, James Duncan, Ben Dungan, Bob French, Bob Harbaugh, Vince Hink, Andy Jernee, Ed Keenan, Jim Kirk, George T. Lafferty, Lizanne Kelly LeVine, John Loeper, Bill Maher, Doris and Bob Marts (Senior Studio), Edna Streaker May, Mike Monihan, John Nieveen, Tom Oves, Bob Schneider, Bill Shea, Lyn Smith, Rodger W. Smith, Mark Soifer, and Irene Williams.

Lastly, I thank the following organizations for their help, pictures, and information for this book: the Ocean City Lifesaving Museum, the Ocean City Historical Museum, the *Ocean City Sentinel*, the National Archives, and the Temple University Urban Archives.

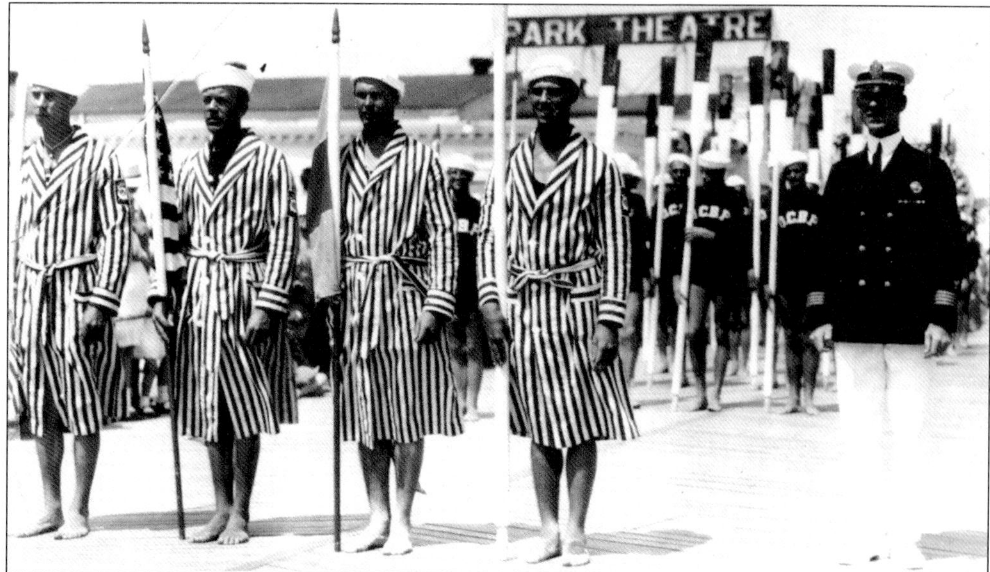

Jack G. Jernee (right), captain of the Ocean City Beach Patrol, leads a large detachment of Ocean City lifeguards in the parade held on July 4, 1929. The parade celebrated the opening of the new concrete-based boardwalk between 2nd and 6th Streets. The lifeguards marched, carrying their oars, to much applause from the crowd.

Introduction

Ocean City Beach Patrol is the story of the hundreds of brave men and women who have risked their lives to save and protect people enjoying the waters off the coast of Ocean City. For more than 100 years, they have been paid by the city to guard bathers, but they actually trace their roots back much farther to the U.S. Life-Saving Service.

The U.S. Life-Saving Service (USLSS) was officially organized in 1871 by the federal government. Its mission was to rescue the men, women, and children who found themselves in deadly peril as their ships foundered off the treacherous coast between Sandy Hook and Cape May. Any number of problems may have caused accidents at sea: the lighthouse warning system may have failed for some reason; a light may not have been visible during a winter storm or fog; or another disaster such as a fire on board may have occurred, instantly putting a ship in severe trouble. Often, a ship in distress would deliberately head toward land to avoid sinking in deep water far offshore, but guiding a small lifeboat through rolling waves or surviving freezing air and water temperatures while clinging to parts of the ship was practically impossible. The U.S. Life-Saving Service was designed to go to the rescue from shore.

Lifesaving stations were set up every few miles along the coast and were manned during the fall, winter, and spring when most shipwrecks occurred. The men at each station patrolled their designated strip of the coast on the lookout for ships in distress. Each man carried a token that he passed on to the next man, assuring that everyone patrolled his entire area for the full time of his watch. When not on duty, the men drilled continuously to hone their skills and perfect their equipment, much of which they invented on the job. Their dependable surveillance and daring heroism saved many people, although unfortunately, many of their own lives were lost.

When Ocean City was founded by Methodist ministers in 1879, only four buildings existed on the island: three U.S. Life-Saving Service stations and the home of Parker Miller and his family. Miller was there as an agent of marine insurance companies, which that hired him to report shipwrecks, to deter people from scavenging from the ships, and to protect the interests of the shipping merchants.

Within 20 years, Ocean City had grown into a major seaside tourist destination. As its popularity grew, so did the daring of those venturing into the ocean waters, and by the late 1890s, several drownings had occurred. Something *had* to be done.

An outcry, led by the local newspapers and businesses, called for the city to hire men to protect the bathers. A few men were already serving as lifeguards, most notably Joseph P. Krauss, who patrolled the surf in front of the large hotels. His only remuneration came from donations by grateful bathers he had rescued and from benefits held at the end of summer on his behalf.

In 1898, the city finally heeded the call and hired three men, Krauss, George Lee, and William Scull, to patrol the surf and to assist bathers when needed. Krauss was named captain of the lifeguards, a position he held until the spring of 1910. The lifeguards were paid $40 per month and worked each day from 9:00 a.m. to 3:00 p.m. Ocean City was the first municipality in Cape May County, and one of the few in the country, to pay for bather protection. Alfred R. Smith, who became a paid lifeguard in 1899, succeeded Krauss as captain in 1910.

In 1920, the city hired former member of the U.S. Life-Saving Service Jack G. Jernee as captain of the lifeguards. He is credited with building the Ocean City Beach Patrol into one of the finest lifesaving squads in the country. Thomas A. Williams, a lifeguard since 1922, took over as captain when Jernee joined the navy in the summer of 1942. Under Williams, the patrol increased greatly in the number of guards and the number of beaches protected. George T. Lafferty, a former member of the Ocean City Beach Patrol and a retired Navy man, was appointed captain when Williams retired in the spring of 1962. Lafferty built the beach patrol into an athletic powerhouse in South Jersey, winning a record number of intercity competitions held with the 15 beach patrols from Brigantine south to Cape May Point. Under the recent leaders, the Ocean City Beach Patrol has continued to grow and has continued its excellent record of bather safety and distinction in athletic competitions.

Much has changed since Joseph P. Krauss left his footprints in the sand of Ocean City, but not the lifeguards' dedication to bather protection.

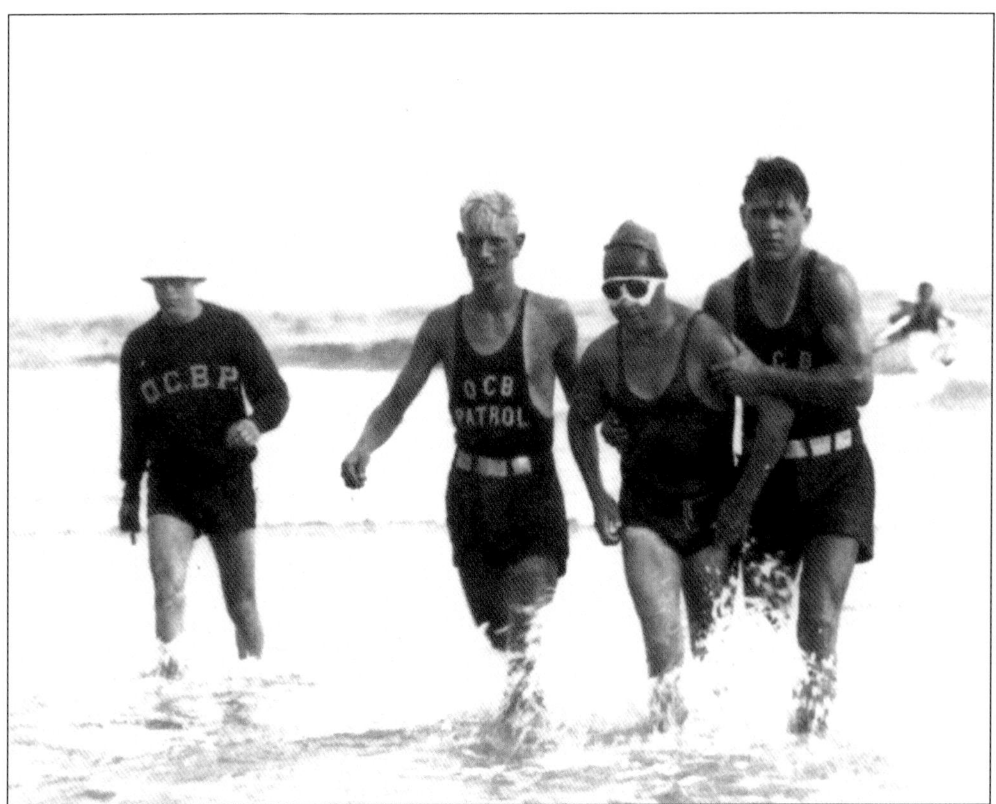

On August 6, 1926, Gertrude Ederle became the first woman to swim the English Channel, and she set off an orgy of swimmers hoping to emulate her feat—but they were swimming the Atlantic Ocean! The lifeguards were very busy during the end of that summer, rescuing would-be long distance swimmers. Here, the lifeguards rescue a swimmer who obviously had higher hopes than his stamina allowed.

One

The Life-Saving Service and the Coast Guard

The U.S. Life-Saving Service had its beginning in New Jersey in 1848, when Congress first appropriated money to provide for surfboats and other equipment necessary for the preservation of life and property from shipwrecks off the coast of New Jersey. Huts were placed on the beaches to shelter distressed mariners and to contain the boats and other rescue apparatus that volunteers, including local fishermen, used in case of shipwreck. The U.S. Life-Saving Service, however, was not fully organized with paid surf men until 1871. A keeper and crew of seven, chosen from those fishermen most distinguished in the use of boats, were assigned to each station. They patrolled the coast, and although they were powerless to prevent shipwrecks, they were instrumental in saving many lives. The tools they used to do this—the breeches buoy, Lyle guns, life vests, and surfboats—were very primitive but very successful.

The U.S. Revenue Cutter Service, which had been organized in 1790 by Alexander Hamilton for the purpose of enforcing the customs laws on the high seas, merged with the U.S. Life-Saving Service in 1915 to form the U.S. Coast Guard.

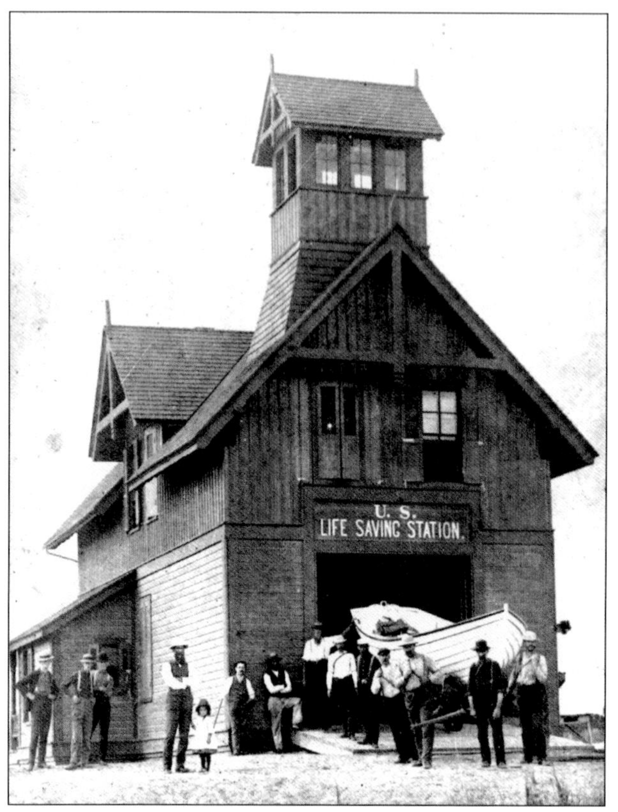

The first professional lifeguards on the island of Ocean City were the men of the U.S. Life-Saving Service, but they did not work in the summer. During the winter, they spent the day watching the ocean looking for trouble from the tower of their station, built in 1885 on the ocean's edge at the corner of 4th Street and Atlantic Avenue. Then, from sunset to sunrise, they patrolled the desolate windswept beach on foot.

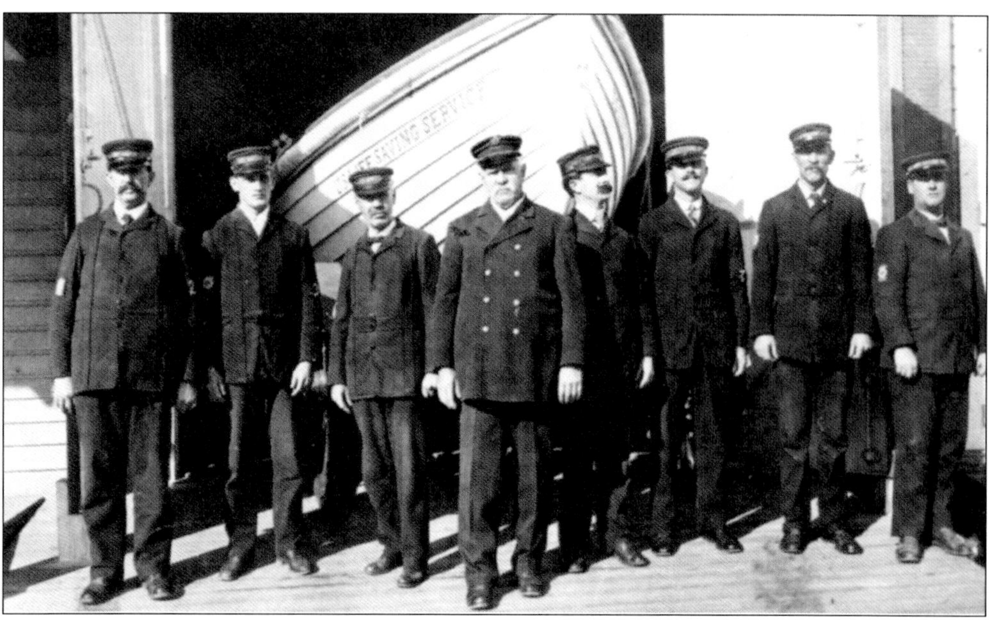

In 1898, J. Mackey Corson (center) was captain of the Ocean City Life-Saving Service. He is pictured with his lifeguard crew, from left to right, Melvin Corson, Townsend Godfrey, Philip S. Hand, William Garrettson, Enoch Clouting, Mulford Jeffries, and E. B. Campbell.

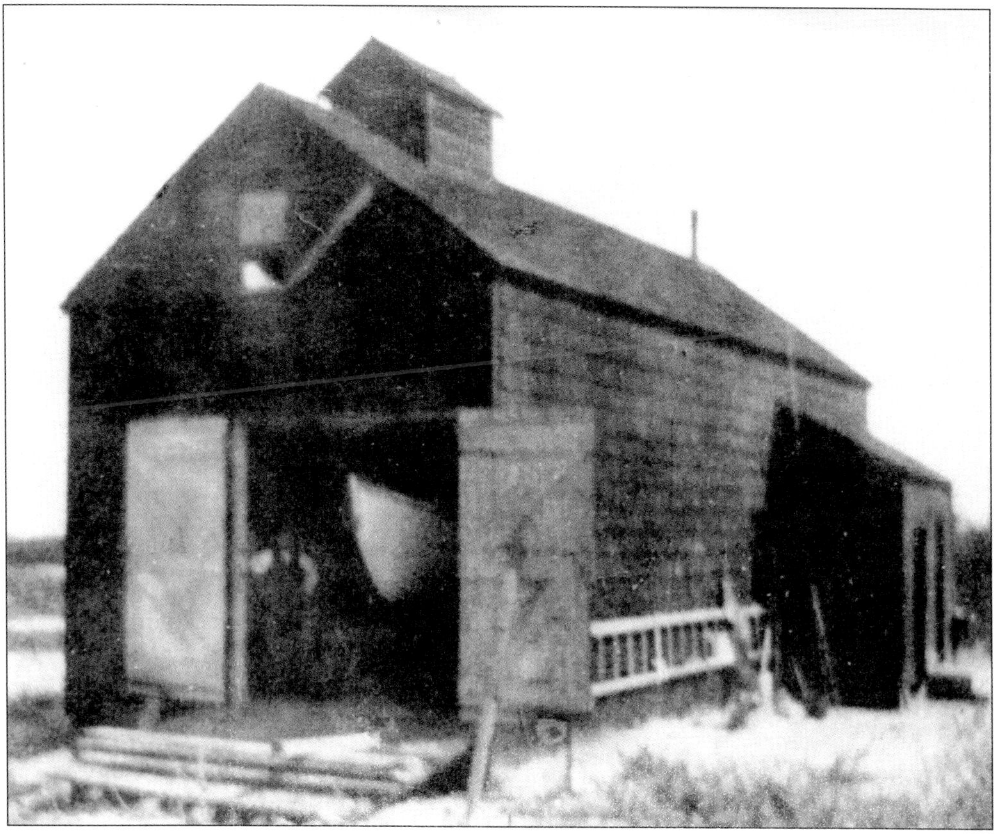

This is an example of the earliest lifesaving stations built on the island. This one was located at the south end of the island. Similar stations were built at the middle and north end.

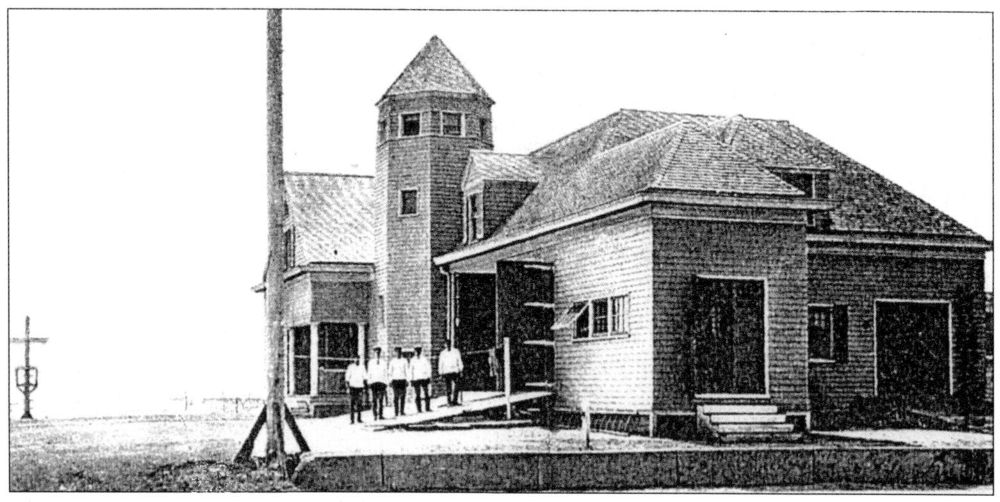

This station, at 36th Street and the beach, was built in 1899 to replace the earlier station. A station very similar to this was also built in 1899 at 58th Street.

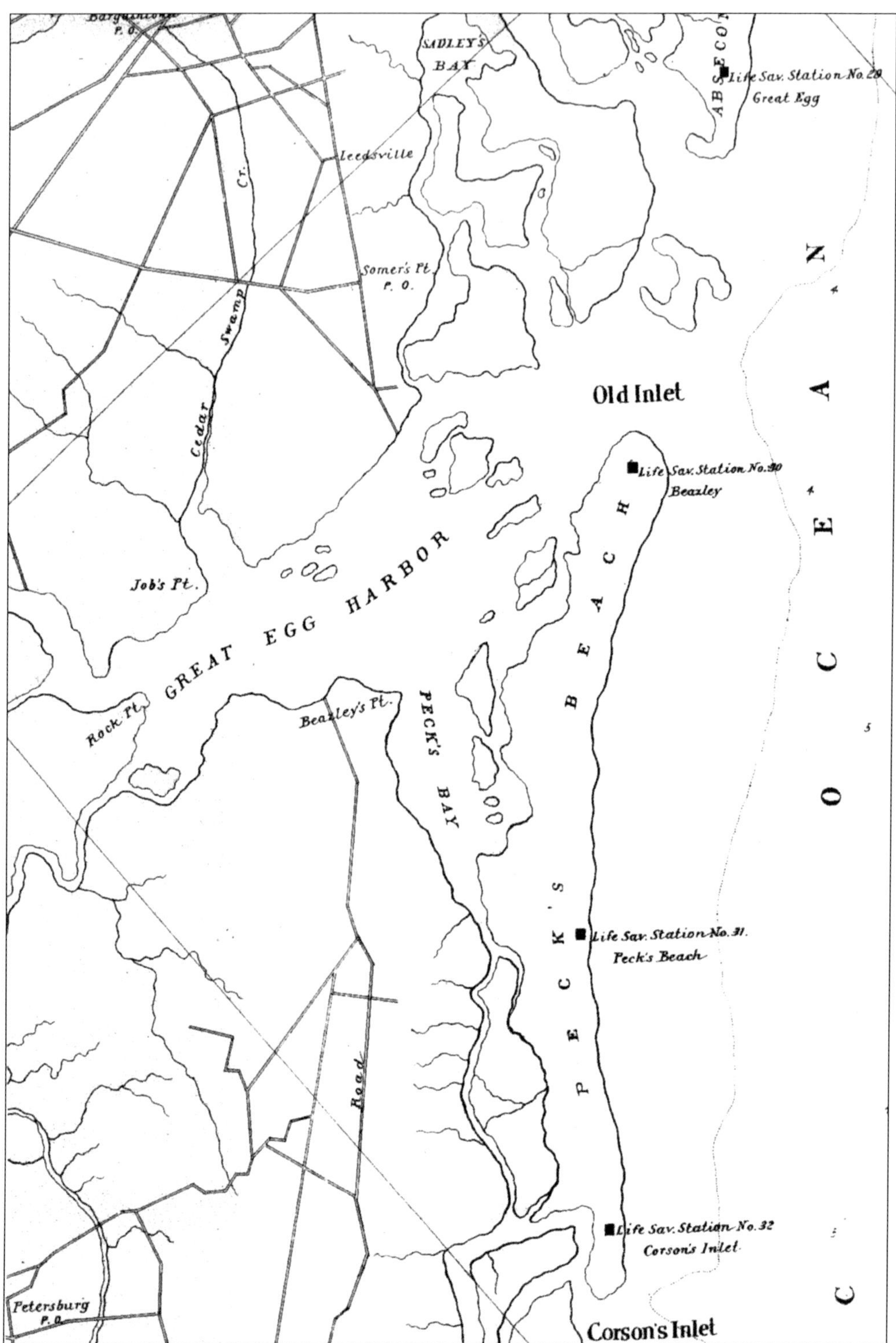

This 1878 map shows the locations of the three lifesaving stations on the island of Peck's Beach one year before the founding of the resort.

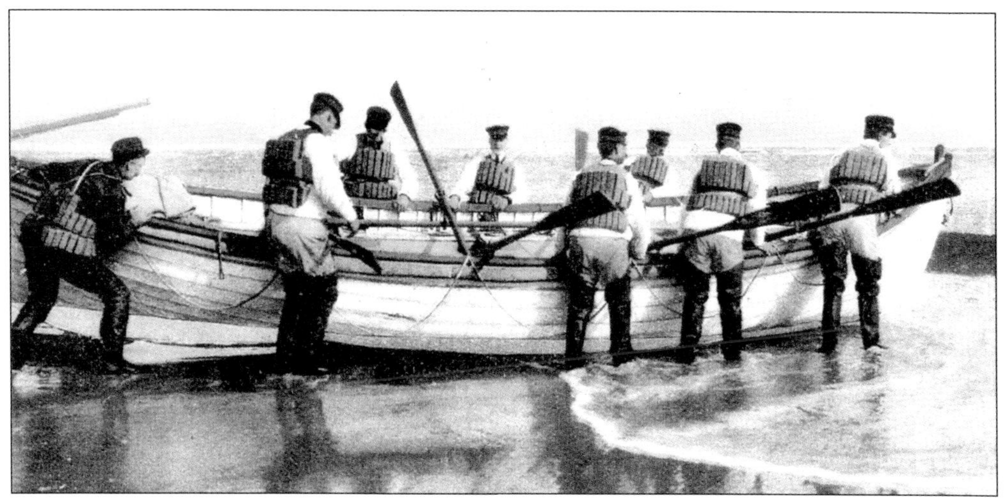

The men of the Ocean City Life-Saving Service prepare to launch their surfboat on the 4th Street Beach in 1896.

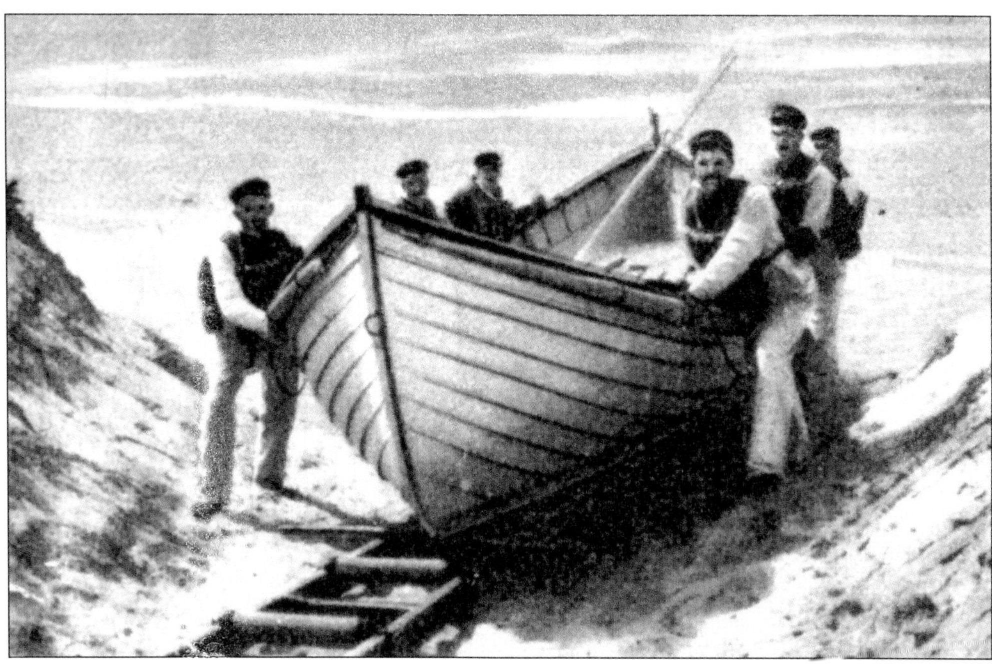

The men of the Ocean City Life-Saving Service return from a practice drill.

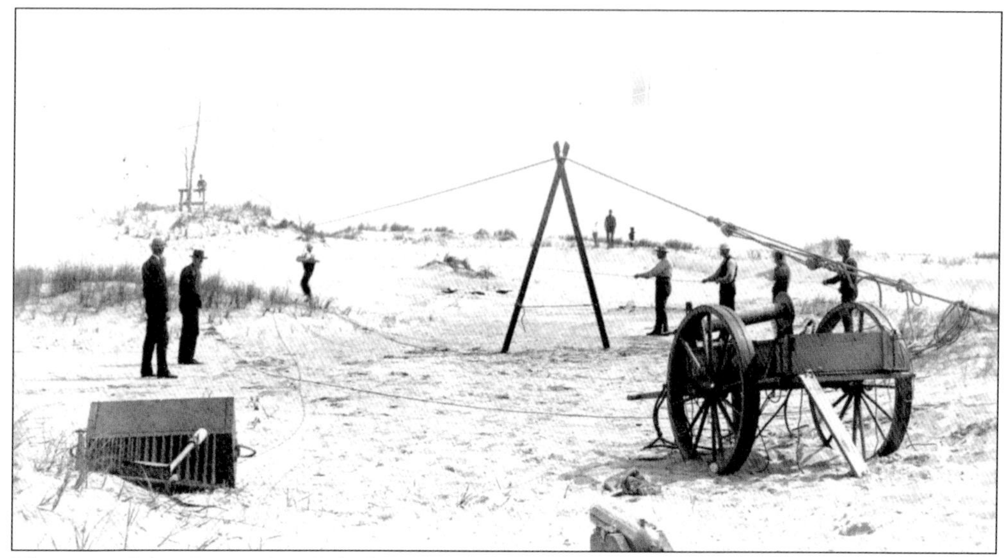

The men of the Ocean City Life-Saving Service practice with the breeches buoy. A breeches buoy was a large pair of canvas pants (breeches) stitched to a cork-filled lifesaving ring. Victims of ship disasters were placed in it one by one and carried by rope over the waves to the beach.

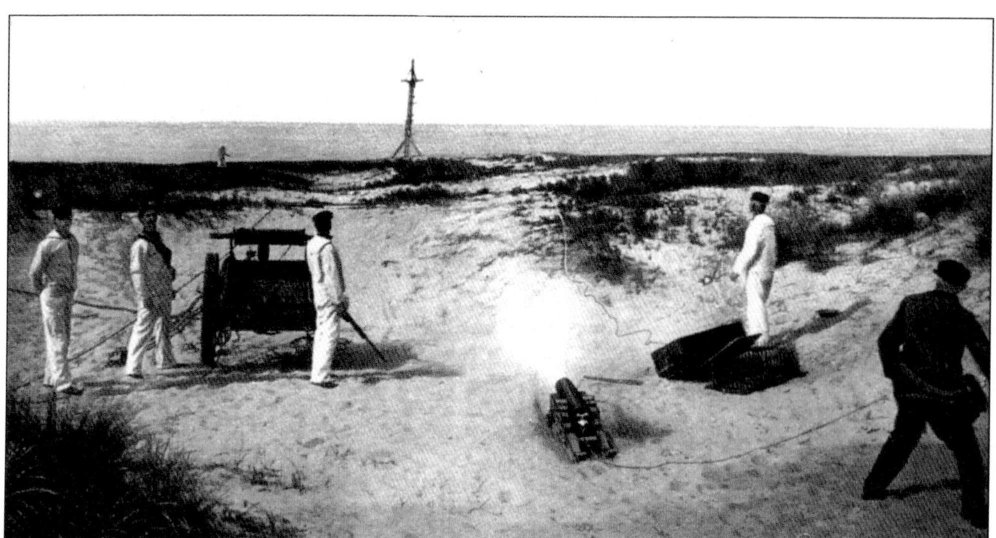

The men are firing a Lyle gun, which shot a window weight–sized projectile with an attached line up to 500 feet to a ship in distress. The ship's crew then pulled the line, which had a stronger line attached to it, and fixed the heavy line to one of the masts. The lifesaving crew on shore set up a wooden frame from which they then could send the breeches buoy to the ship.

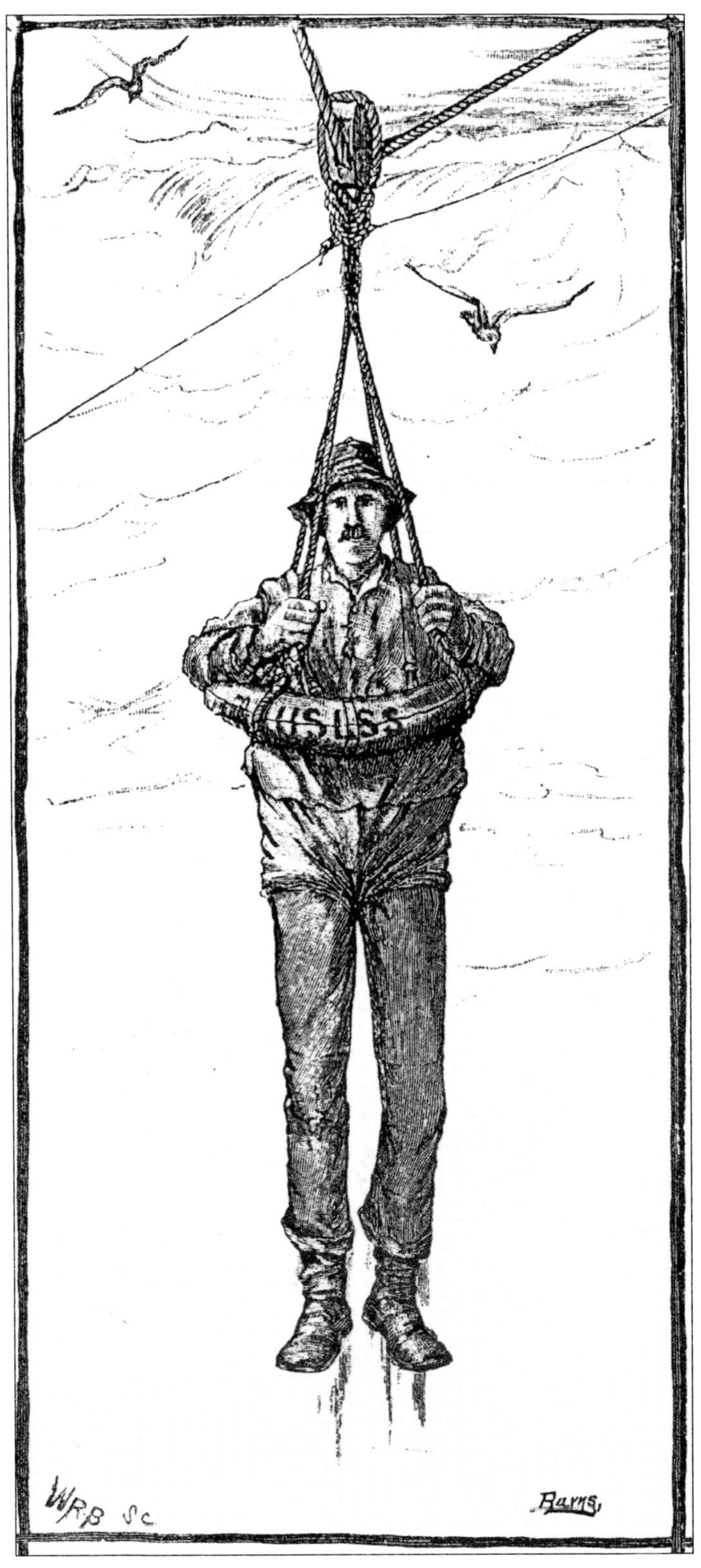

This illustration shows a breeches buoy in action.

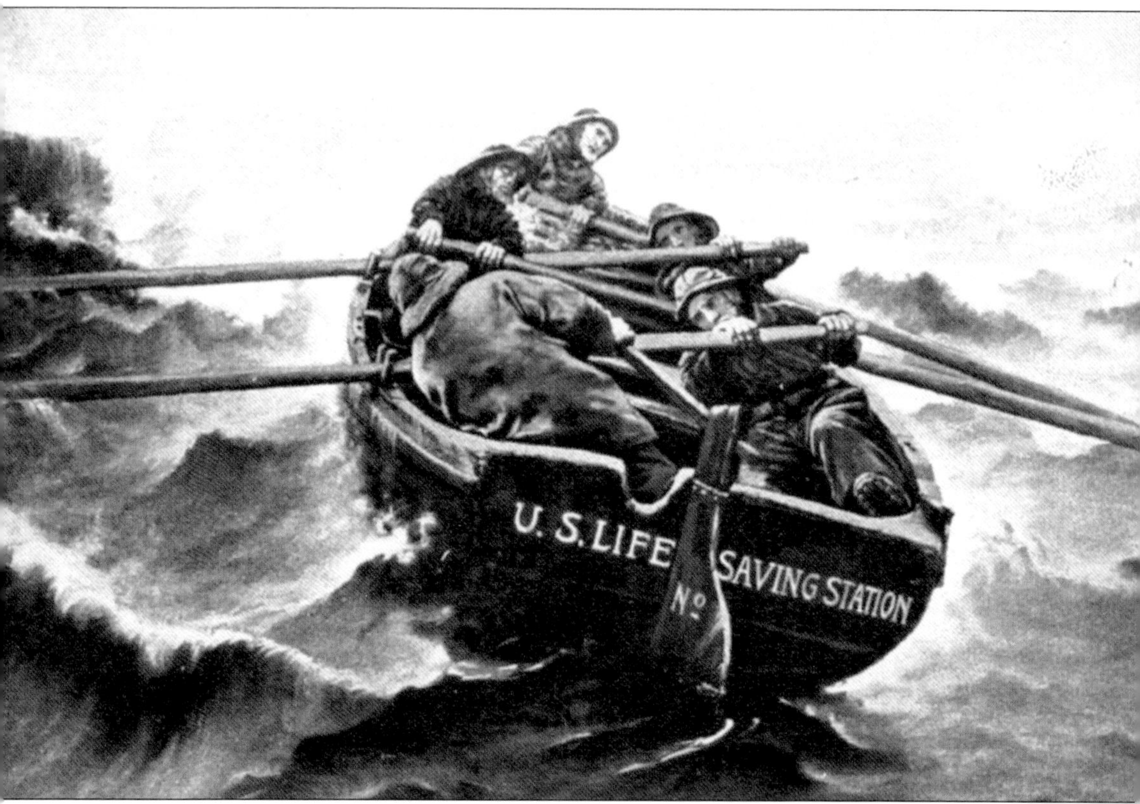

Men of the lifesaving service starting out to a rescue, which may be that of the crew of the *Henry May*, shipwrecked off the northern end of Ocean City in 1897. The October 9, 1897, issue of the *Ocean City Ledger* reported, "It takes brave men to go out on the ocean in a small boat when the wind and waves are as strong as they were last Saturday and Sunday. But the crew of our Life Saving Station are brave men, and the way they risked their lives to save others last Sunday morning proved it. . . . All of Saturday night they watched the light which the crew of the *Henry May* had fastened to the wreck, and, as soon as day dawned they put out in their boat. The waves rose so high that at times our men could not see even the tops of the houses at Ocean City. But finally the wreck was reached in safety, and it was learned that not a soul was lost. . . . It was with much difficulty that the rescued men were taken into the boat and the return trip made. Willing hands helped them to land, and many a fervent 'Thank God' was heard when it was found that all were saved. . . . The saving of the lives of five human beings is no small thing, and the Ocean City Life-Saving Crew are deserving of much praise."

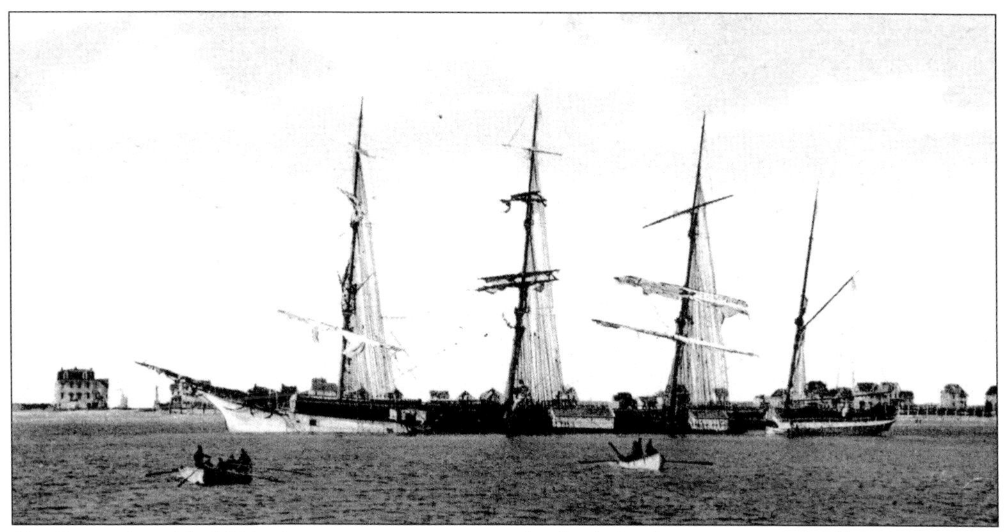

On December 15, 1901, during a raging storm, the bark *Sindia* ran aground off 17th Street at 2:30 in the morning. Distress signals from the ship were immediately answered by the men of the Ocean City and Peck's Beach Life-Saving Stations. A breeches buoy was tried but was unsuccessful. So, surfboats manned by Ocean City Capt. J. M. Corson and his crew, and Peck's Beach Capt. A. C. Townsend and his crew went out at sunrise. After four trips, they had rescued the entire crew of 33 men.

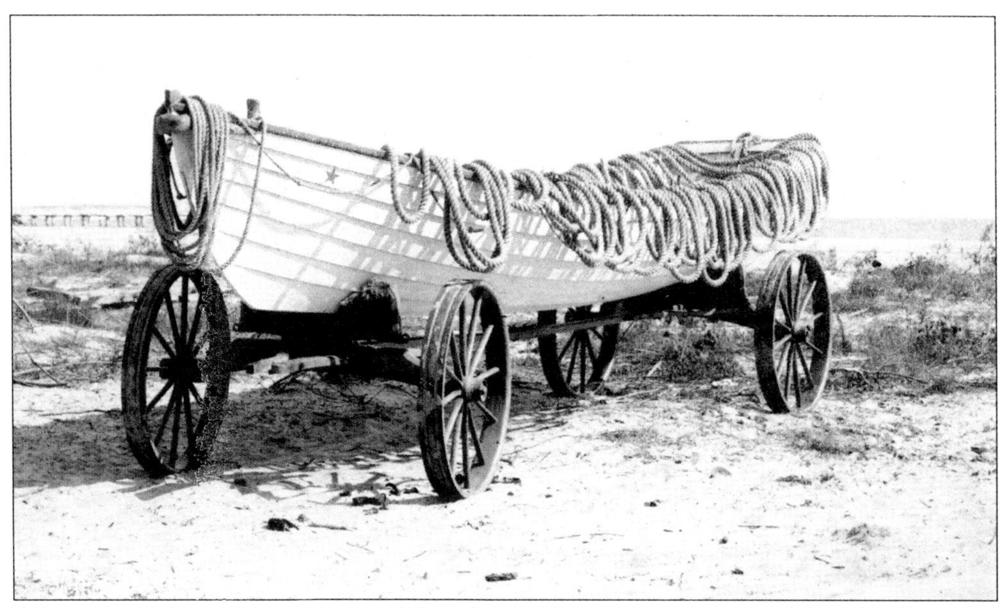

After rescues, the surf men were careful to clean and dry their equipment. Here, they have laid their ropes out to dry.

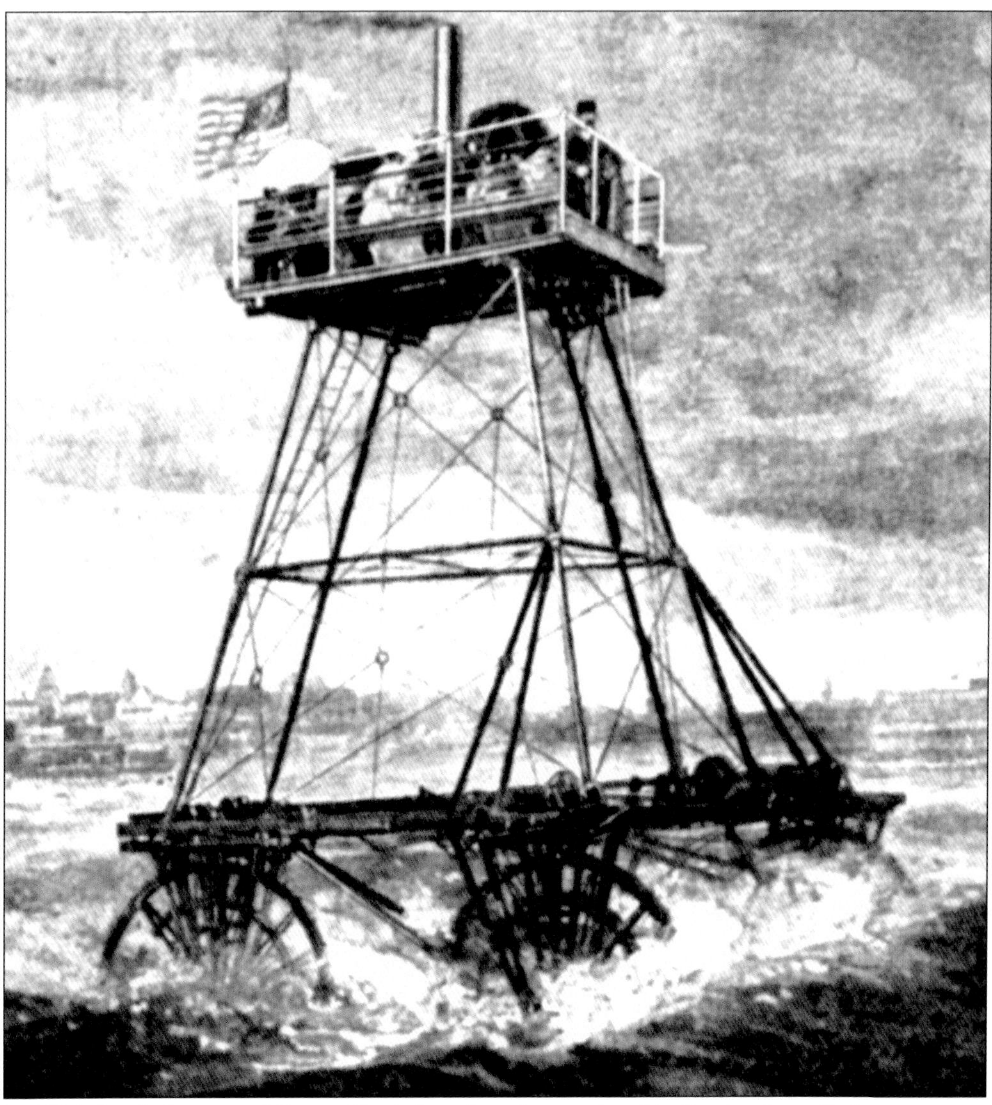

In 1884, Ezra Lake, one of Ocean City's founders, designed and built what he called a sea wagon for use by the men of the U.S. Life-Saving Service. He felt sure it would replace the surfboat. On December 18, 1884, in a well-publicized event that drew hundreds of people to the 4th Street Beach, he took it for its first test in the water. Although the island's top U.S. Life-Saving Service officials watched the test with interest, the contraption was never used by the service and faded into history.

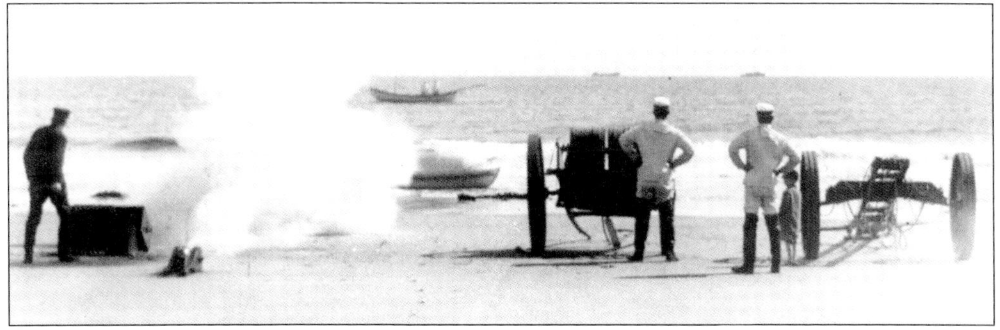

The 36th Street U.S. Life-Saving Service crew practices rescues with the breeches buoy.

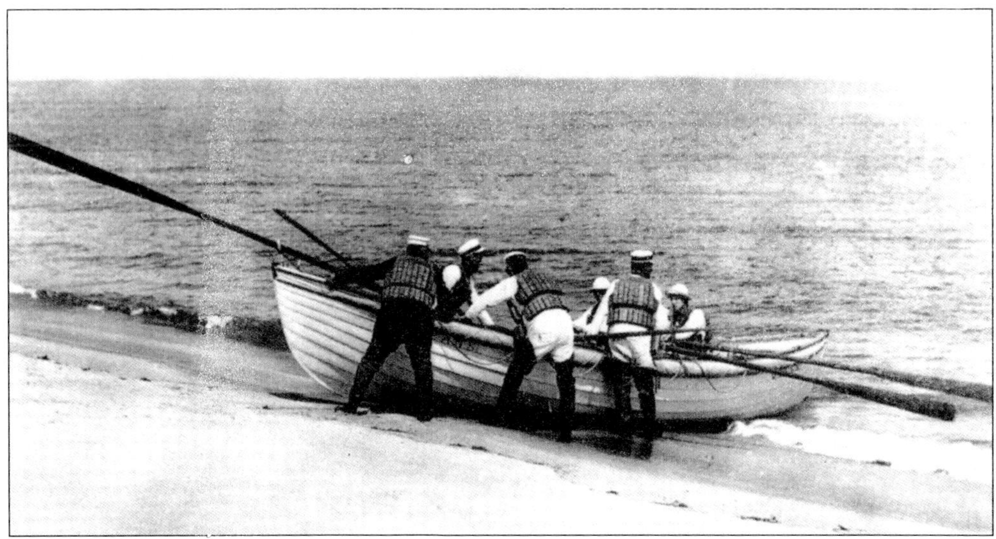

The crews of the U.S. Life-Saving Service had a set weekly routine: Sunday was for rest or religion; Monday was for practice with the breeches buoy and inspection and repair of equipment; Tuesday was for practice with surfboats; Wednesday was for practice with the international code of signals; Thursday was another day for practice with the breeches buoy; Friday was for practice of artificial respiration; Saturday was for house cleaning.

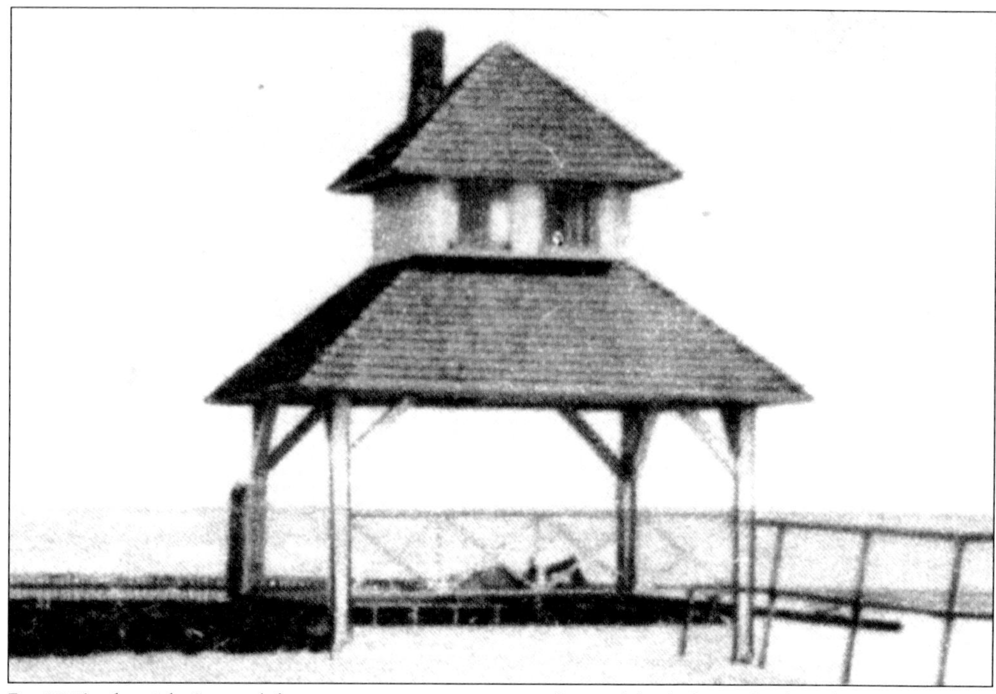

By 1913, the 4th Street lifesaving station was more than a block from the beach, and the men could no longer see the ocean from the tower. That year, the federal government paid local builder Otis M. Townsend $700 to build a lookout tower on the Boardwalk between North and 1st Streets. The area below the tower was for the people to enjoy.

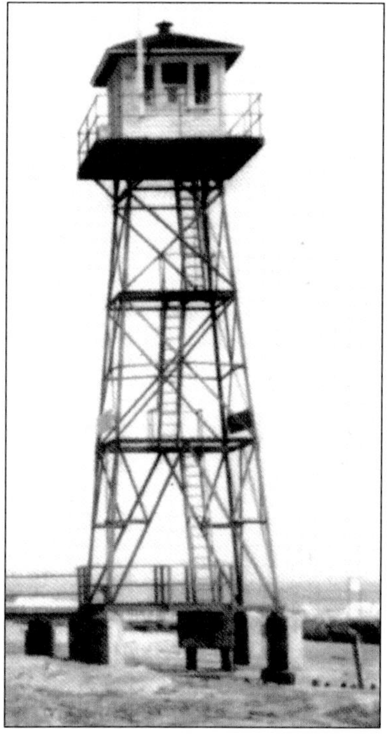

In 1938, the U.S. Coast Guard moved out of the Boardwalk tower into this much higher one on the beach at East Atlantic Boulevard.

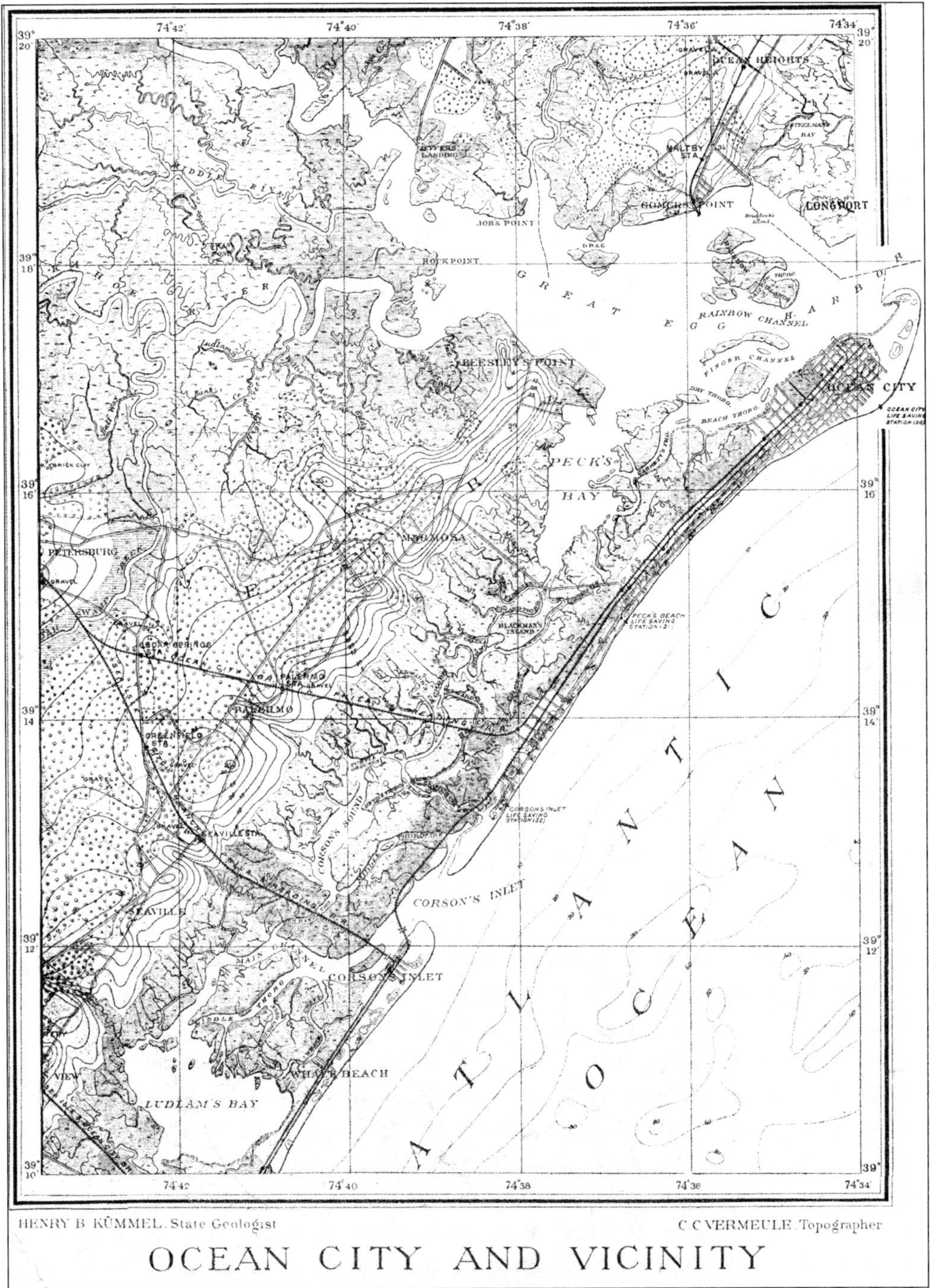

This 1904 map shows how much Ocean City had developed over the past 25 years. The three lifesaving stations—Ocean City No. 30, Peck's Beach No. 31, and Corson's Inlet No. 32—are shown, along with the two railroad lines. Streets have also been laid out.

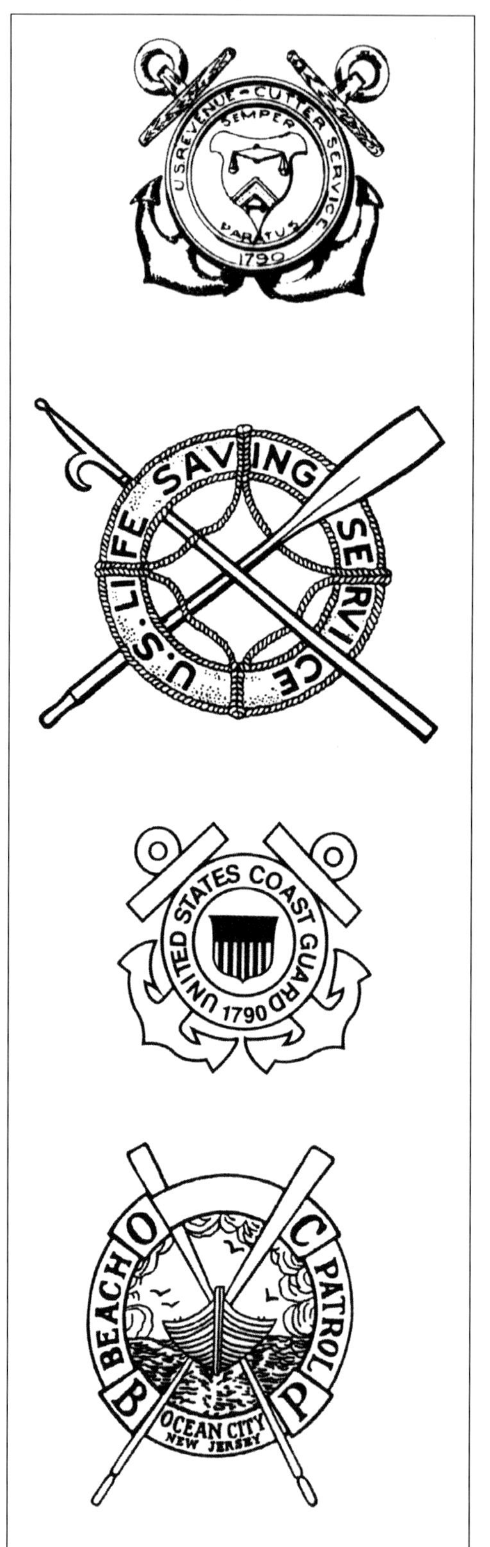

This illustration shows how the Ocean City Beach Patrol emblem evolved from the insignias of the U.S. Revenue Cutter Service, U.S. Life-Saving Service, and U.S. Coast Guard.

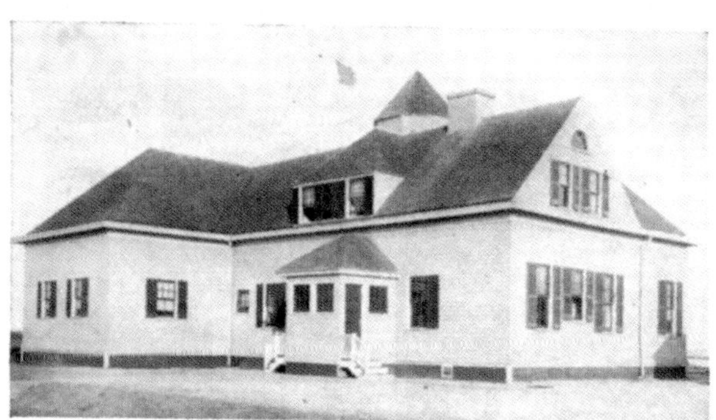

UNITED STATES COAST GUARDS STATION
Thirty-sixth Street

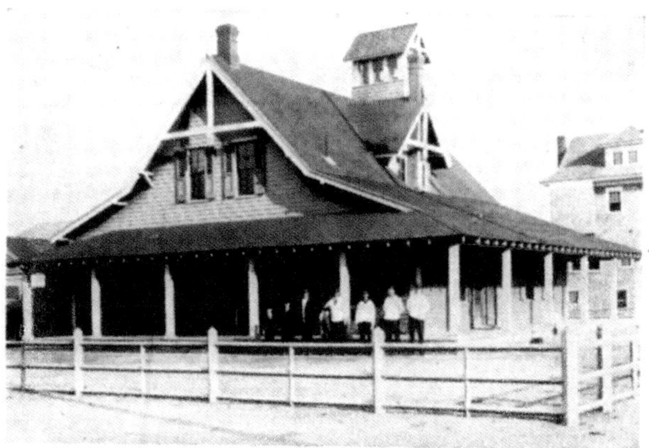

UNITED STATES COAST GUARDS STATION
Fourth Street and Atlantic Avenue

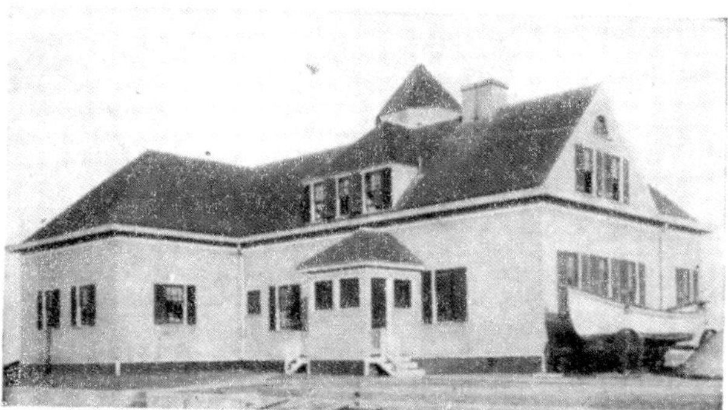

UNITED STATES COAST GUARDS STATION
Fifty-eighth Street and Central Avenue

This picture, taken from a 1915 Ocean City promotional brochure, shows the former U.S. Life-Saving Service Stations renamed as U.S. Coast Guard Stations.

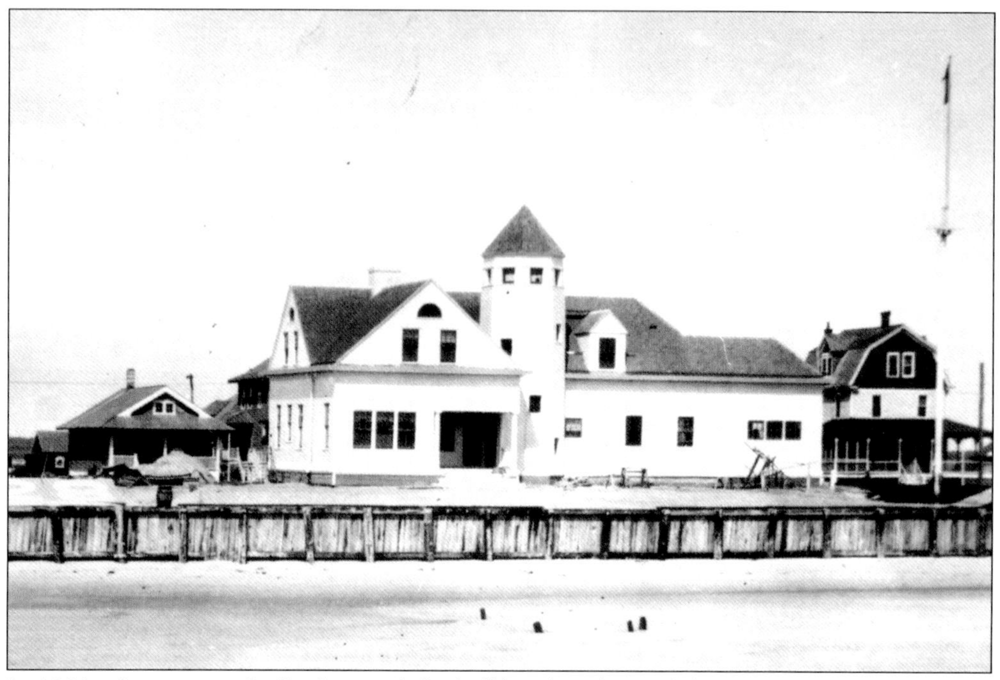

In 1924, after a storm badly damaged the bulkhead in front of the 58th Street Coast Guard Station, the building was dismantled and moved across the inlet to Strathmere, a move opposed by the South Ocean City Association.

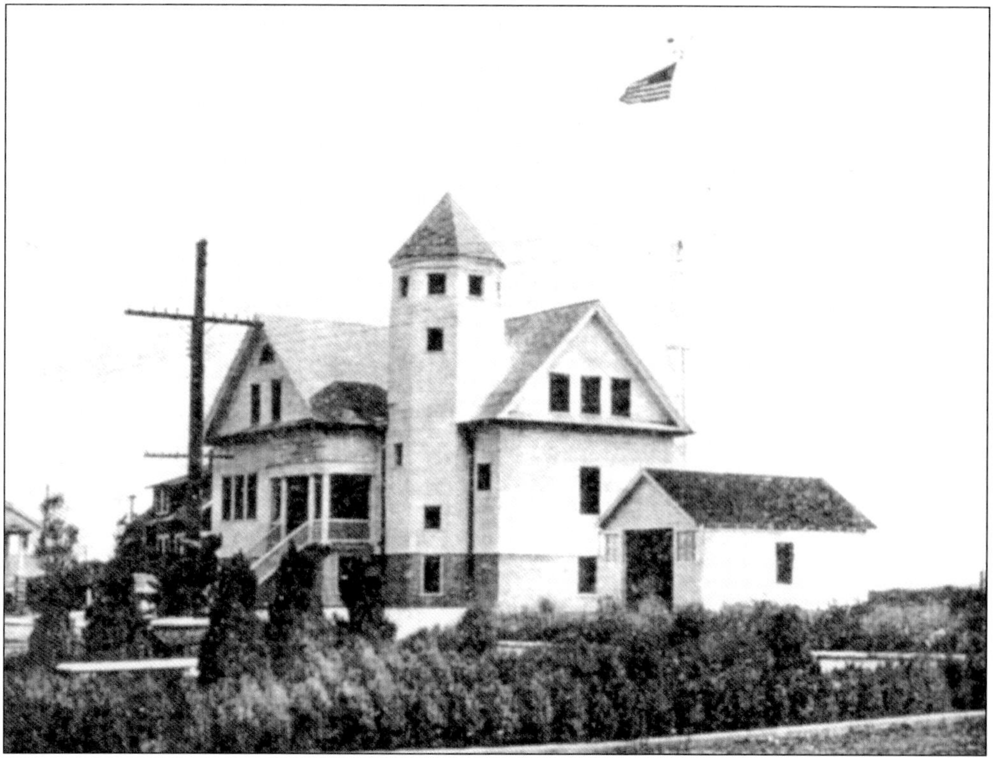

Today, the former 58th Street Coast Guard Station is a private residence in Strathmere.

This World War I memorial honor roll in Ocean City's Memorial Park lists the names of 15 local men who served in the Coast Guard during the war.

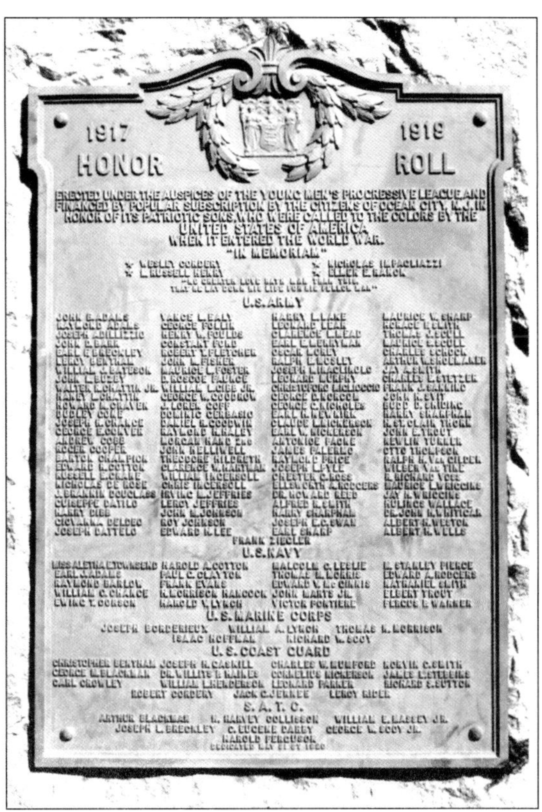

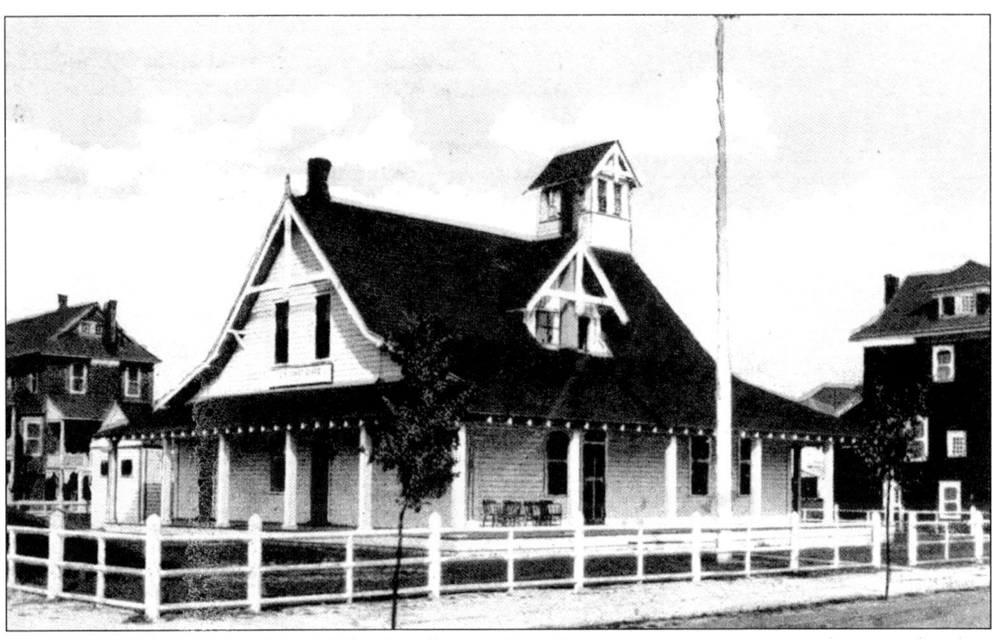

During Prohibition (1920–1933) the Coast Guard was very active in enforcing the law against alcohol. Shown is the main Ocean City Coast Guard Station, at 4th Street and Atlantic Avenue.

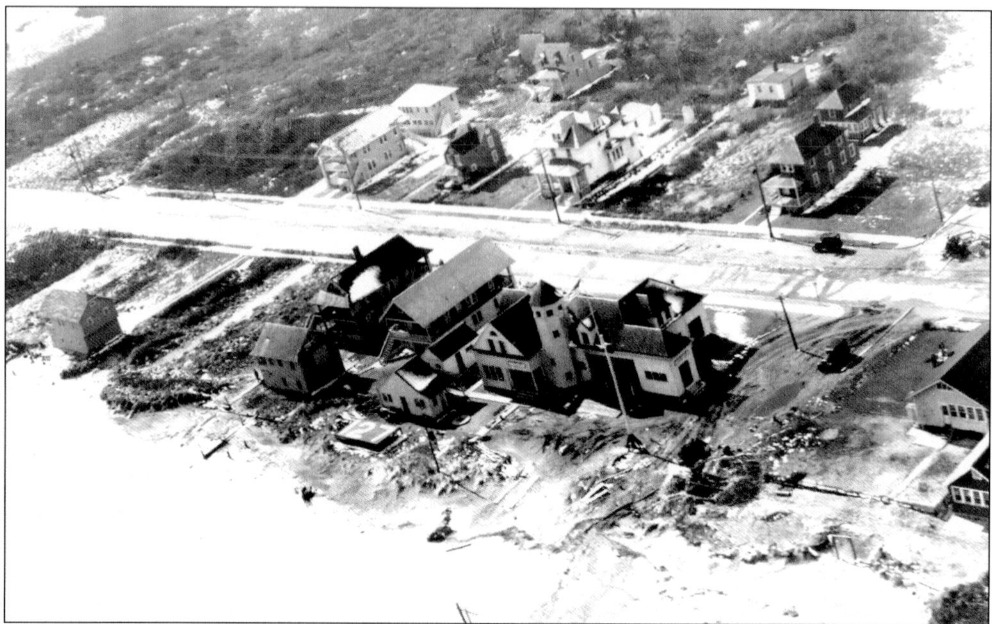

The Peck's Beach Coast Guard Station at 36th Street is shown here in 1931. After World War II, Jack G. Jernee, retired Ocean City Beach Patrol captain, bought the building and opened the Ocean City Academy, a summer camp with a nautical atmosphere for boys 12 to 18 years old. A few years later, he turned it into a hotel, Jernee Manor.

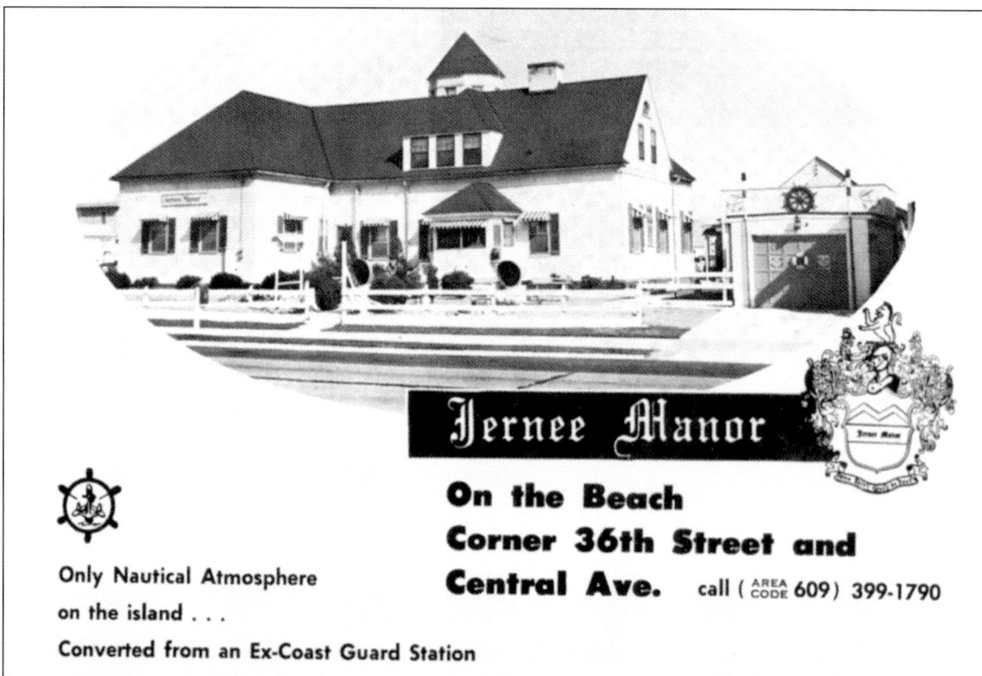

This advertisement for Jernee Manor was in the *1966 Ocean City Vacation Guide*. Some of the hotel guests claimed to have heard ghosts walking in the tower at night. In 1981, members of the Ocean City Beach Patrol tried to save the building from demolition. They hoped to make it into a lifesaving museum, but unfortunately, they were unsuccessful.

On January 1, 1937, the Coast Guard moved into this new building, on North Point Road. This location was chosen because of its easy access to the ocean.

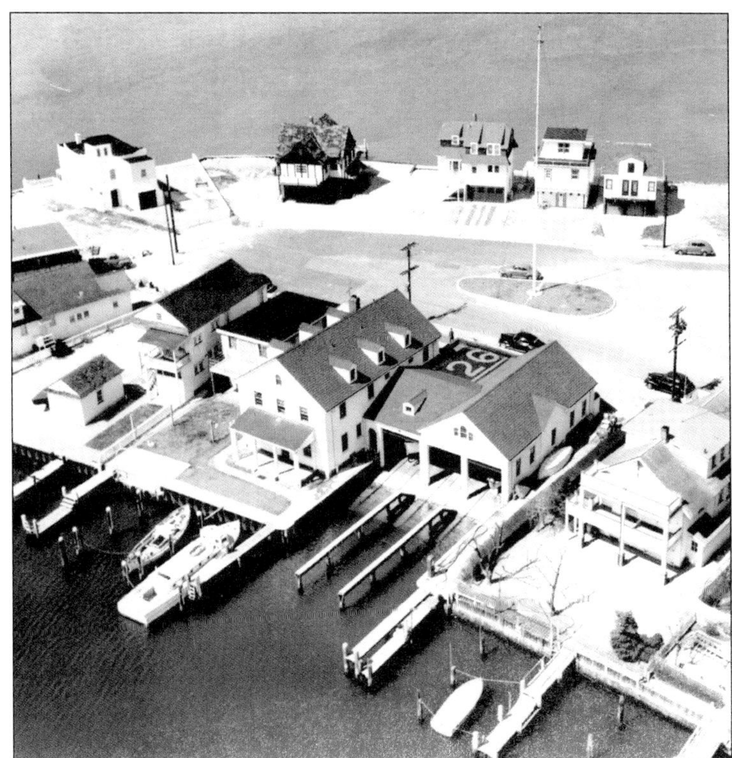

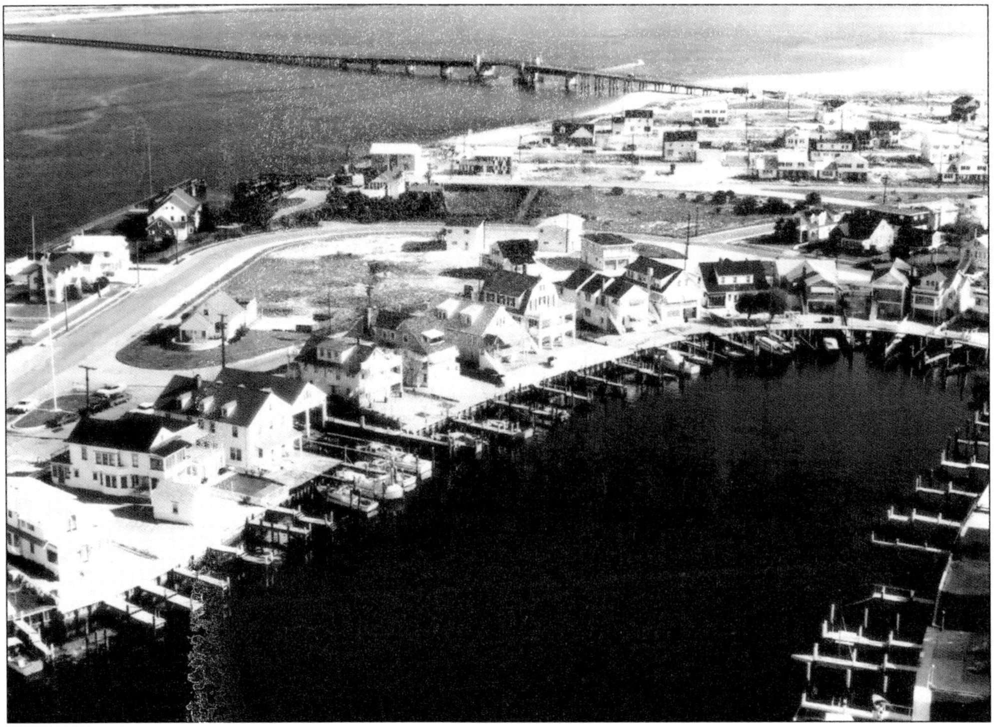

This 1964 aerial view of the North Point Lagoon shows the Coast Guard Station at its North Point Road location

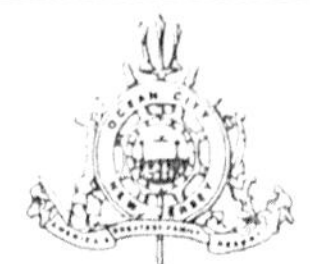

CITY OF OCEAN CITY

AMERICA'S GREATEST FAMILY RESORT

PROCLAMATION

A PROCLAMATION HONORING

UNITED STATES COAST GUARD STATION, GREAT EGG, FOR

125 YEARS OF SERVICE TO THE COMMUNITY

WHEREAS, the United States Coast Guard Station, Great Egg has been established in Ocean City since 1871, eight years before Ocean City was founded, when the community was known as Peck's Beach; and

WHEREAS, the United States Coast Guard has served Ocean City continuously since 1871, providing many vital services; and

WHEREAS, these services include assistance with life saving, protection of the water, protection of water craft, and search and rescue missions; and

WHEREAS, the United States Coast Station, Great Egg has worked in harmony with the Ocean City Beach Patrol, Police Department and other municipal agencies; and

WHEREAS, the Coast Guard Station has been responsible for saving hundreds of lives since its inception here in 1871.

NOW, THEREFORE, I, Henry S. Knight, Mayor of the City of Ocean City, New Jersey, on behalf of City Council and our community, gratefully acknowledge the many contributions of the United States Coast Guard Station, Great Egg and look forward to many more years of hosting this outstanding unit of the United States Coast Guard.

Ocean City's Mayor Henry S. Knight signed this proclamation, which at the 1996 lifeguard reunion was presented to Coast Guard PO Jeffrey Valentine and Seaman William Hillyer by Fred Miller and John McShane, president and vice president, respectively, of the Ocean City Beach Patrol Administration Association.

Two

Early Lifeguards

"Lifeguard Krauss to the rescue!" was the shout as a floundering bather struggled in the waves in the 1890s. Joseph P. Krauss patrolled the beaches between 8th and 11th Streets as far back as 1893, working for donations. He would row a boat back and forth, helping swimmers reach shallow water. When city officials decided to hire paid lifeguards in 1898, they hired Krauss as captain and George Lee and William Scull as his crew. The wreck of the *Sindia* off the 17th Street Beach in December 1901 caused much extra work for the lifeguards. The four-masted bark was imbedded in the sand not far from the beach. Young people were attracted to the wreck, and many found themselves in trouble while trying to swim out to it.

As Ocean City increased in popularity and more people came to the city, more lifeguards were needed to protect the bathers; so, more were hired. By 1910, when lifeguard Alfred R. Smith was appointed captain, there was a crew of 18 guards. At that time, Krauss was appointed as superintendent of lifeboats, a position he held until his death in 1924.

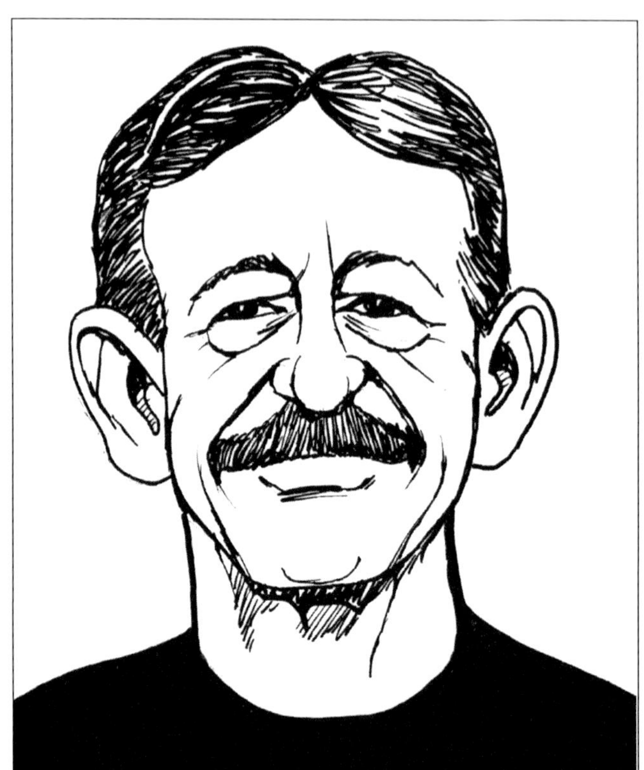

Lifeguard Joseph P. Krauss, the first Ocean City lifeguard, was posthumously inducted into the Ocean City Beach Patrol Hall of Fame. The Hall of Fame was started by the lifeguards in 1975 to recognize outstanding members of the patrol.

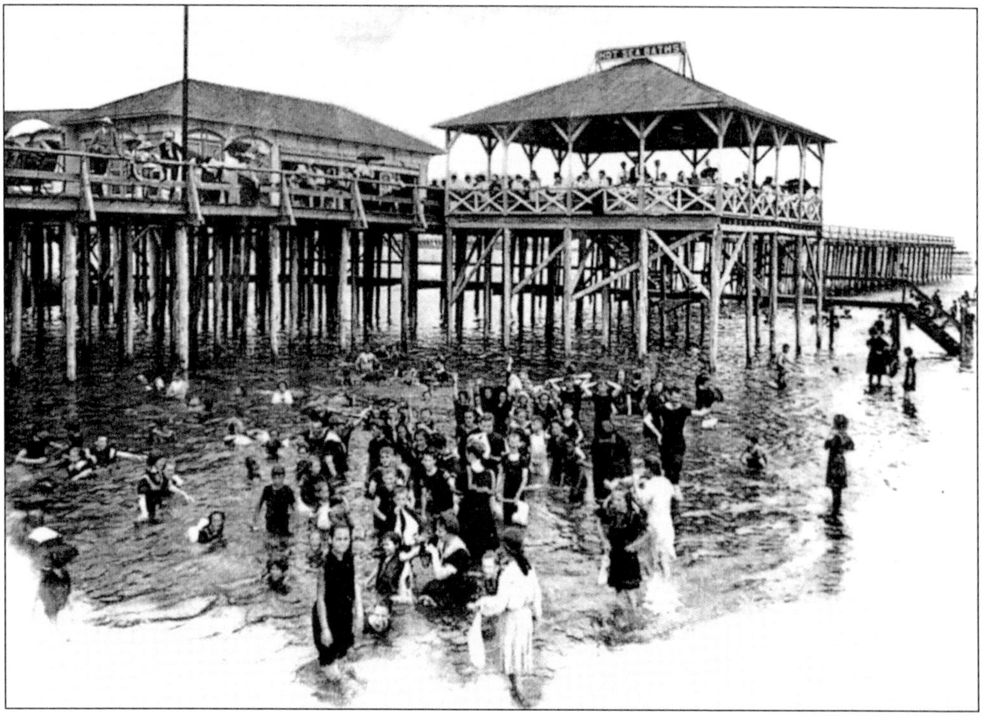

At the end of the 19th century, many people were discovering the enjoyment and healthful benefits of ocean bathing.

In 1887, the restriction in Ocean City against Sunday bathing was relaxed. This illustration from a 1959 Philadelphia newspaper poked fun at the ordinance still firmly on the books in 1882, when George G. Lenning waded into the surf on Sunday, July 30. Lenning was promptly arrested and fined $5 when he returned to the beach.

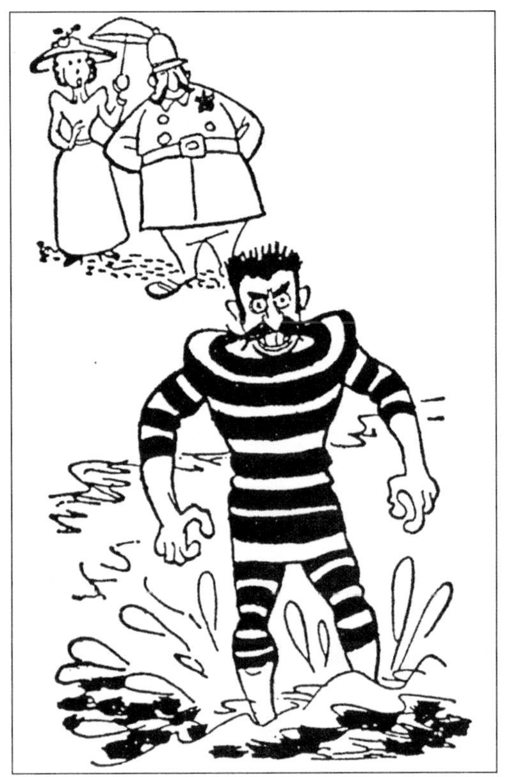

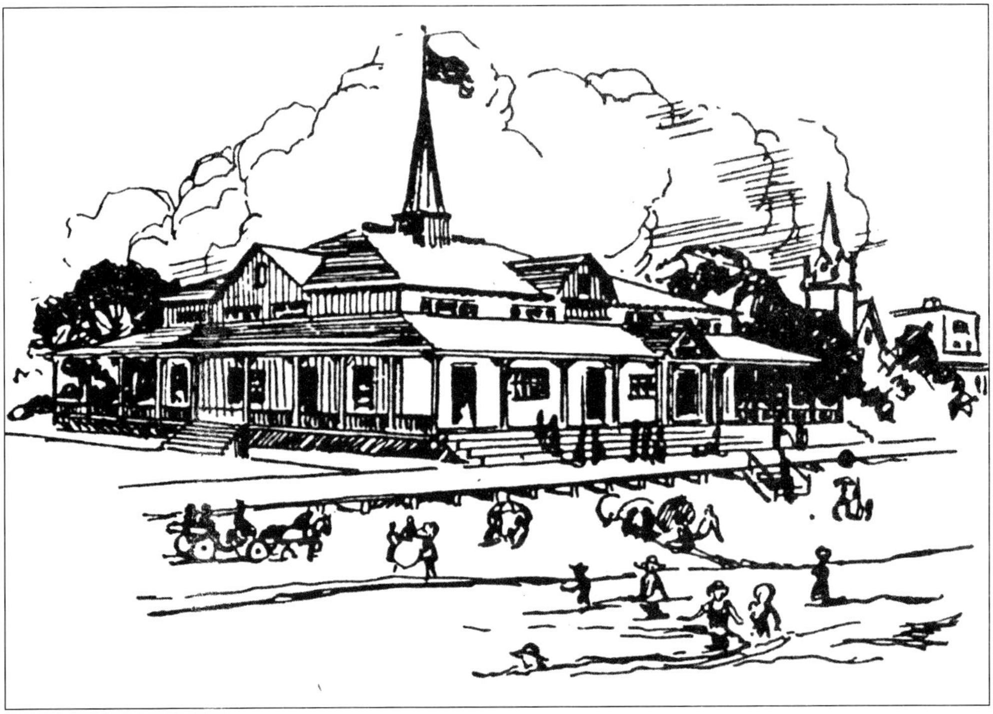

The Excursion House was built at 11th Street and the beach in 1887, as the first amusement center and bathhouse in Ocean City. The beach in front of it was a popular bathing beach.

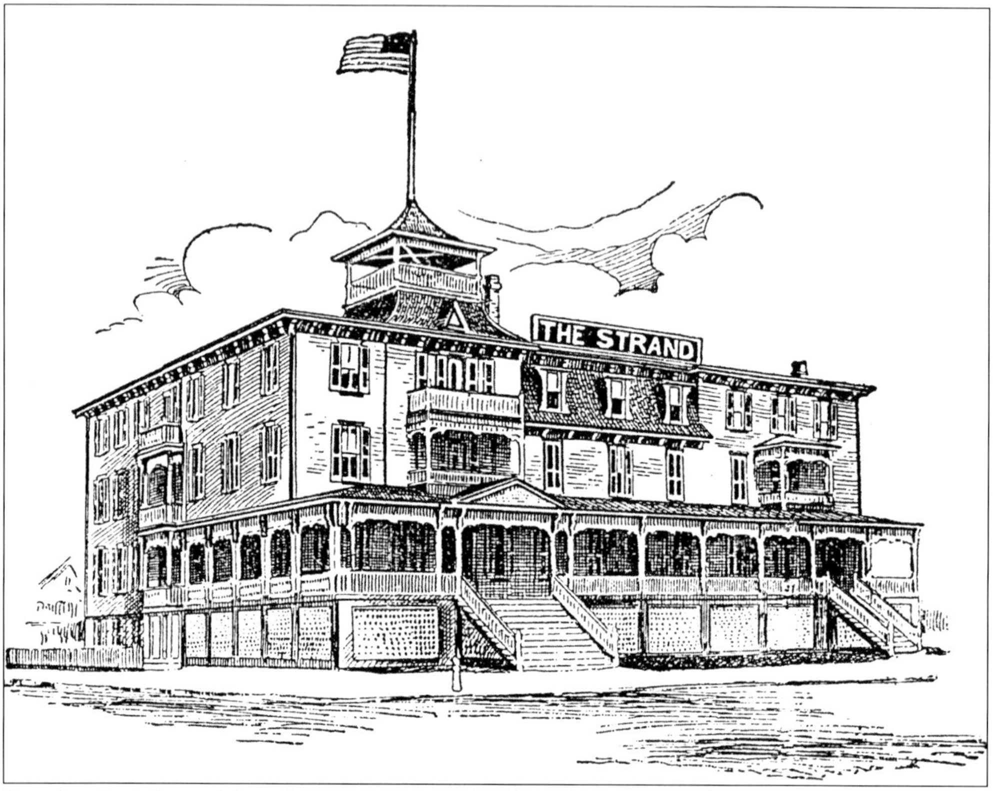

Benefits for lifeguard Joseph P. Krauss were held at the close of the summer of 1894 at the Strand Hotel, pictured here.

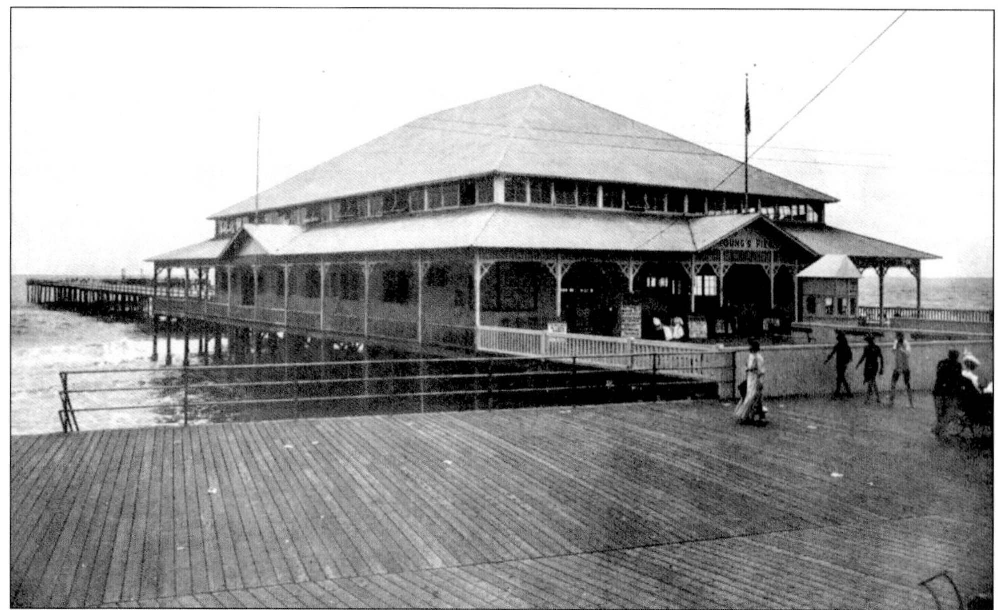

A benefit held for the lifeguards at Young's Pier in 1904 drew the ire of Joseph Champion, Ocean City's mayor, who felt that the city's wages for the lifeguards made such benefit affairs no longer necessary.

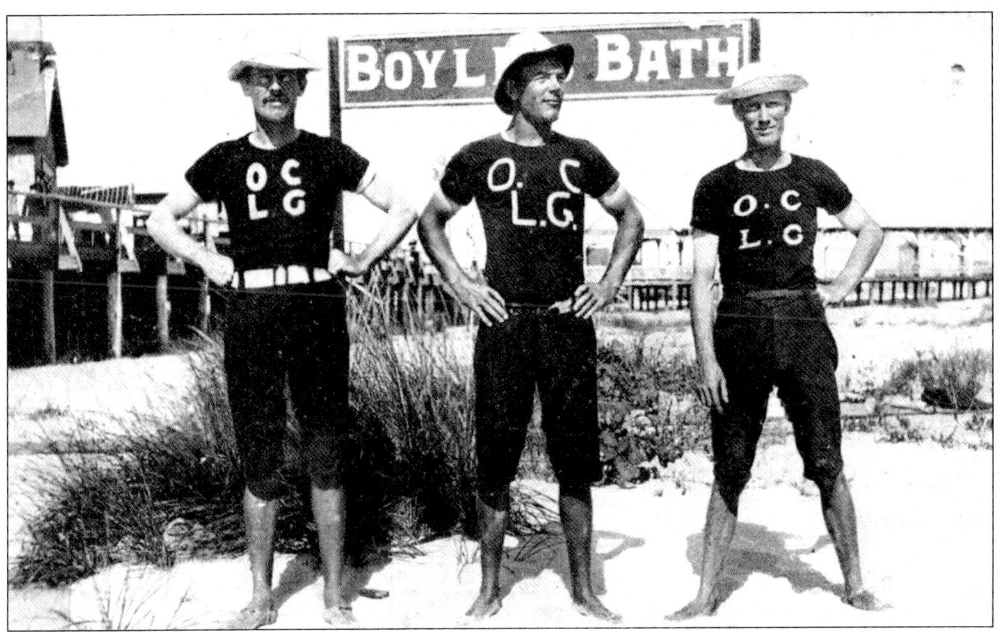

Somers Cameron (left), Alfred R. Smith (center), and Willard Steelman pose proudly in their lifeguard uniforms in 1902.

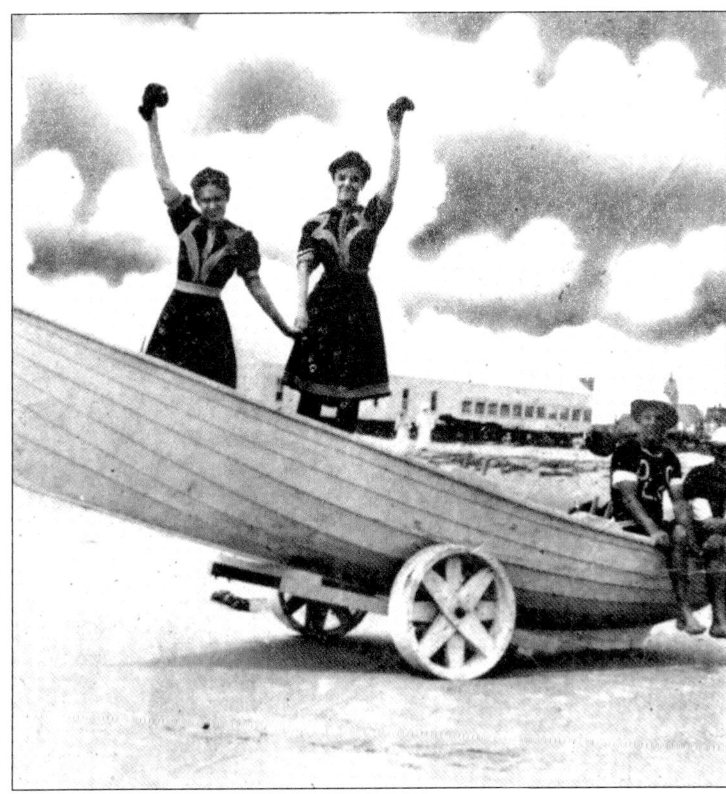
Lifeguards often attract young women admirers, and these two were happy to have their picture taken in the lifeboat with guards Al Smith and Walter Foster.

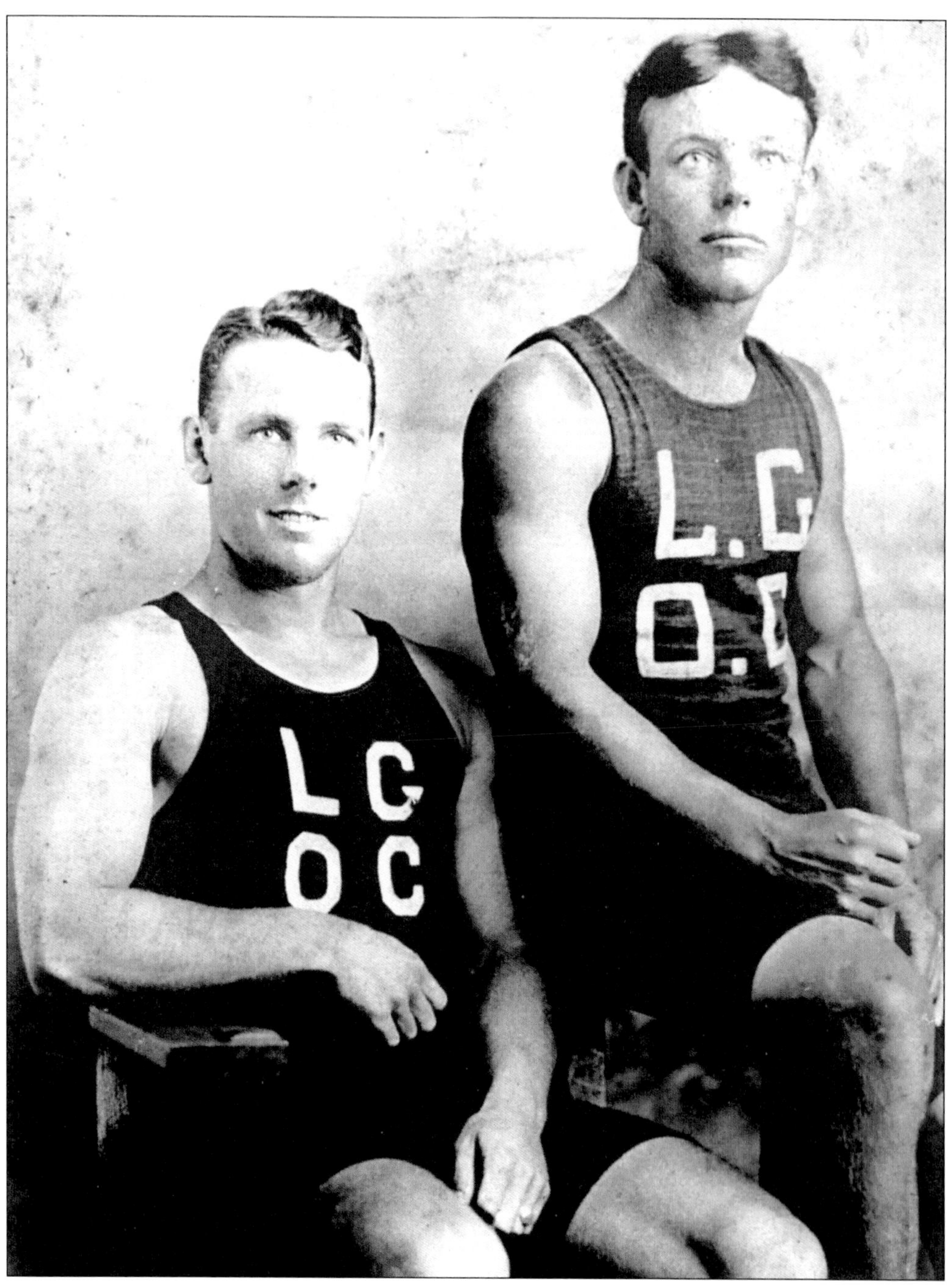

Pictured are lifeguards Walter Foster (left) and Alfred Smith. Smith was given a medal by the city for rescuing two people within one hour in 1899. He was appointed captain of the lifeguards in 1910. In 1918, during World War I, he rose to the rank of captain in the U.S. Army. In 1900, Foster was also awarded a medal for heroism in his lifeguard duties. He became an Ocean City policeman. His son, Preston Foster, became a well-known movie actor.

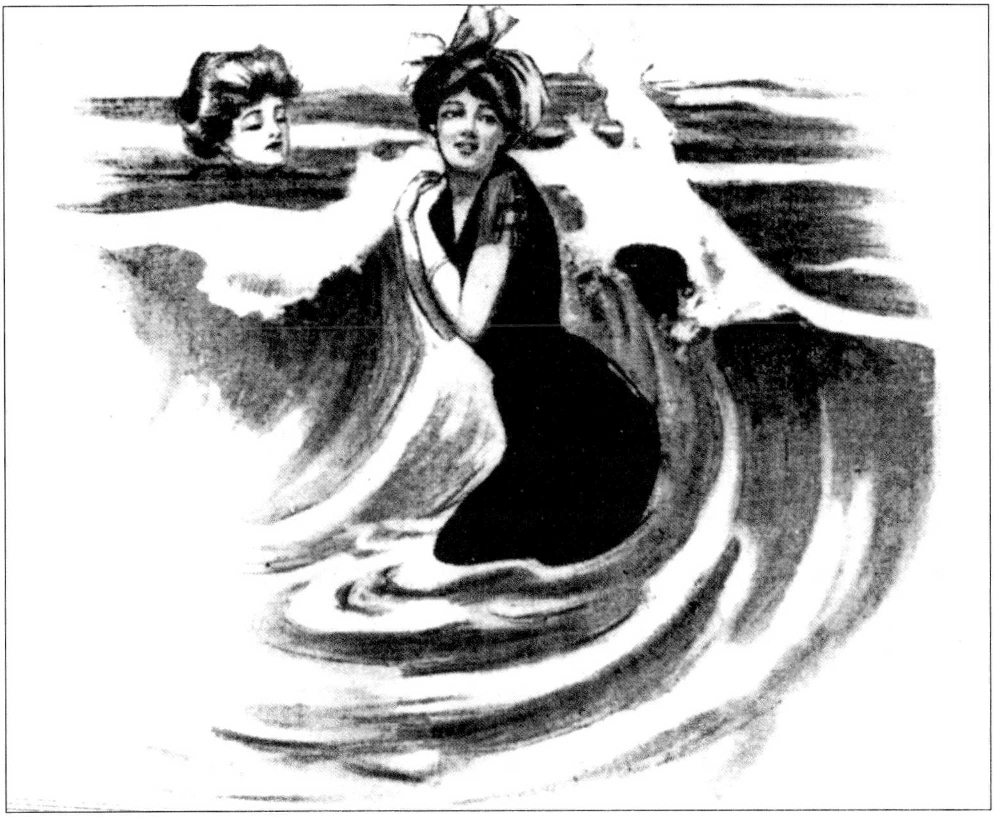

This illustration appeared in the *Ocean City Guidebook of 1910*, accompanied by an article entitled "Ocean City's Ideal Beach." The article lauded the beach at Ocean City and the safety and healthful benefits of the ocean, including the "constant and most efficient lifeguard service."

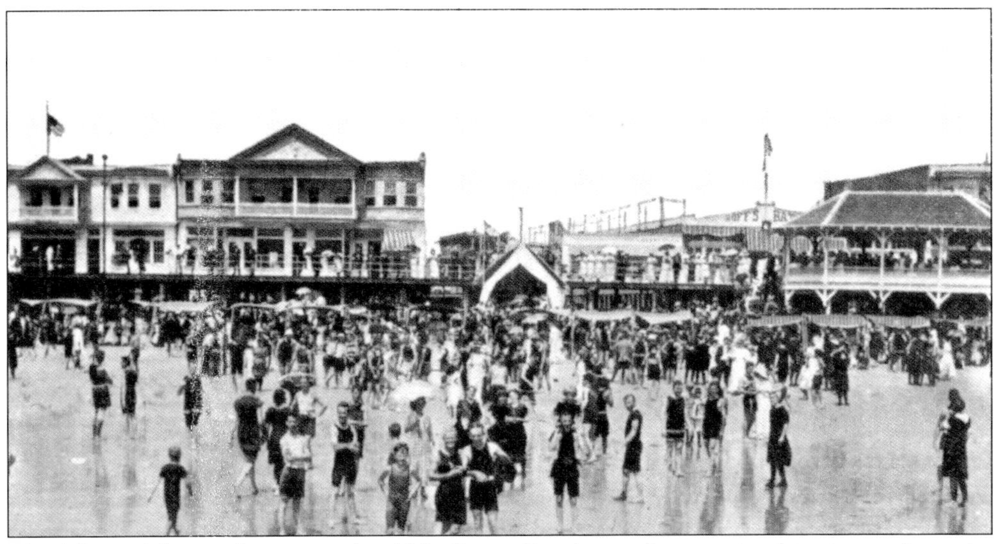

The lifeguard hospital tent on the 10th Street Beach can be seen in this picture from the summer of 1912. Dr. J. Garrison was in charge at the time.

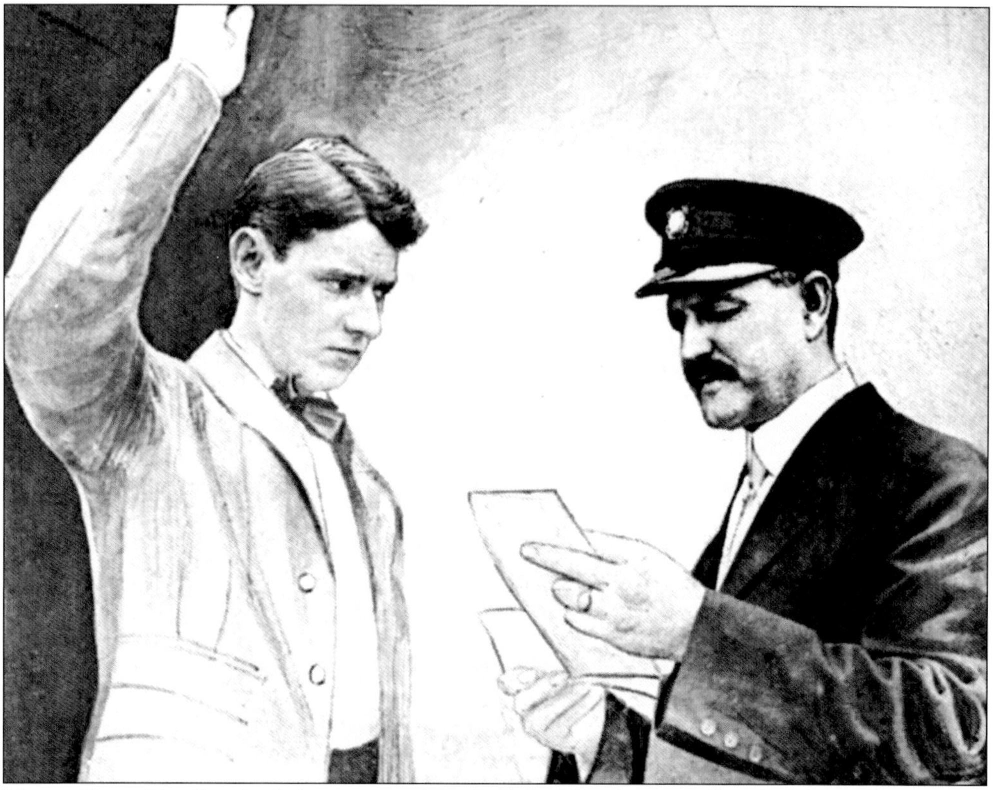

Mayor Harry Headley (right) swears in Marshall Earl Reid as an official U.S. mail carrier on August 3, 1912, before Reid made the first airmail flight in New Jersey. Lifeguards cleared the 10th Street Beach of people so it could be used as a takeoff and landing strip for Reid's plane.

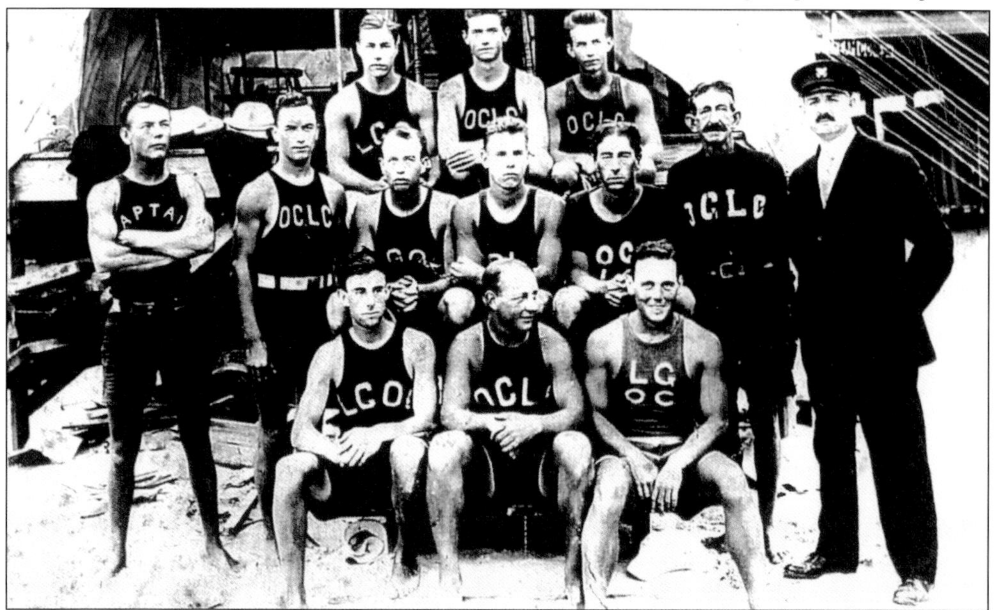

Before swearing in Marshall Reid, Mayor Harry Headley (right) poses with the Ocean City lifeguards and Capt. Alfred R. Smith (left) in front of their 10th Street tent.

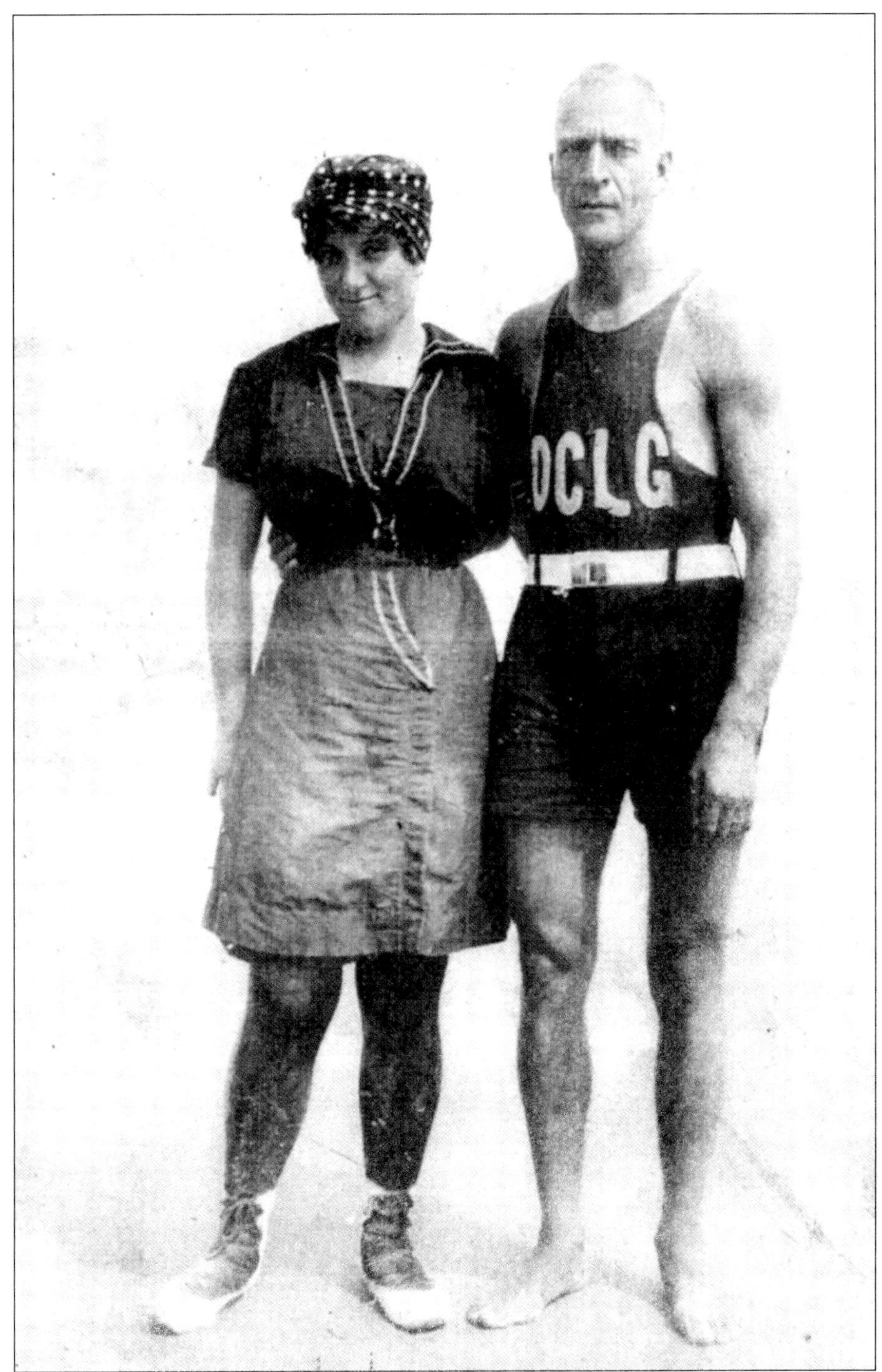

Reuben Oves, an Ocean City lifeguard from 1910 to 1917, poses here with his wife, Mary. He was physical director for the Pennsylvania Railroad YMCA. Following his father into the beach patrol in 1951 was Tom Oves, who taught physical education in Wildwood. His son, Chris Oves, began his career in the beach patrol in 1984 and taught in the Egg Harbor Township school system. Both Tom and Chris Oves were champion rowers for the Ocean City Beach Patrol.

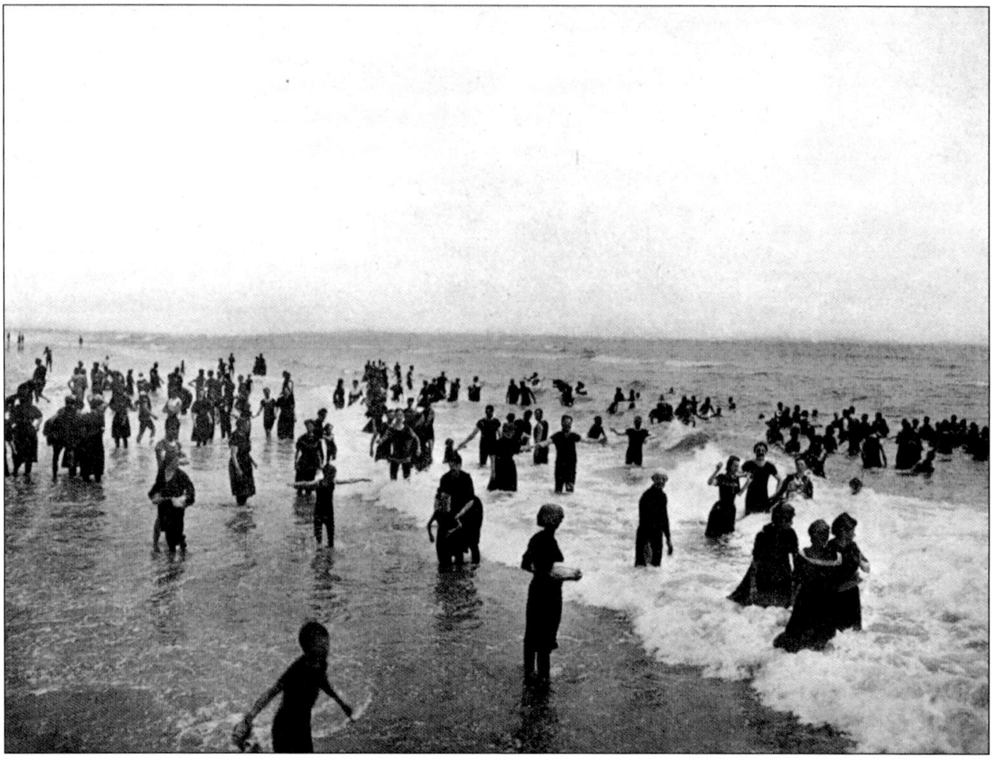

A 1912 publicity brochure touted Ocean City's safe beaches.

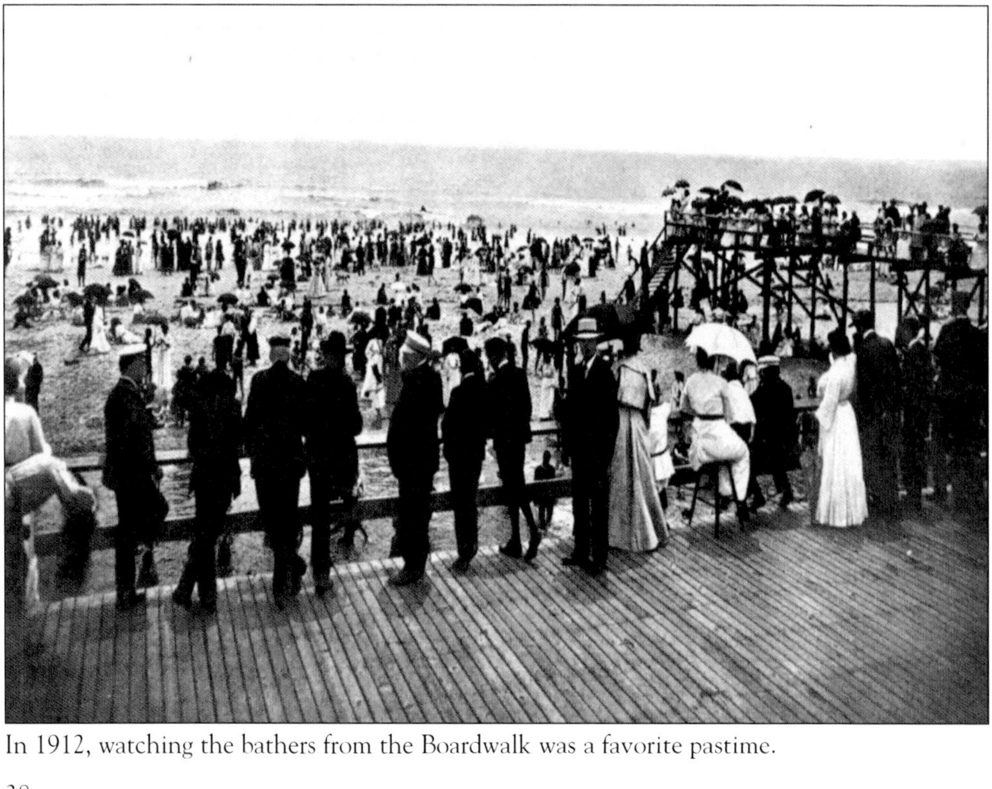

In 1912, watching the bathers from the Boardwalk was a favorite pastime.

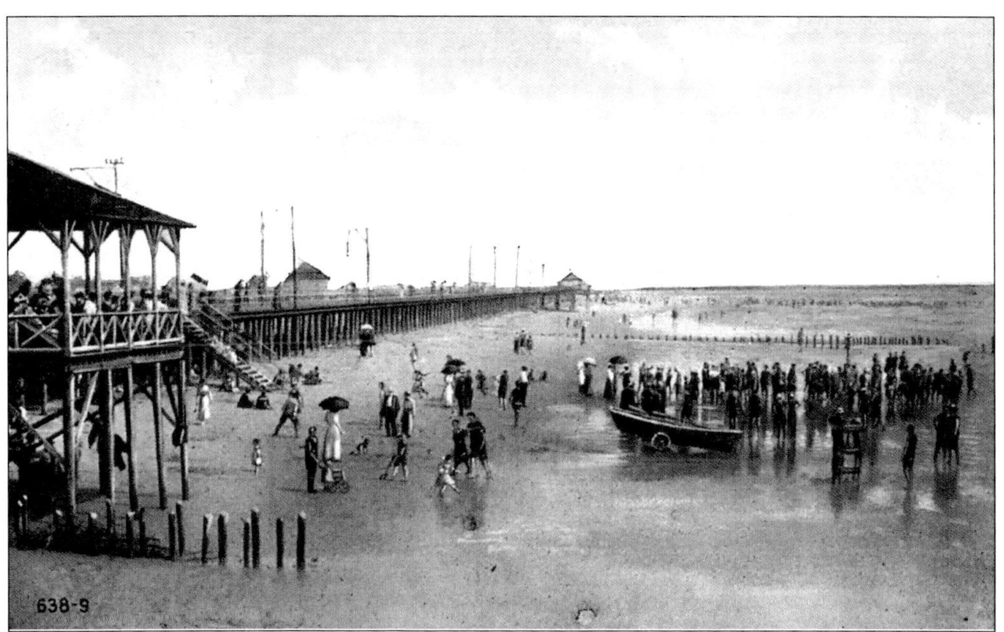

This view looking northward from 8th Street shows the lifeboat, rescue can on its stand, and crowded beach during the summer of 1915.

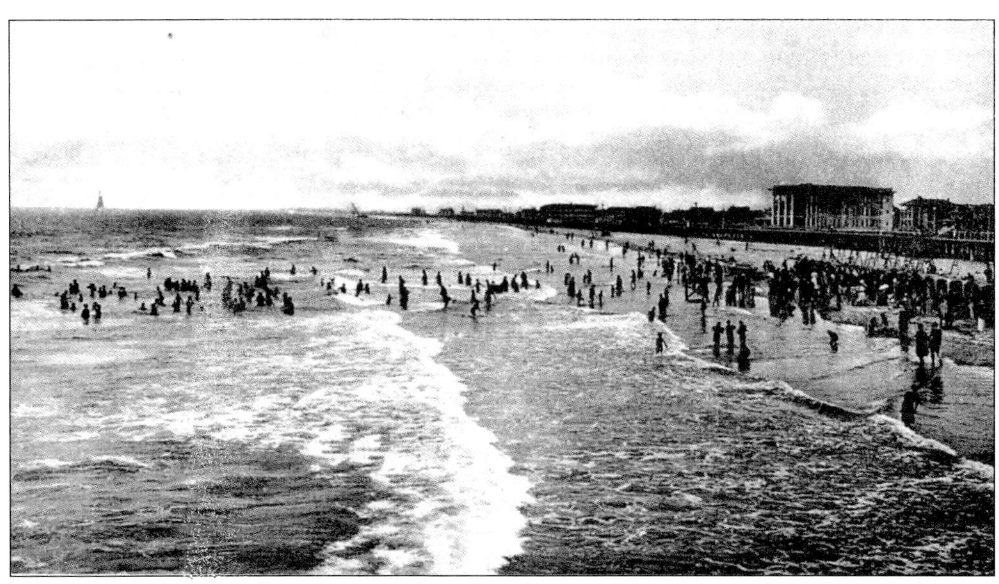
This view looking southward from 9th Street shows a lifeguard stand, lifeboat, and crowd of bathers.

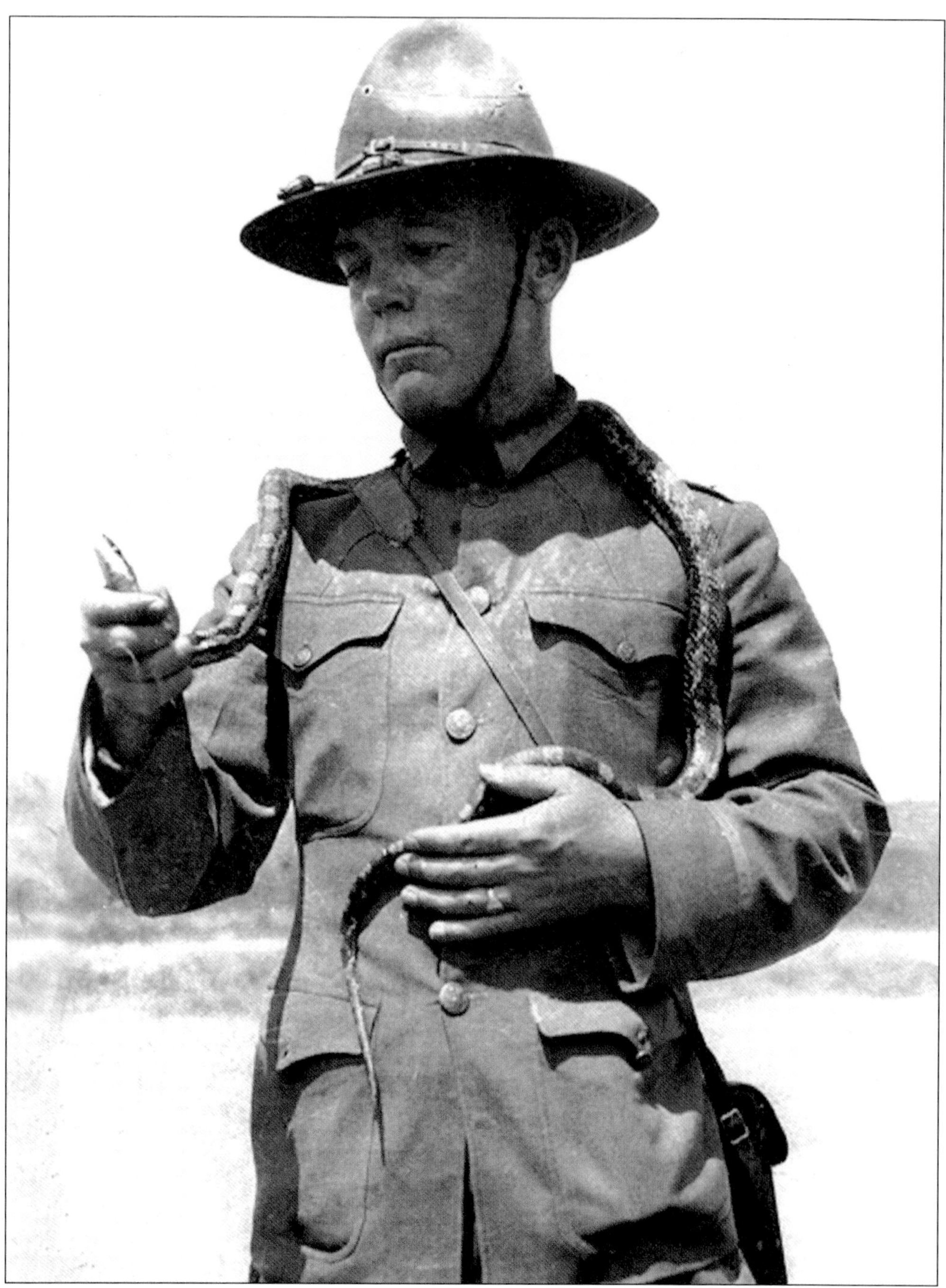

At Fort McClelland during World War I, Capt. Alfred R. Smith demonstrates how to handle snakes, which were often found in the trenches. A lifeguard from 1899 to 1919, he was captain of the lifeguards from 1910 to 1919 (except during his 1917–1918 army stint). His name is engraved on the World War I monument in Ocean City's Memorial Park. Smith was inducted posthumously into the Ocean City Beach Patrol Hall of Fame in 1995.

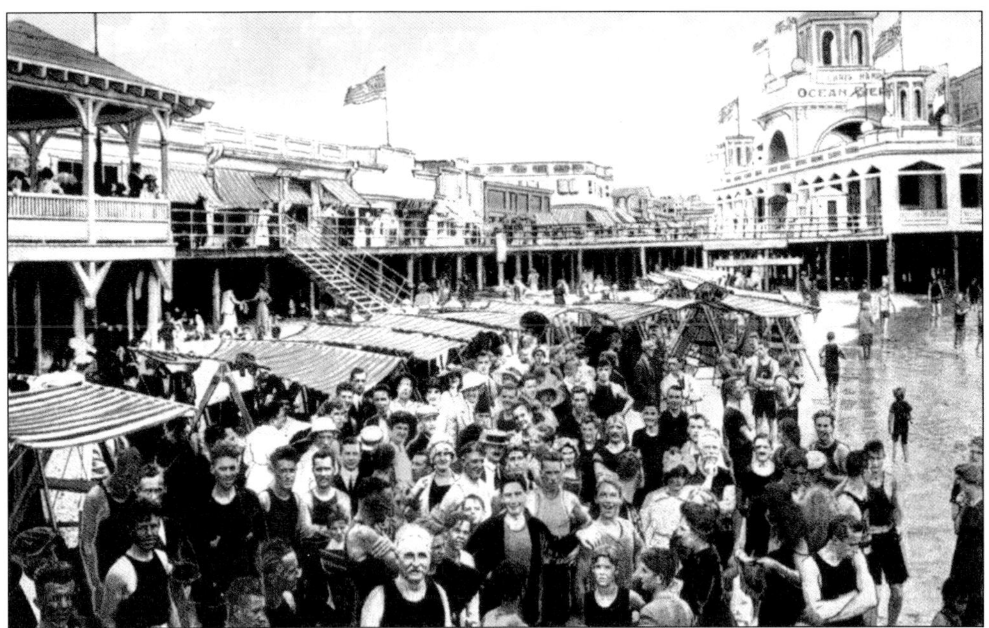

During the summer of 1917, the 10th Street Beach was the site of the lifeguard headquarters and the most popular beach in town.

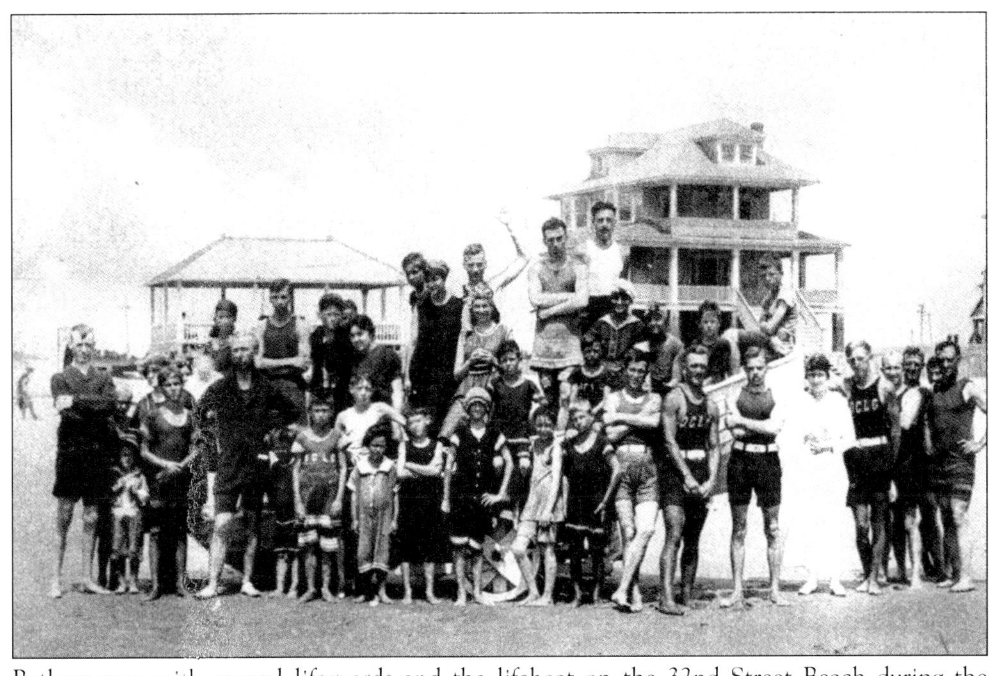

Bathers pose with several lifeguards and the lifeboat on the 32nd Street Beach during the summer of 1917.

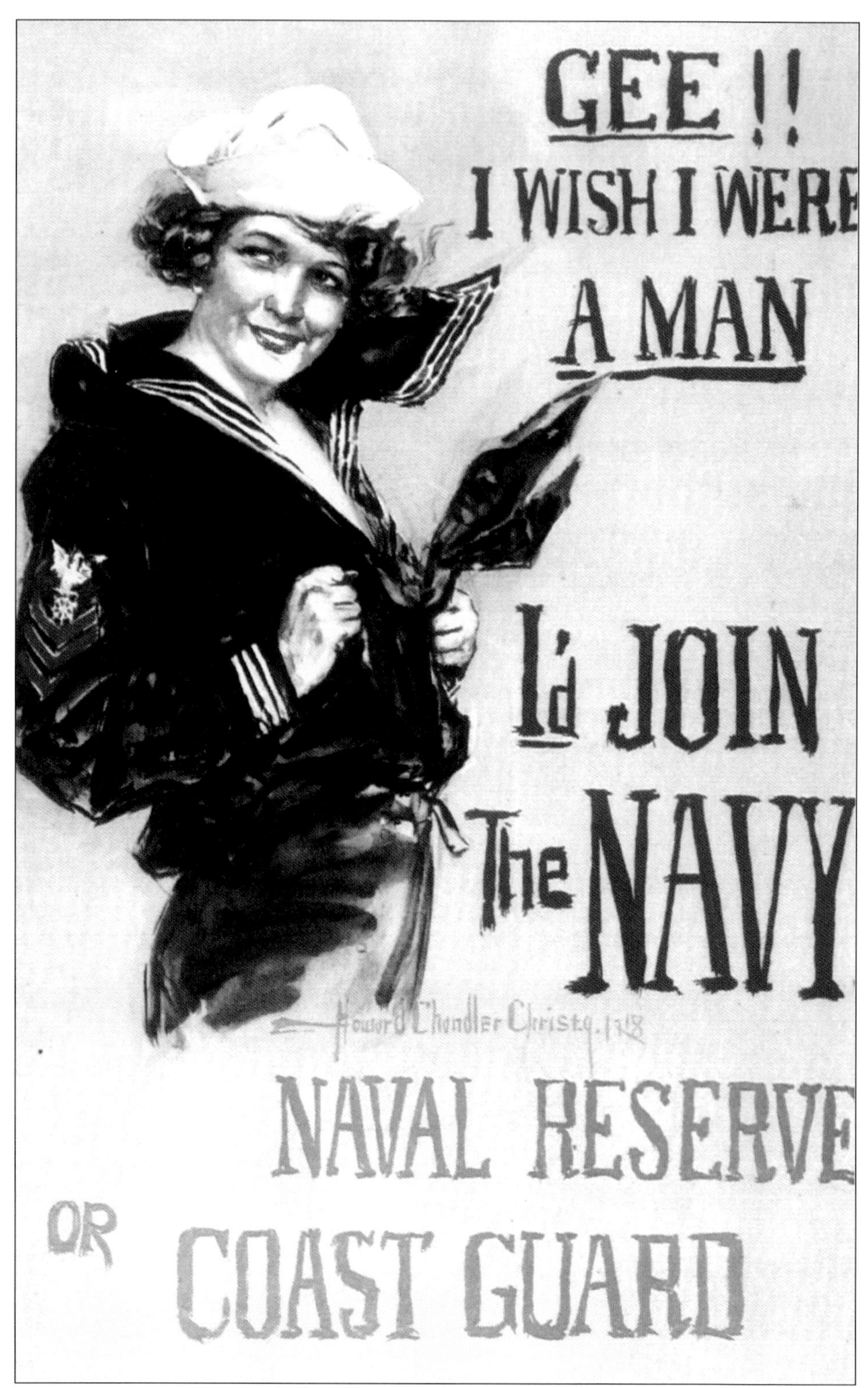

During World War I, this recruiting poster hung in the Ocean City Post Office.

Three

The Jernee Years

Jack G. Jernee was appointed captain of the Ocean City lifeguards in 1920, and one of the first things he did was to change the name to the Ocean City Beach Patrol, the name still used. He used the experience he gained in the U.S. Life-Saving Service and the U.S. Coast Guard to build the Ocean City Beach Patrol into one of the finest lifesaving squads in the country. During his tenure, the Ocean City Beach Patrol received national attention for its lifesaving skills, athletic prowess (National Lifeguard Champions in 1933, 1934, and 1935), giant water shows, and flag ceremonies held each day at the Music Pier.

Jernee developed a close relationship with wealthy Philadelphia businessman John B. Kelly, who had built a summer home for his family at 26th Street in 1931. Kelly was a former Olympic rowing champion and often joined the lifeguards for a row in the ocean. During the Depression, whenever the city was unable to provide equipment for the beach patrol, John Kelly stepped in with needed financial support.

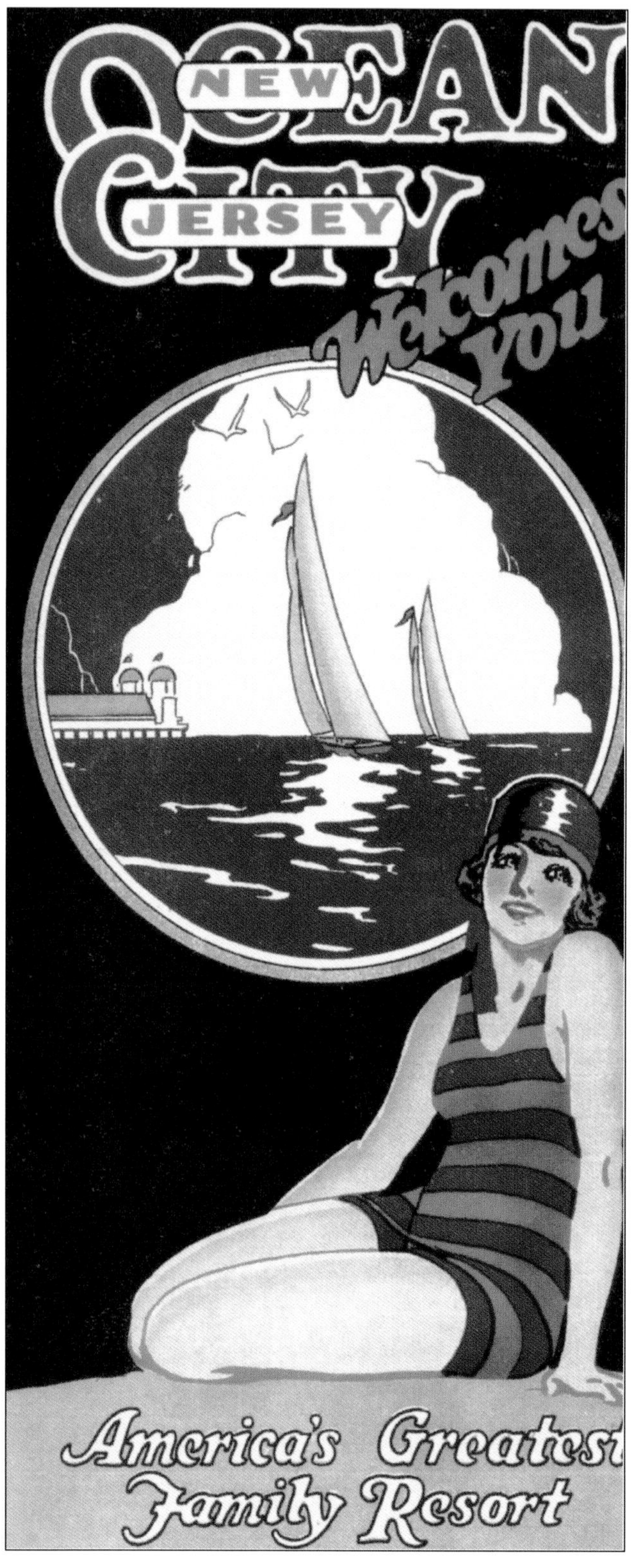

In 1920, the Ocean City Chamber of Commerce chose the city's new slogan, "America's Greatest Family Resort." Resort officials embraced this motto, and it has graced all publicity booklets and brochures ever since.

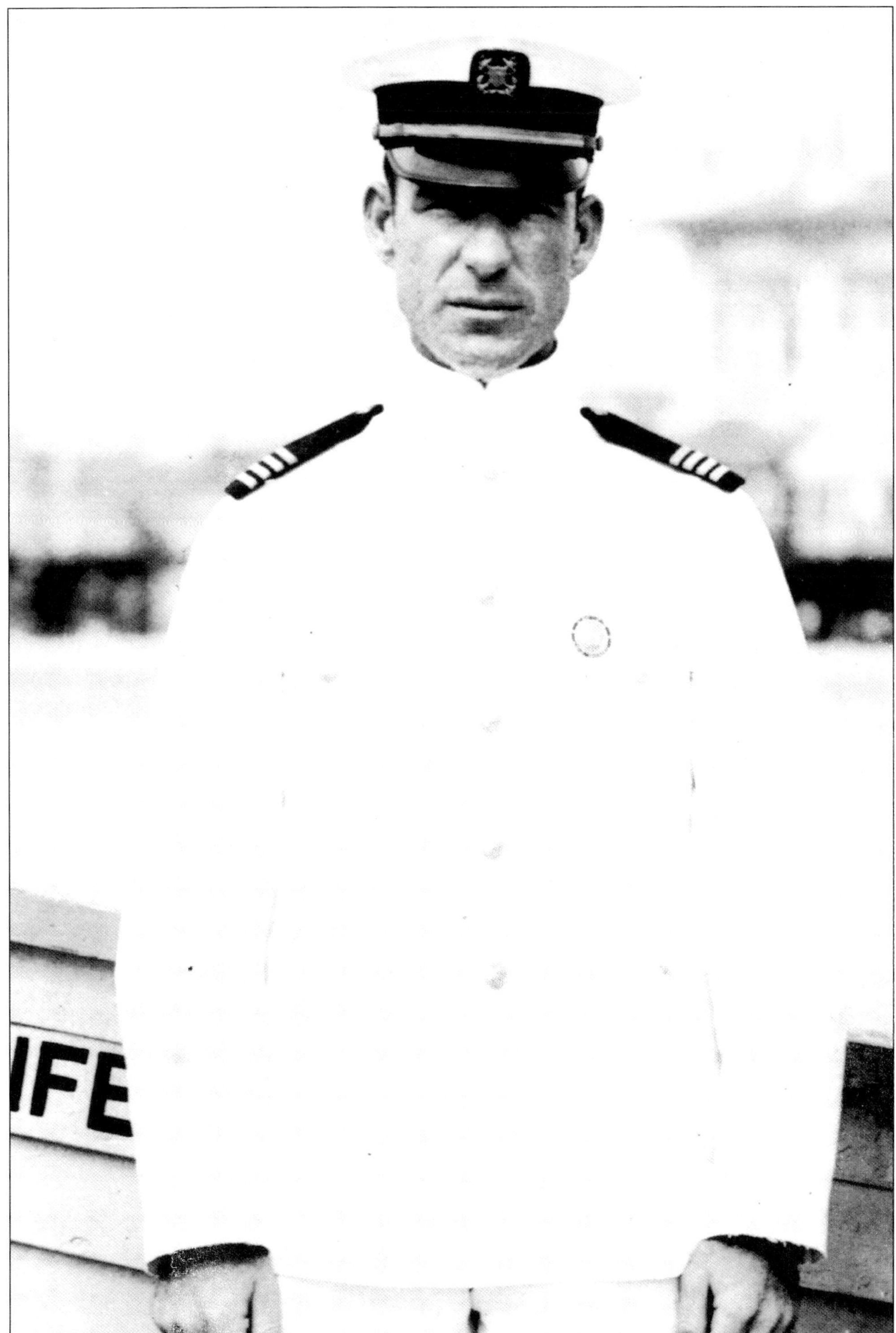

In 1920, when Alfred R. Smith resigned his position as captain of the Ocean City lifeguards to join his family's business, the city appointed Jack G. Jernee (above) as captain.

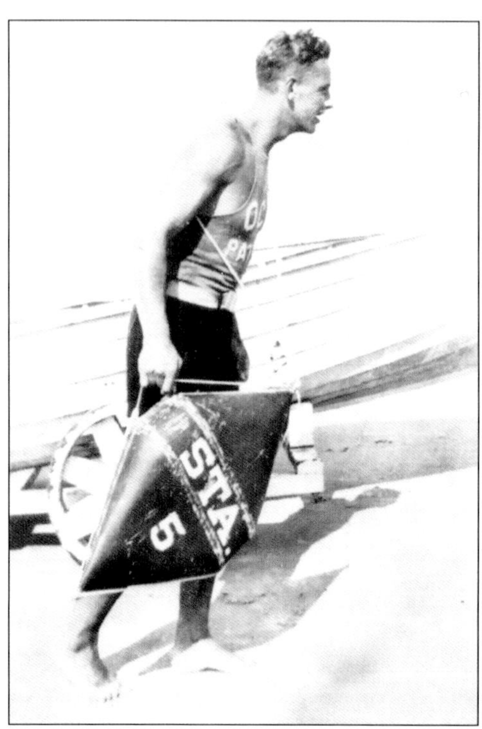

Lifeguard William Young performs a lifesaving drill using the can buoy flotation device.

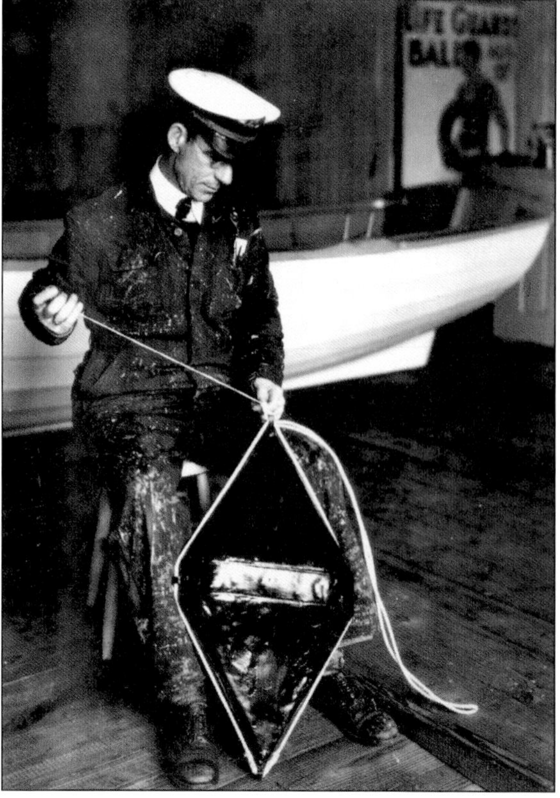

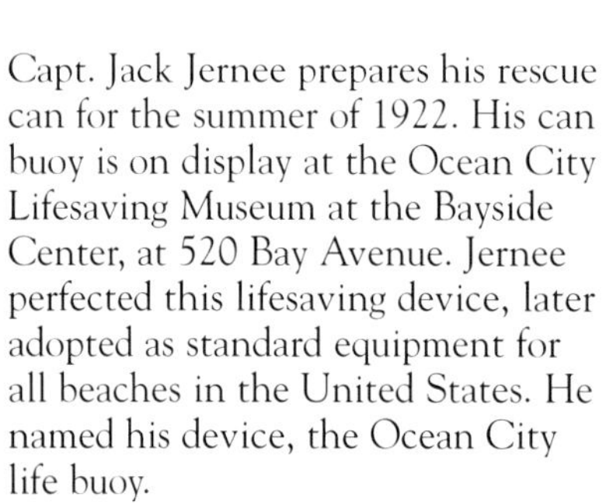

Capt. Jack Jernee prepares his rescue can for the summer of 1922. His can buoy is on display at the Ocean City Lifesaving Museum at the Bayside Center, at 520 Bay Avenue. Jernee perfected this lifesaving device, later adopted as standard equipment for all beaches in the United States. He named his device, the Ocean City life buoy.

During the summer of 1923, a group of public-spirited citizens led by Jack Jernee, Ocean City Beach Patrol captain, decided to revive the bay carnival. Called the Night in Venice Boat Parade, it had been started in 1907 and held for several summers. This 1923 royal barge carried Bay Carnival queen Jeannette Darby and her court.

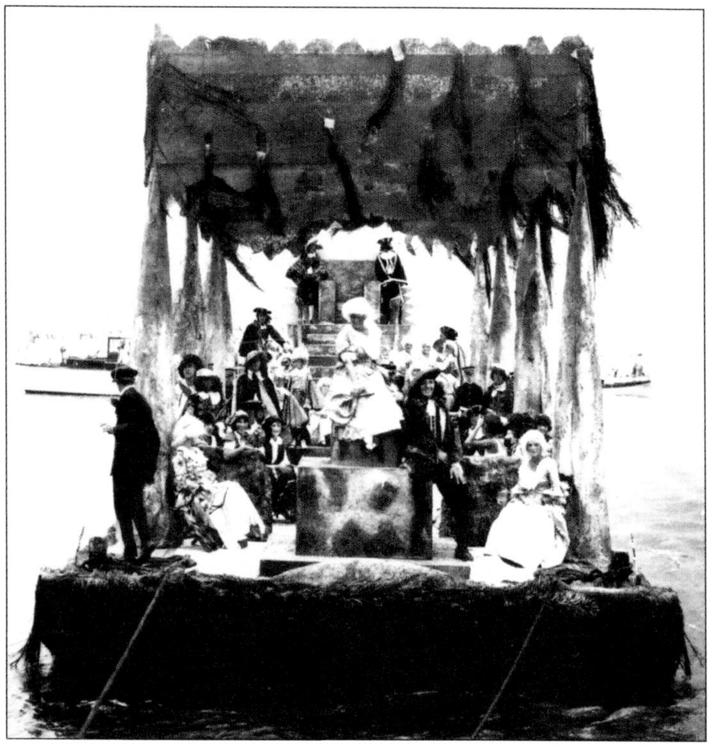

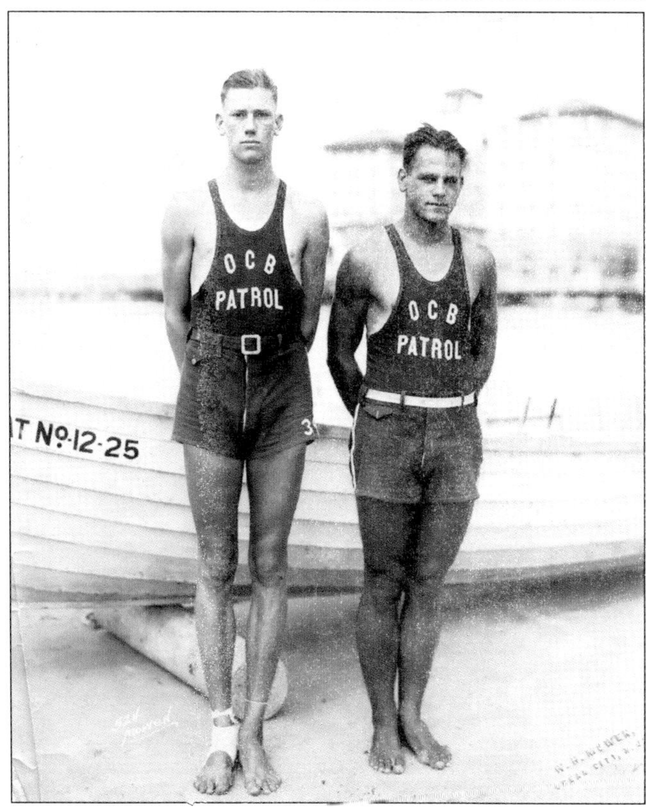

Lockwood Miller (left) and Lee Johnson were Ocean City Beach Patrol doubles rowing champions.

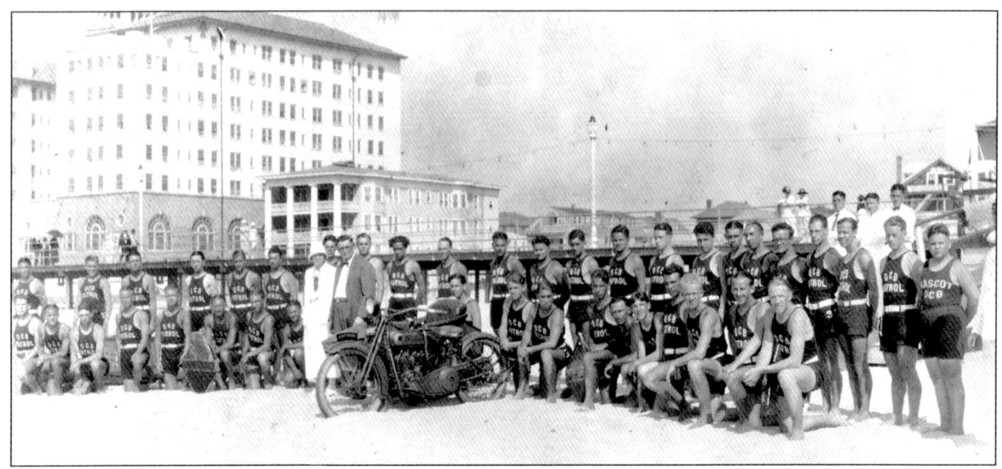

The lifeguards pose in front of their 10th Street tent in the summer of 1924. In front are, from left to right, beach surgeon Dr. Marcia V. Smith, Mayor Joseph G. Champion, and Capt. Jack G. Jernee. The local lifeguards still refer to their zone headquarters as tents.

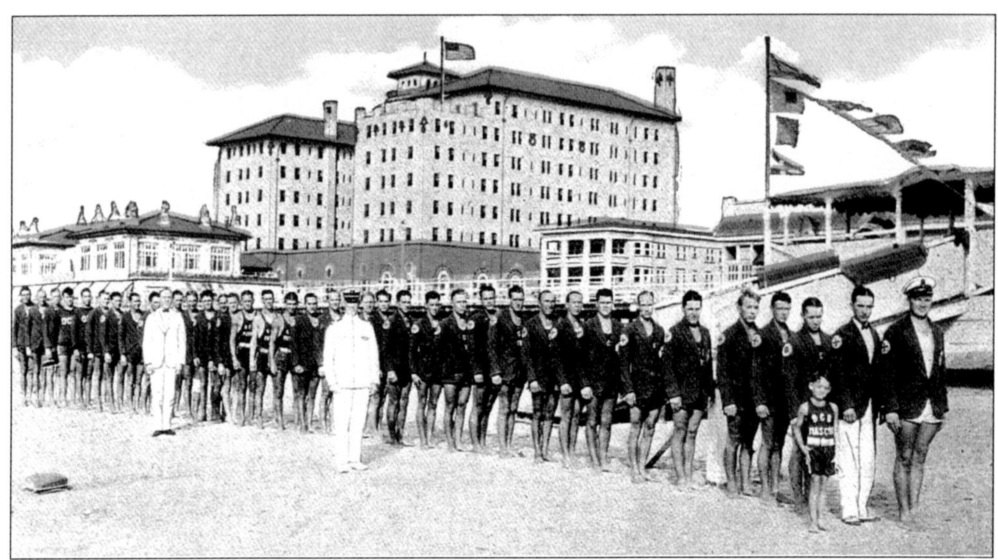

This is the Ocean City Beach Patrol of 1926. Pictured next to Capt. Jack Jernee (right) are assistant beach surgeon Dr. Welsh and the beach patrol's young mascot, Kenneth O. Snow.

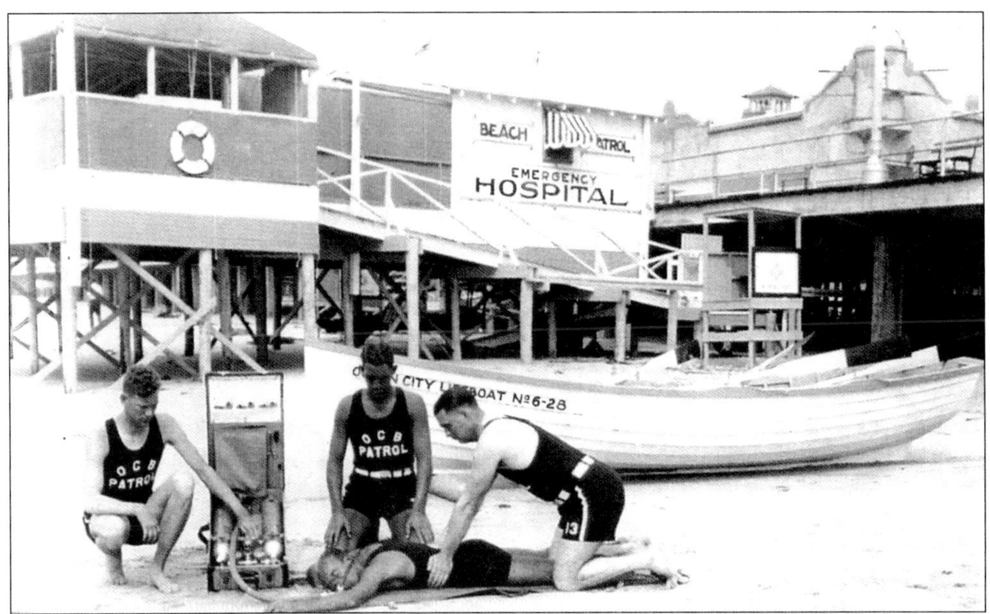

Ocean City lifeguards practice their resuscitation skills on the 10th Street Beach in 1928. Techniques have changed since then but not the lifeguards' commitment to saving lives.

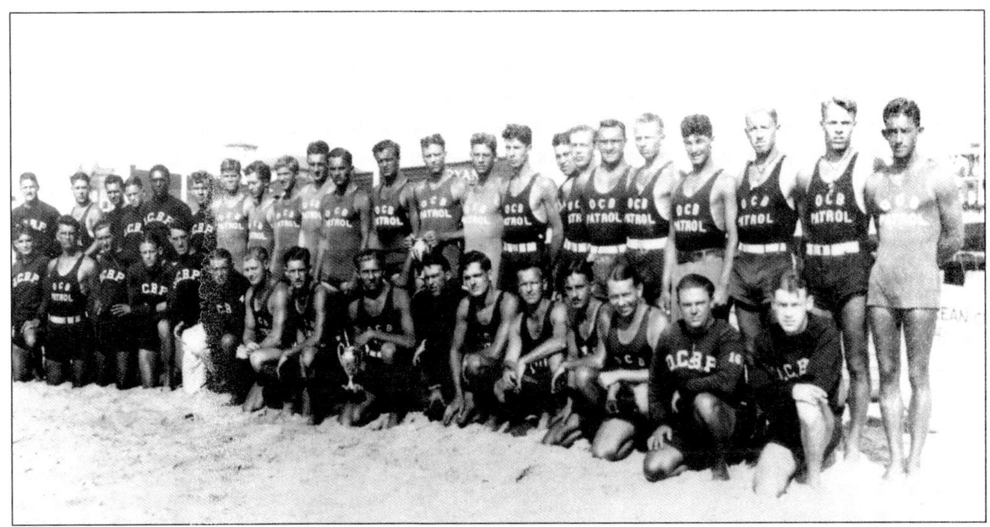

The first African American lifeguard on the Ocean City Beach Patrol was Alvin Thompson (standing fifth from the left). He was on the patrol from 1928, the date of this picture, through the summer of 1937. No one ever drowned on his watch, although many of his rescues were so dramatic they were reported in the local newspaper. In August 1930, he was voted the most outstanding guard of the week by the Ocean City Real Estate Board and given a $10 award.

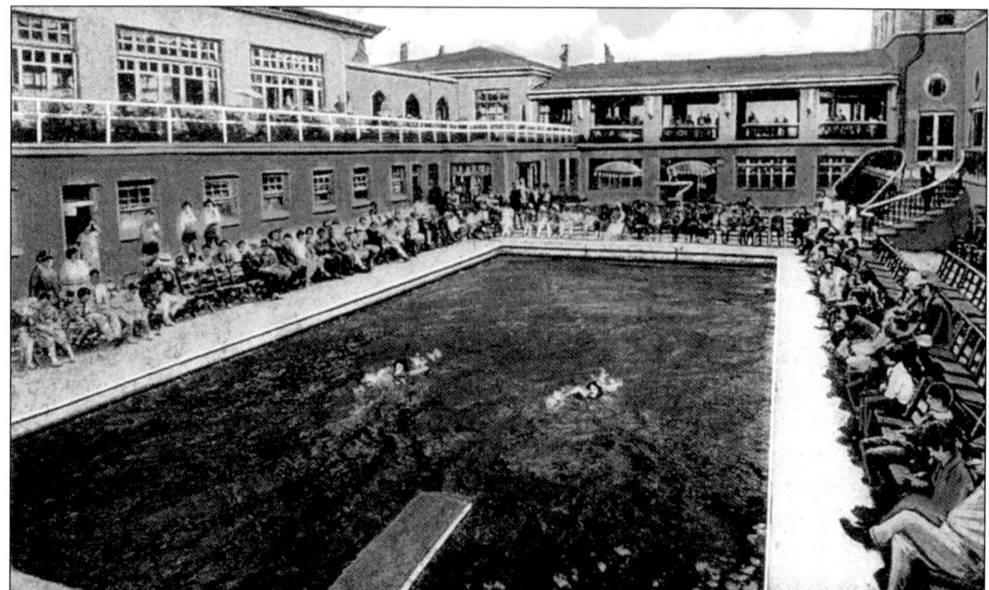

The first swimming pool at the Flanders Hotel opened on May 30, 1924. The new pool drew hundreds of visitors every day, and large crowds attended the aquatic shows put on by members of the Ocean City Beach Patrol. On Saturday evening, August 23, the pool area was packed with spectators watching the lifeguard intra-squad swim championship.

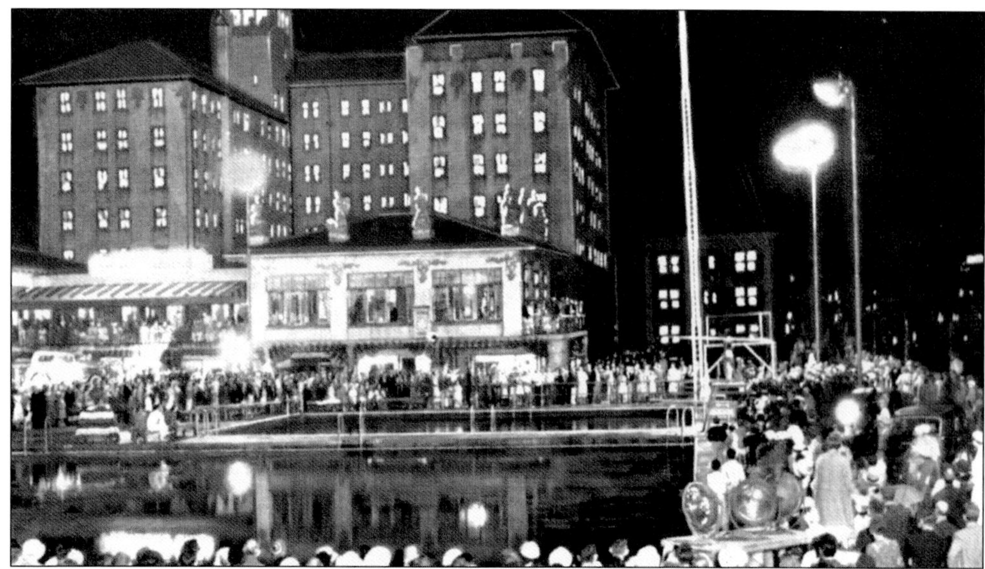

In 1929, the Flanders Hotel opened three more swimming pools, and the era of the Ocean City Beach Patrol's giant water shows began. As this photograph shows, the bleachers surrounding the largest pool were always filled with people who were there to watch the exciting water spectaculars designed by Capt, Jack Jernee to educate, thrill, and entertain.

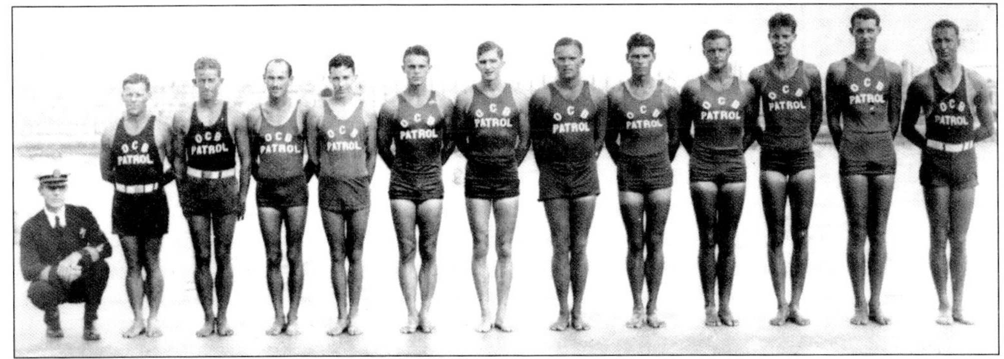

The 1930 Ocean City Beach Patrol swim team trained at the Flanders Hotel pool before reporting for work. From left to right are Capt. Jack Jernee, Pep Smith, Frank McKee, Marley Fitzgerald, Ed Kelly, Ed Bardo, Frank Holt, Bill Brown, Fran Hoffman, Robert Beatty, Bill Ennis, Bill Briggs, and John Gooley.

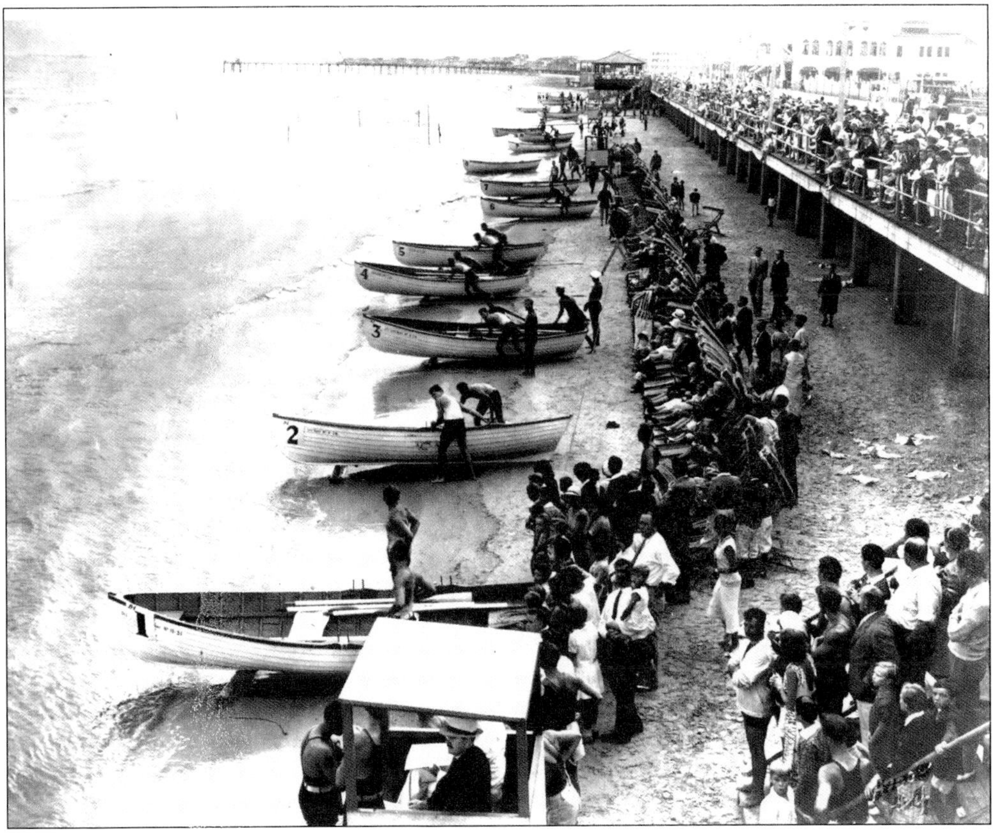

These Ocean City lifeguards have their boats lined up for a 1931 intra-squad doubles rowing championship. Charles Kieffer and Bert Loeper won this race.

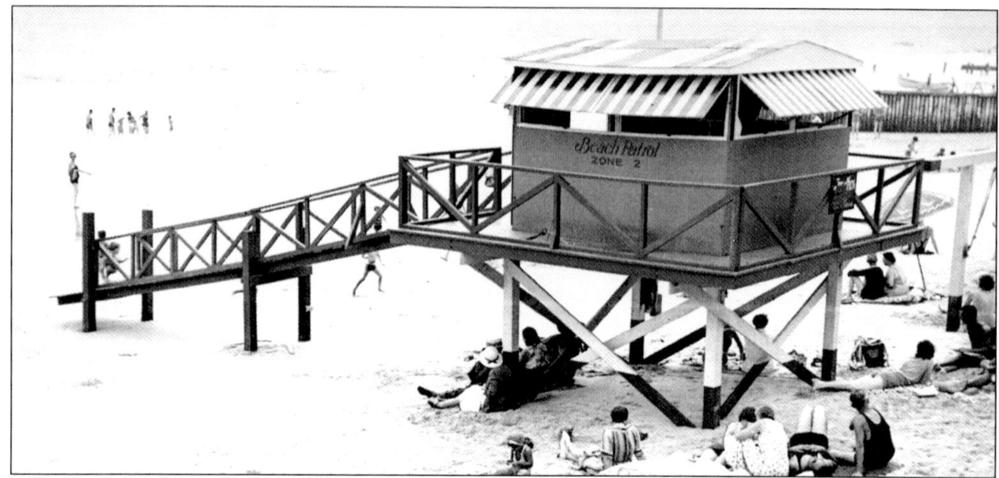

The main beach patrol headquarters was located on 10th Street, but each lifeguard zone had a tent like this one. The lifeguards used these zone tents to store rescue equipment and first aid supplies.

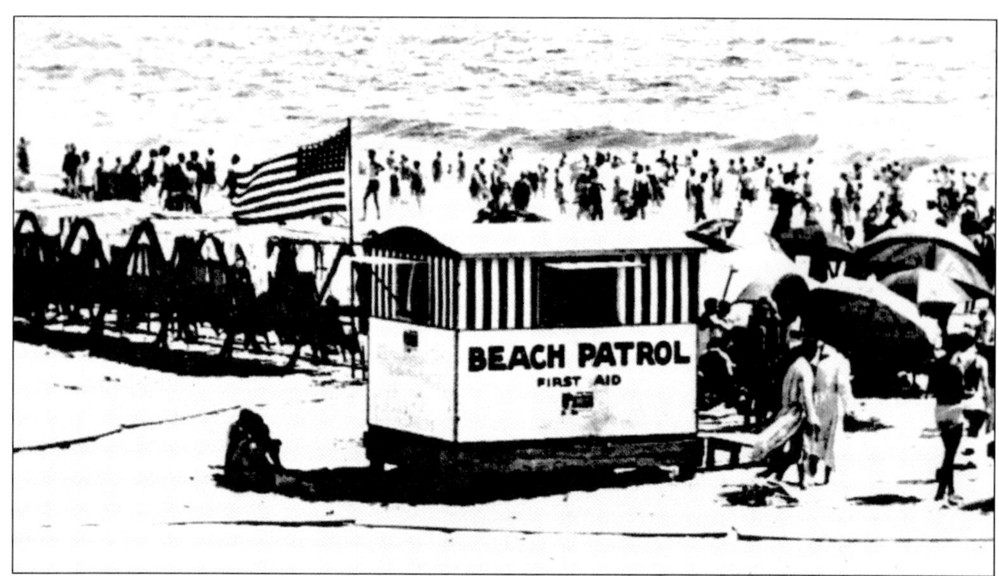

This is a picture of another, more portable first-aid tent used by the lifeguards.

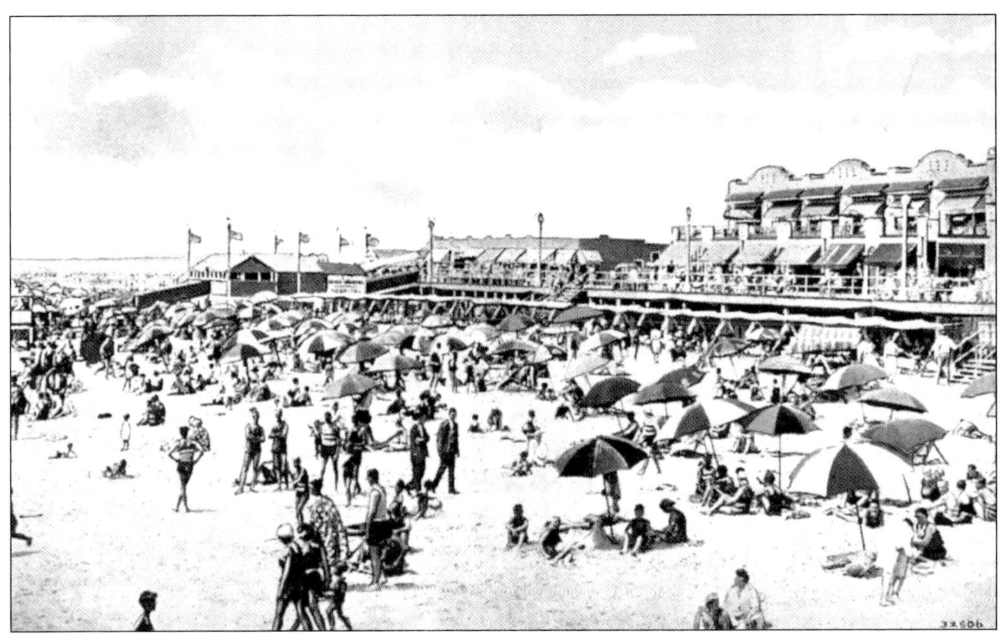

This view of the beach at 4th Street shows the lifeguard tent on the beach and a lifeguard stand. This tent was washed away during a storm in 1932.

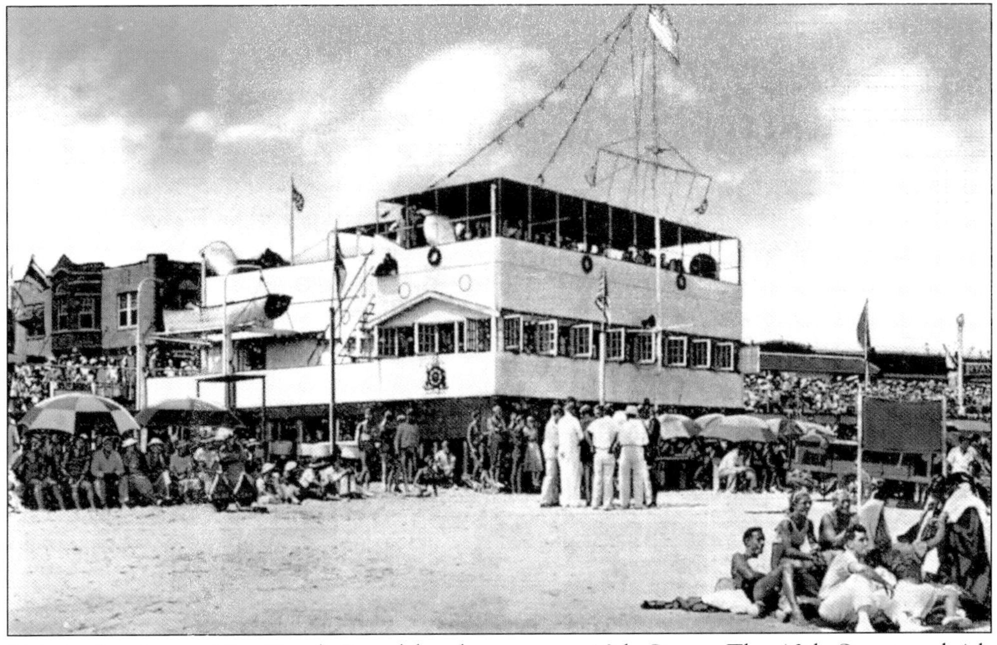

This is the Ocean City Beach Patrol headquarters at 10th Street. The 10th Street and 4th Street Beaches were two of the busiest beaches in the city. The 10th Street headquarters was destroyed in the March 1962 storm.

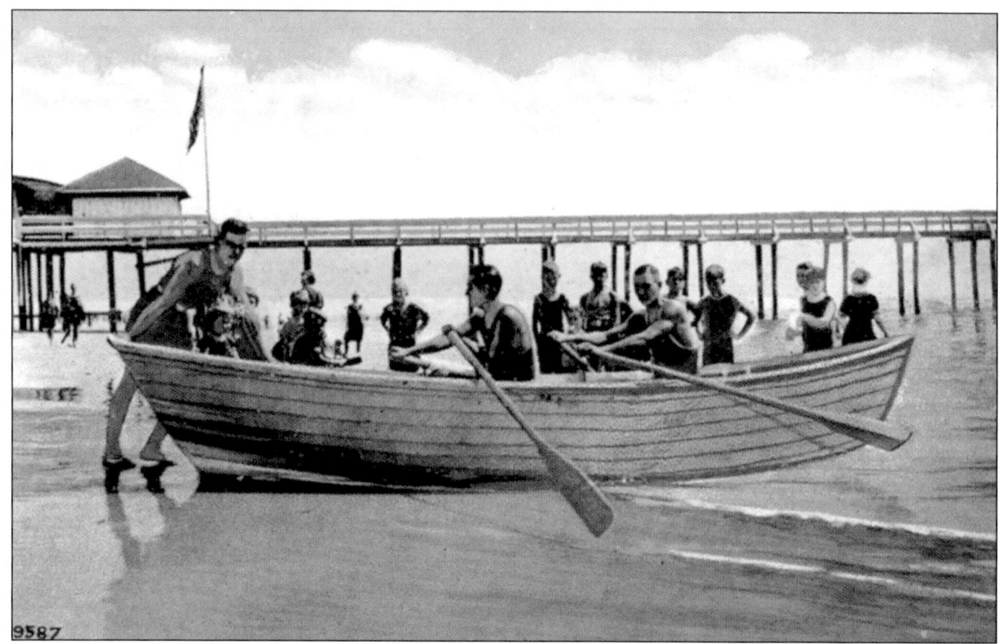

The Angler's Club Fishing Pier, seen behind the lifeguards and their boat, was washed away in the same 1932 storm that destroyed the 4th Street lifeguard tent.

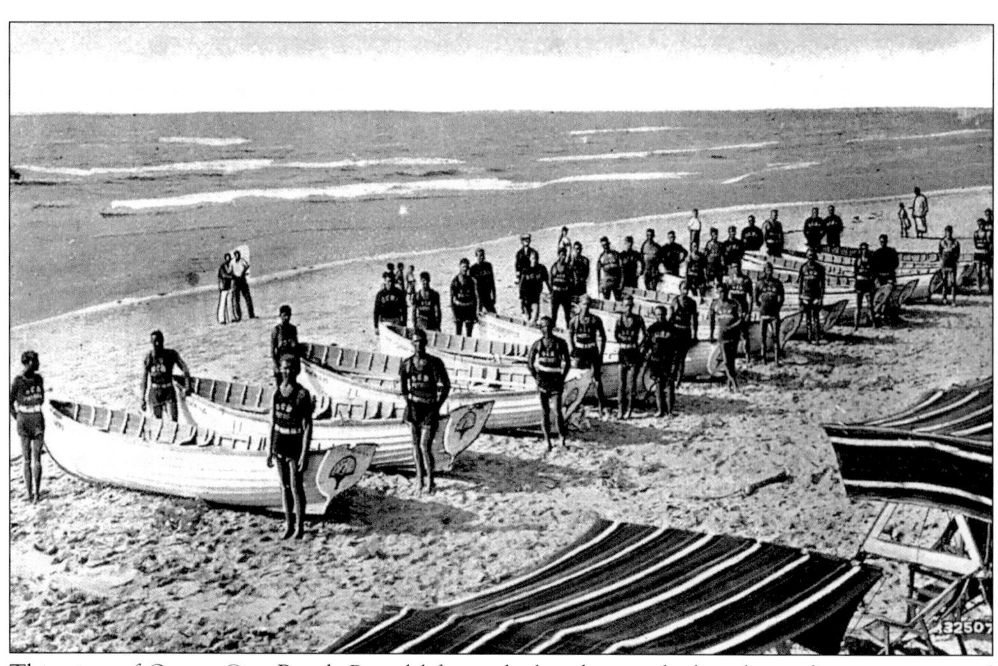

This view of Ocean City Beach Patrol lifeguards, lined up with their boats for an intra-squad rowing race, was a popular picture postcard in the 1930s.

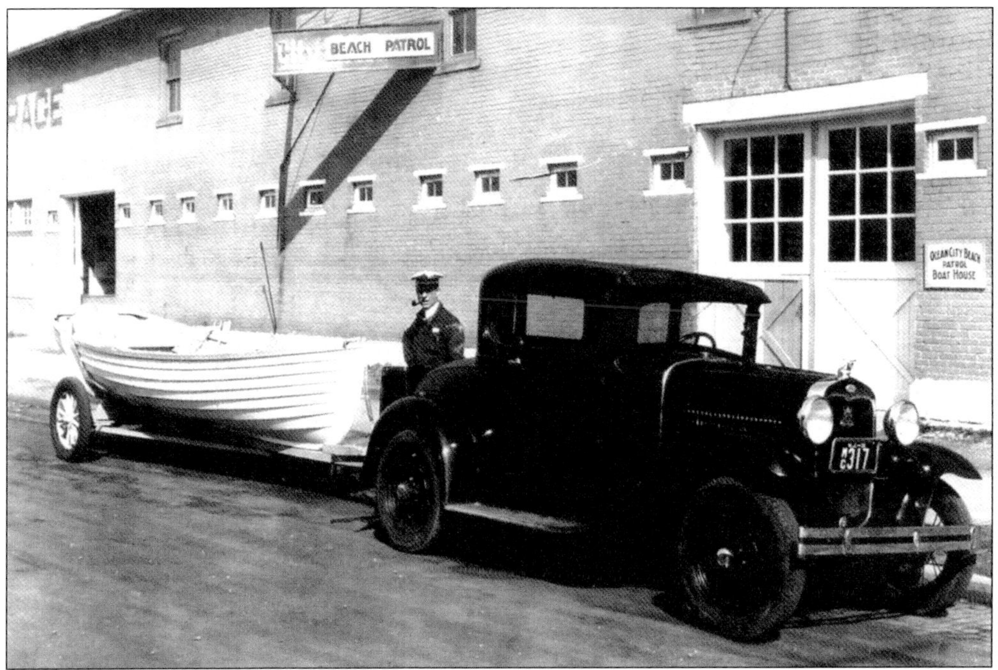

Capt. Jack Jernee hitches a lifeboat to the Ford Model A in front of the beach patrol's winter headquarters, at 7th Street and Haven Avenue, on Saturday, May 30, 1931. The lifeboat is going to the 10th Street Beach, where veteran lifeguards Harry Thorning, Ralph Clayton, and Marley Fitzgerald are stationed.

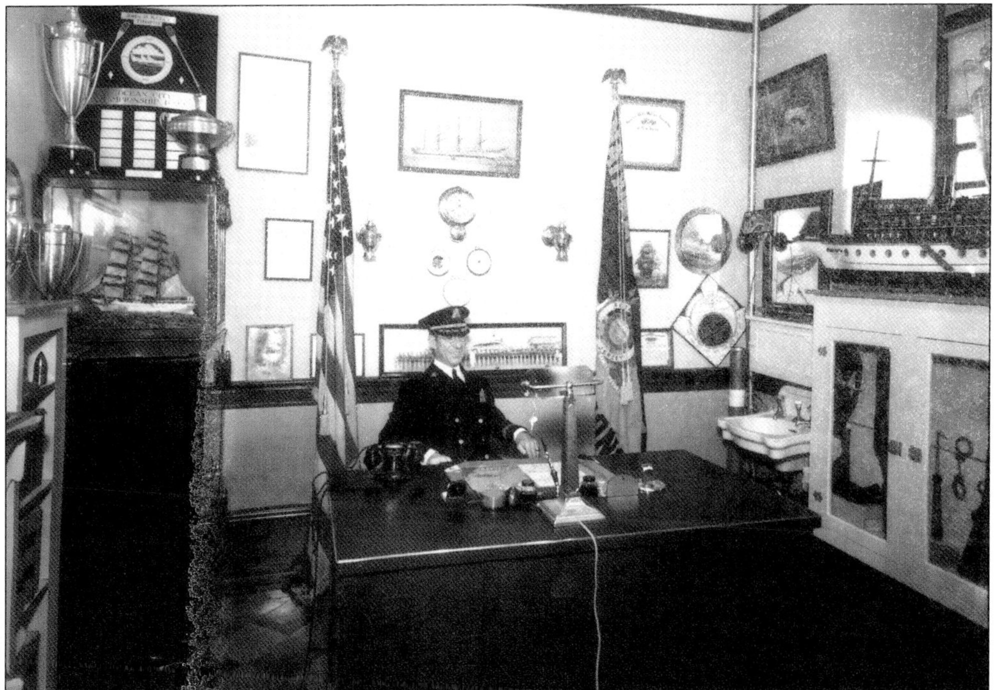

From 1933 to 1935, Jack Jernee served not only as the captain of the Ocean City Beach Patrol captain but also as the city's chief of police. Here, he sits in his office in city hall.

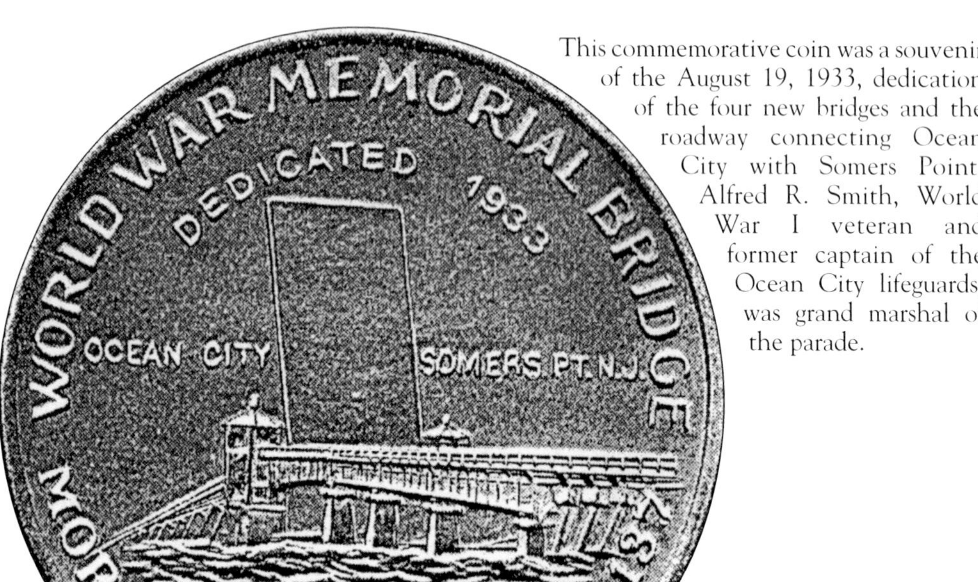

This commemorative coin was a souvenir of the August 19, 1933, dedication of the four new bridges and the roadway connecting Ocean City with Somers Point. Alfred R. Smith, World War I veteran and former captain of the Ocean City lifeguards, was grand marshal of the parade.

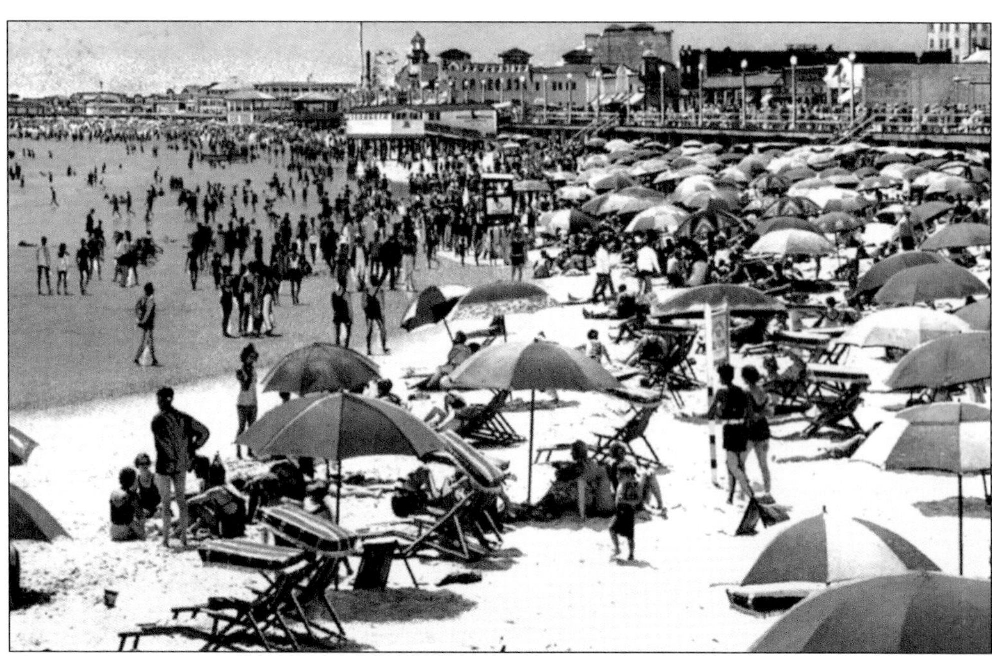

In this crowded beach scene, viewed from the Music Pier looking southward, the lifeguard stand and 10th Street headquarters can be seen. Crowds like this are still seen almost every day of the summer near the Music Pier.

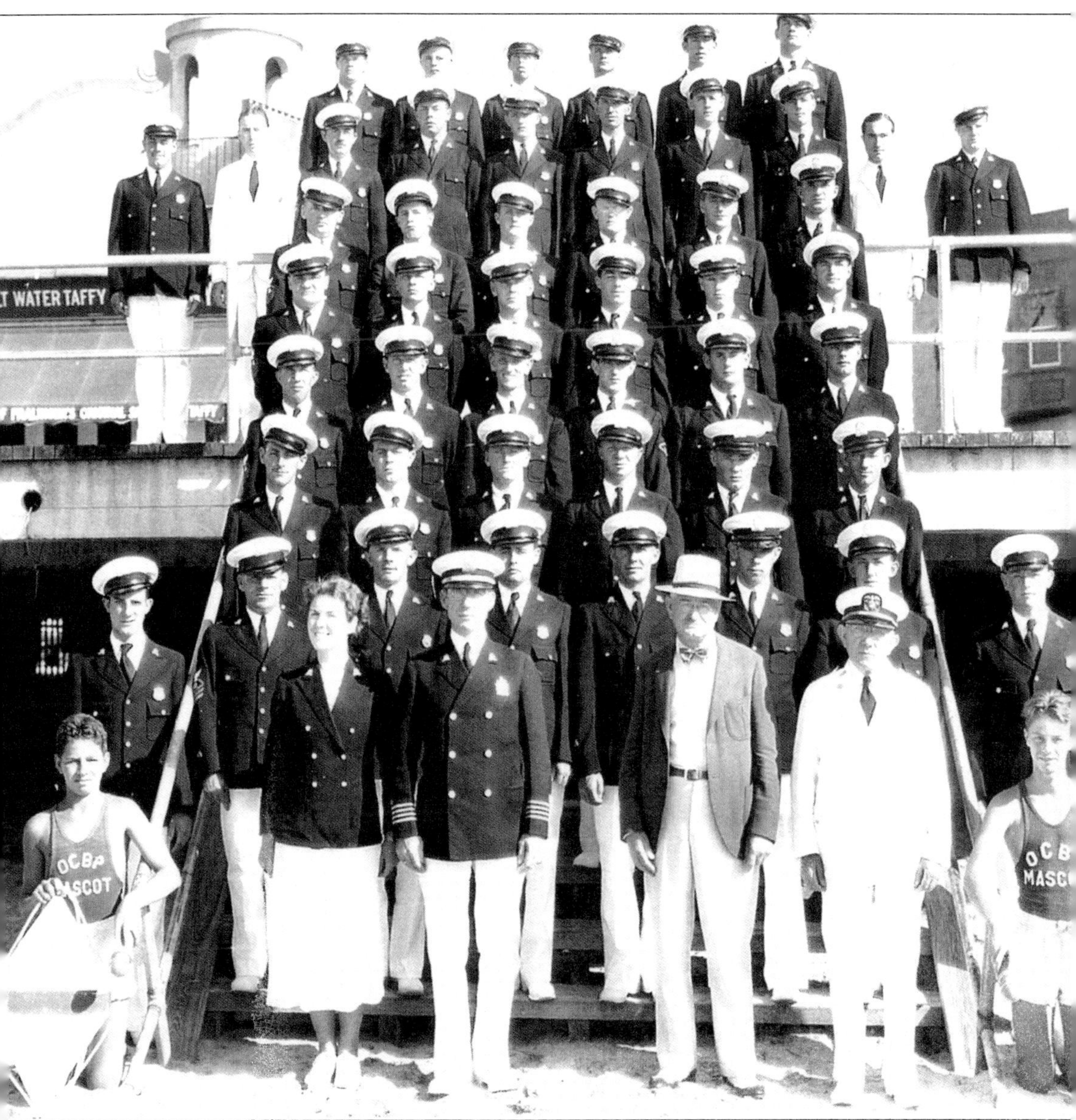

During the summer of 1933, Capt. Jack Jernee and his lifeguards wore two hats. Earlier that year, Mayor Harry Headley appointed Jernee chief of police, a position he held for three years. During the day, the lifeguards protected folks east of the Boardwalk; at night they put on their police uniforms, as shown here, and protected folks west of the beach.

Attend Ocean City's Greatest Celebration

National Life Guard Tournament Races

— Thursday, July 26th —

17 Crack Life Guard Teams to Compete For National Championship!

NATIONAL LIFE GUARD

8 TOURNAMENT EVENTS 8

Also:

BREECHES BUOY and UPSET DRILLS by U. S. Coast Guard.

ONE-MILE RACE between Coast Guard Crews for Silver Trophy.

TOM BLAKE, surf board champion of Honolulu in 1931, in demonstration of Surf Board Riding, and Rescue with Surf Board.

— OFF 10th STREET BEACH —

Tournament Events Begin at 1:30 p. m., off 10th st. Beach. Bleacher seats on Boardwalk Now on Sale, at 20c Each

Life Guard Water Circus

— IN FLANDERS POOL —

Beginning at 8 p. m.

Formal Ball

— IN FLANDERS BALL ROOM —

At 9:30 P. M.

Including FLOOR SHOW; BUFFET SUPPER AT 11 P. M.

One Ticket Admits to All

Seat on Hotel Balcony for Water Circus

(With Distinguished Visiting Guests)

Formal Ball and Buffet Supper

Tickets $2.50 Each

Many Distinguished Visitors to Attend - -

INCLUDING

Mr. and Mrs. James Roosevelt

Son and Daughterin-Law of the President

Hon. Ernest Lee Jahncke

Former Assistant Secretary of the Navy Under President Hoover

Rear Admiral H. G. Hamlet

Commander of the U. S. Coast Guards, Washington, D. C.

Hon. Harold G. Hoffman

New Jersey Commissioner of Motor Vehicles

And Many Other Prominent Figures in Civic, Military and Naval Affairs

Tickets for Bleacher Seats and Also for Evening Events Now on Sale at 10th St. Beach Headquarters and at Information Bureau, Music Pier

This is a poster from the summer of 1934, advertising the National Life Guard Tournament Races.

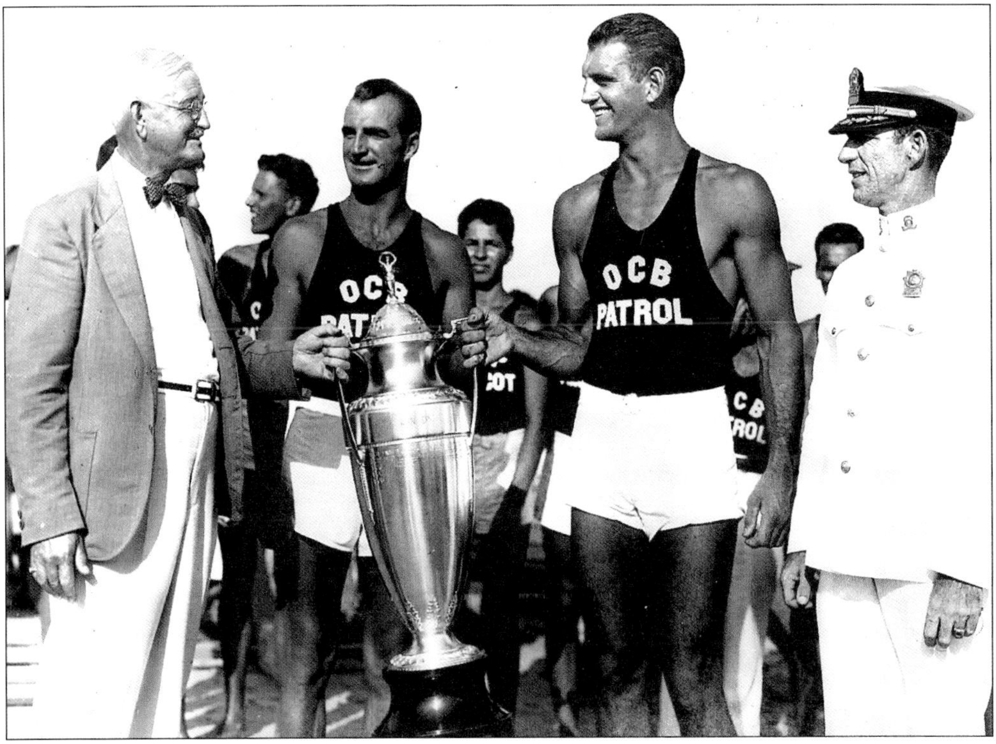

Mayor Harry Headley (left) presents the 1934 National Rowing Championship trophy to Bob Stretch (second from the left) and Bert Loeper. Capt. Jack Jernee looks on.

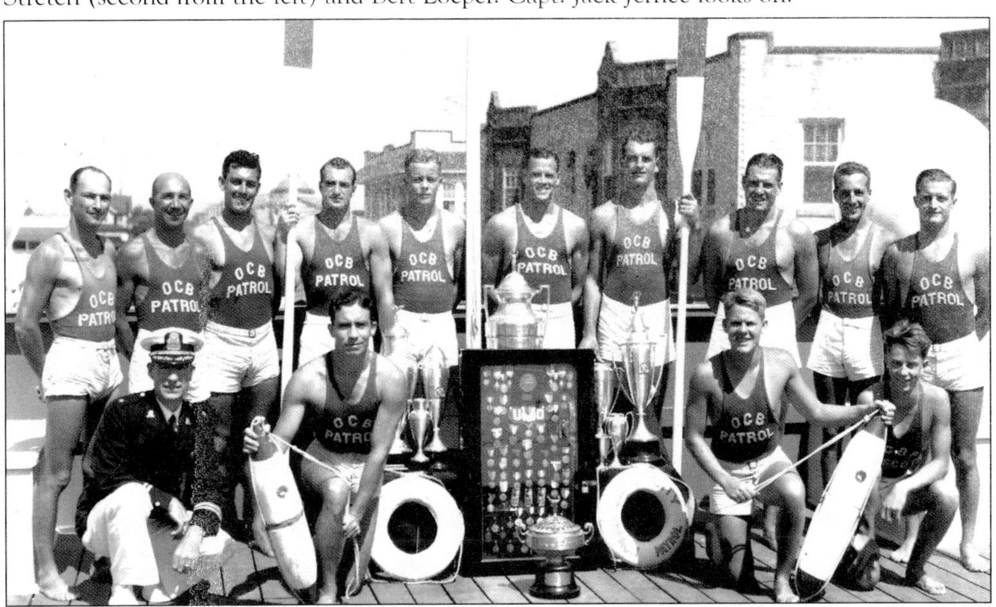

On July 26, 1934, the Ocean City lifeguards won their second straight National Lifeguard Championship. From left to right are the following: (first row) Capt. Jack G. Jernee, Ed Kelly, Howard McAdoo, and Russ Leary; (second row) Marley Fitzgerald, George Hafner, T. John Carey, Bob Stretch, Jim Dougherty, Lew Parlette, Bert Loeper, George Becker, George Dougherty, and Al Reichenbach.

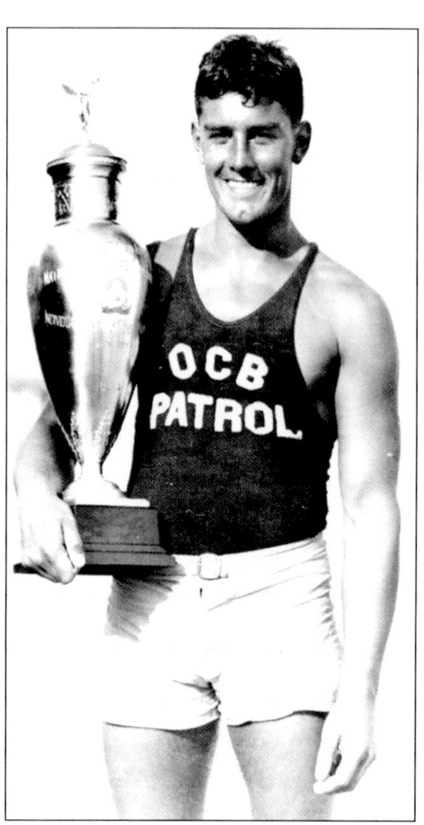

T. John Carey won the Individual National Lifeguard Championship in 1934.

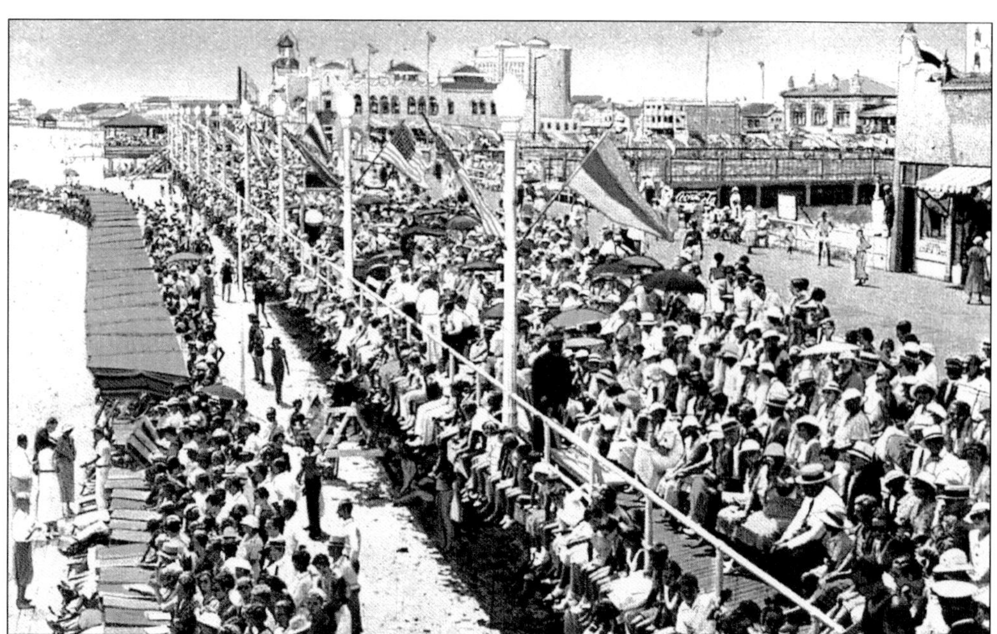

Enormous crowds lined the beach and the Boardwalk to watch the 1934 National Lifeguard Tournament.

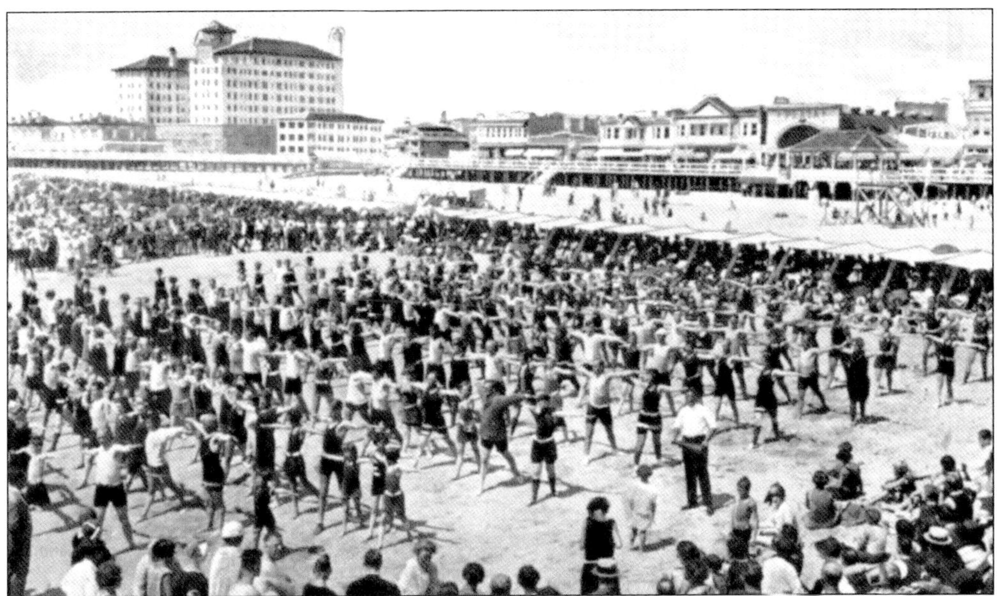

W. Ward Beam, a former member of the Ocean City Beach Patrol, started exercise classes on the beach at 10th Street in 1921.

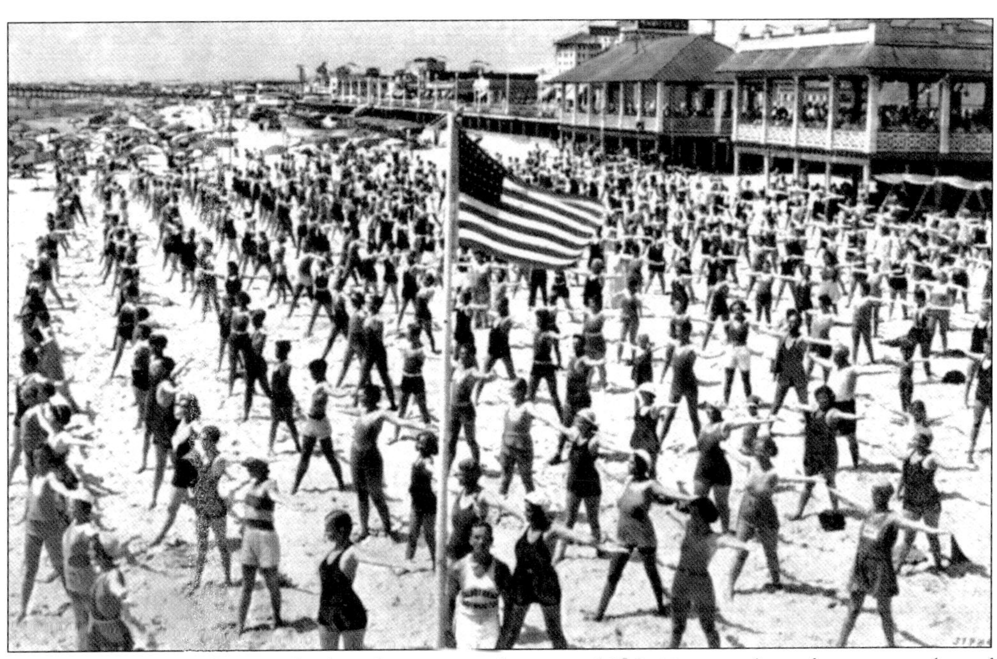

Elmer E. Unger took over the beach exercise classes in 1930. He was also a former member of the Ocean City Beach Patrol.

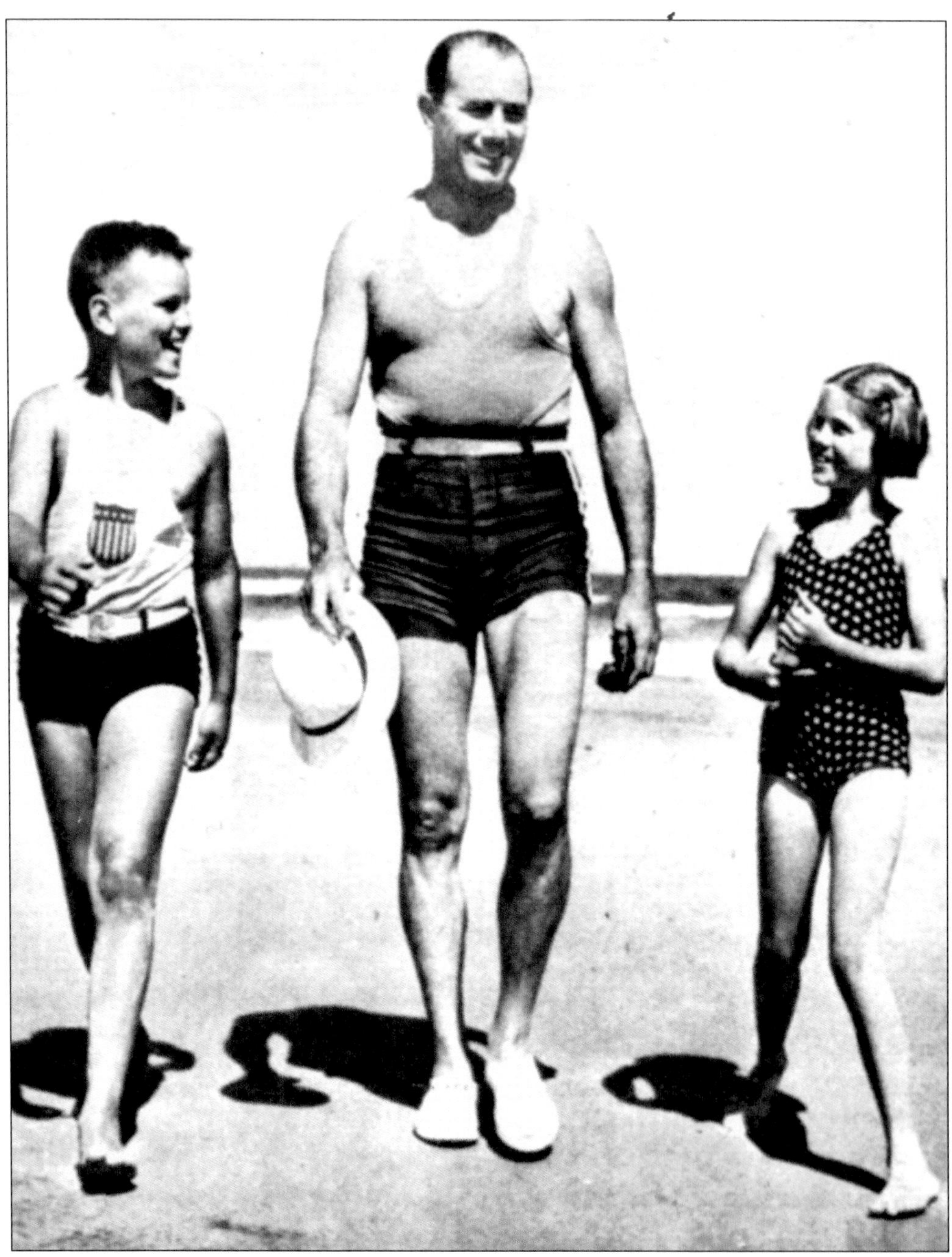

This is a picture from the front page of the July 19, 1938 *Daily Sentinel Ledger*. The caption reads, "Jack Kelly, normally Democratic leader of Philadelphia, but just a happy vacationer when in Ocean City. He spends much of his time here during the summer. The camera caught him with Jack, Jr., and Grace, his two lively children, on the beach, not far from his summer home, 2536 Wesley Avenue." John Kelly and son Jack were both inducted into the Ocean City Beach Patrol Hall of Fame. Daughter Grace Kelly became a movie star and a princess.

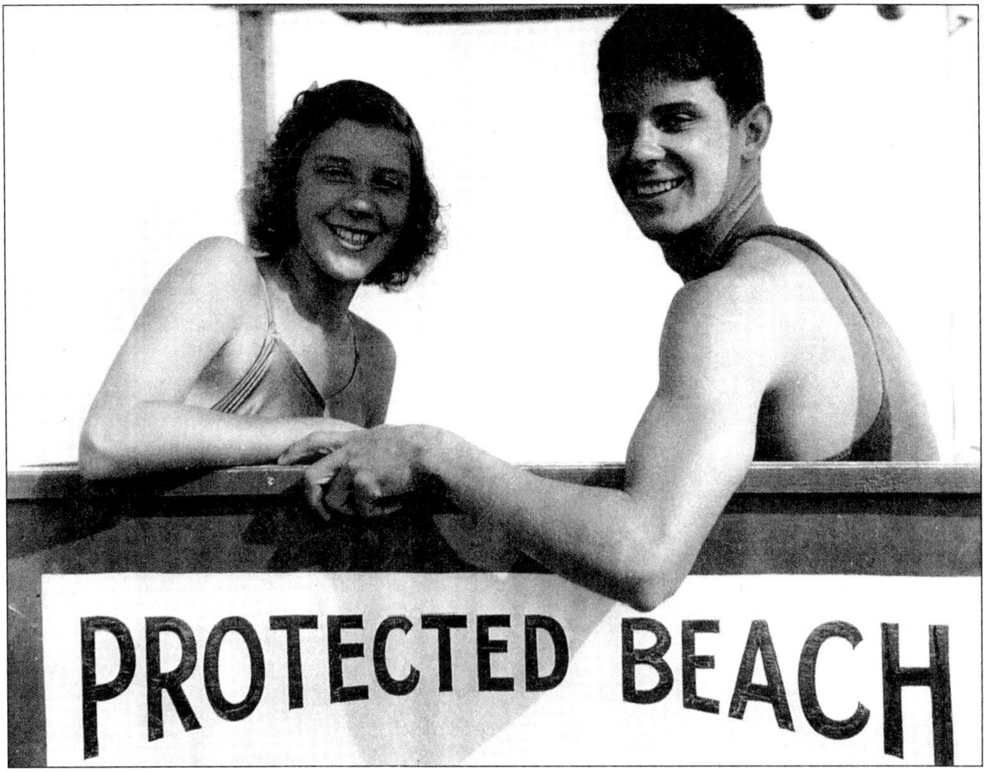

In 1938, the best brother and sister swimmers in New Jersey were Bob and Anne Monihan. It was Bob Monihan's second year on the Ocean City Beach Patrol, but his sister was not eligible since ocean lifeguarding was strictly a male profession in those days. Monihan's father, son, and grandson all served as Ocean City lifeguards.

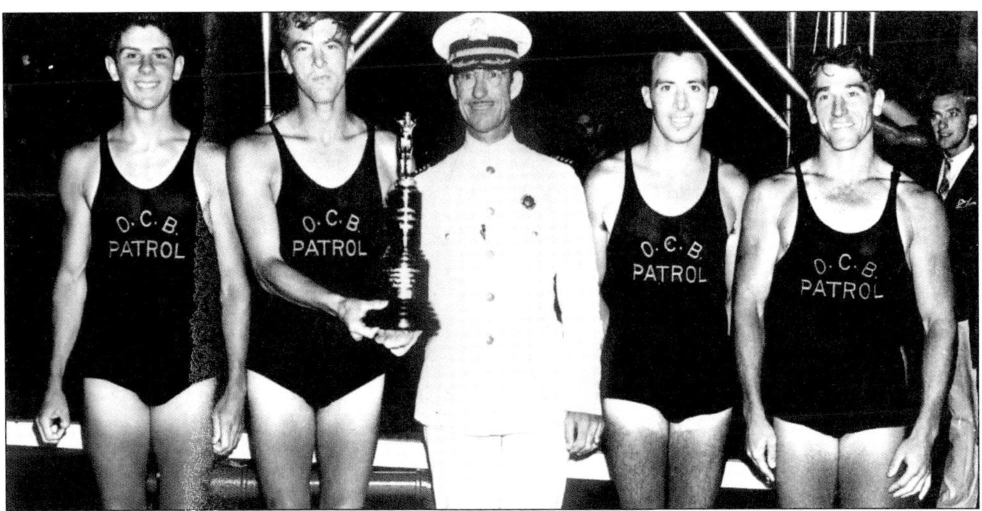

On July 15, 1938, in front of 3,000 cheering spectators at the Flanders Hotel swimming pool, the Ocean City Beach Patrol won the Atlantic Coast Relay Championship for the third year in a row. Flanking Capt. Jack Jernee are, from left to right, Bob Monihan, Reggie Kaithern, Ed Kelly, and Ed Gilbert.

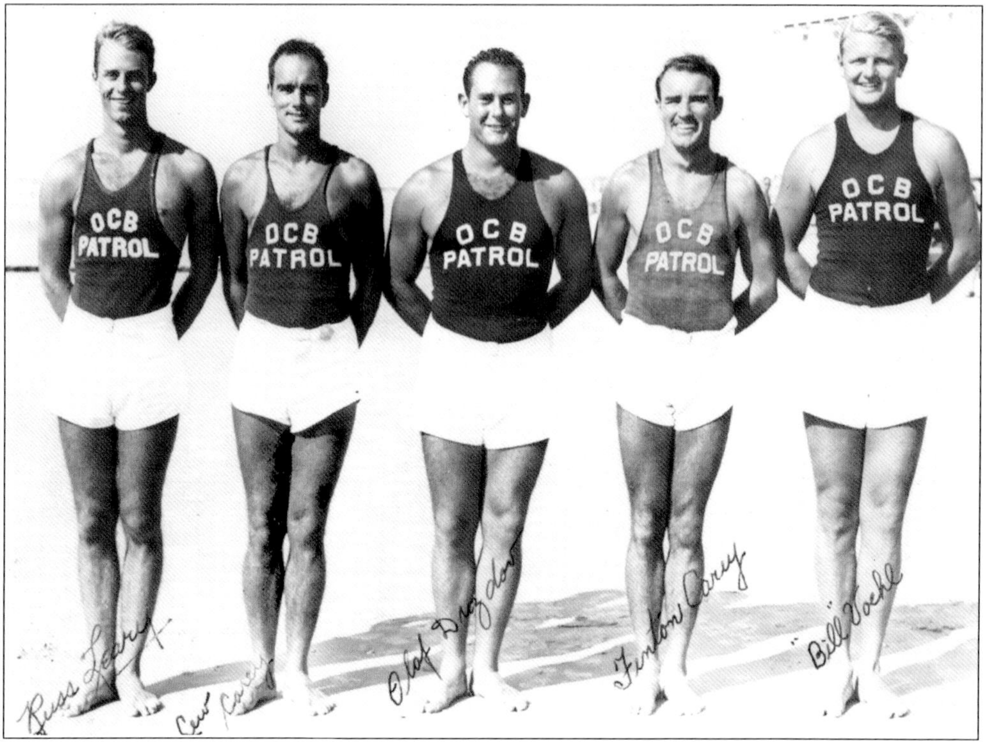

Ocean City Beach Patrol members—from left to right, Russ Leary, Lew Carey, Olaf Drozdov, Fenton Carey, and Bill Voehl—pose for the camera during the summer of 1938.

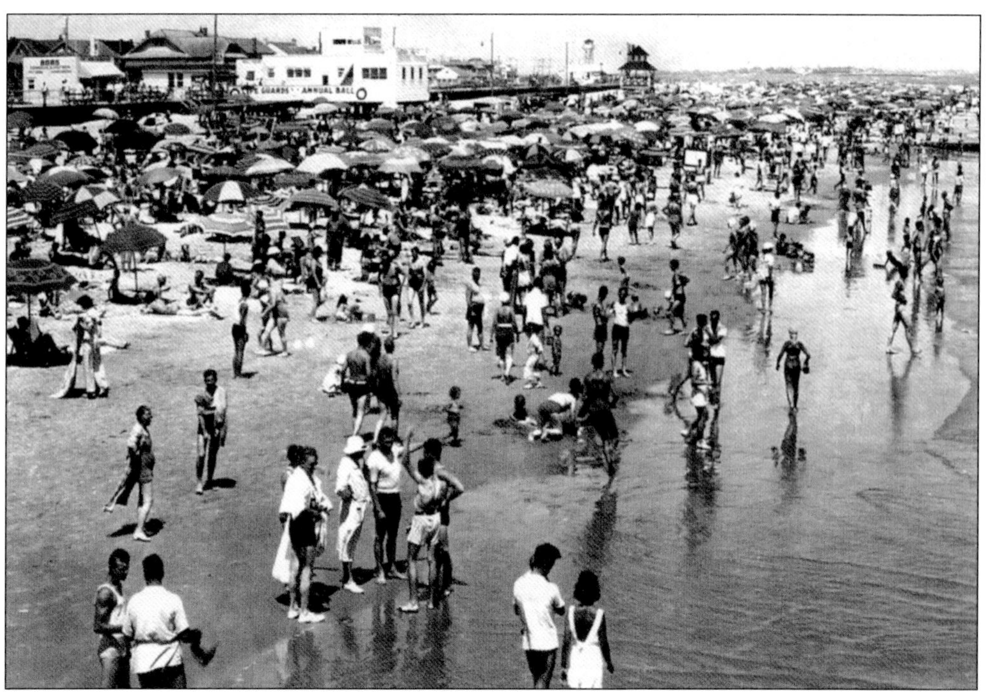

The new beach patrol headquarters on the 1st Street Beach opened for the summer of 1938.

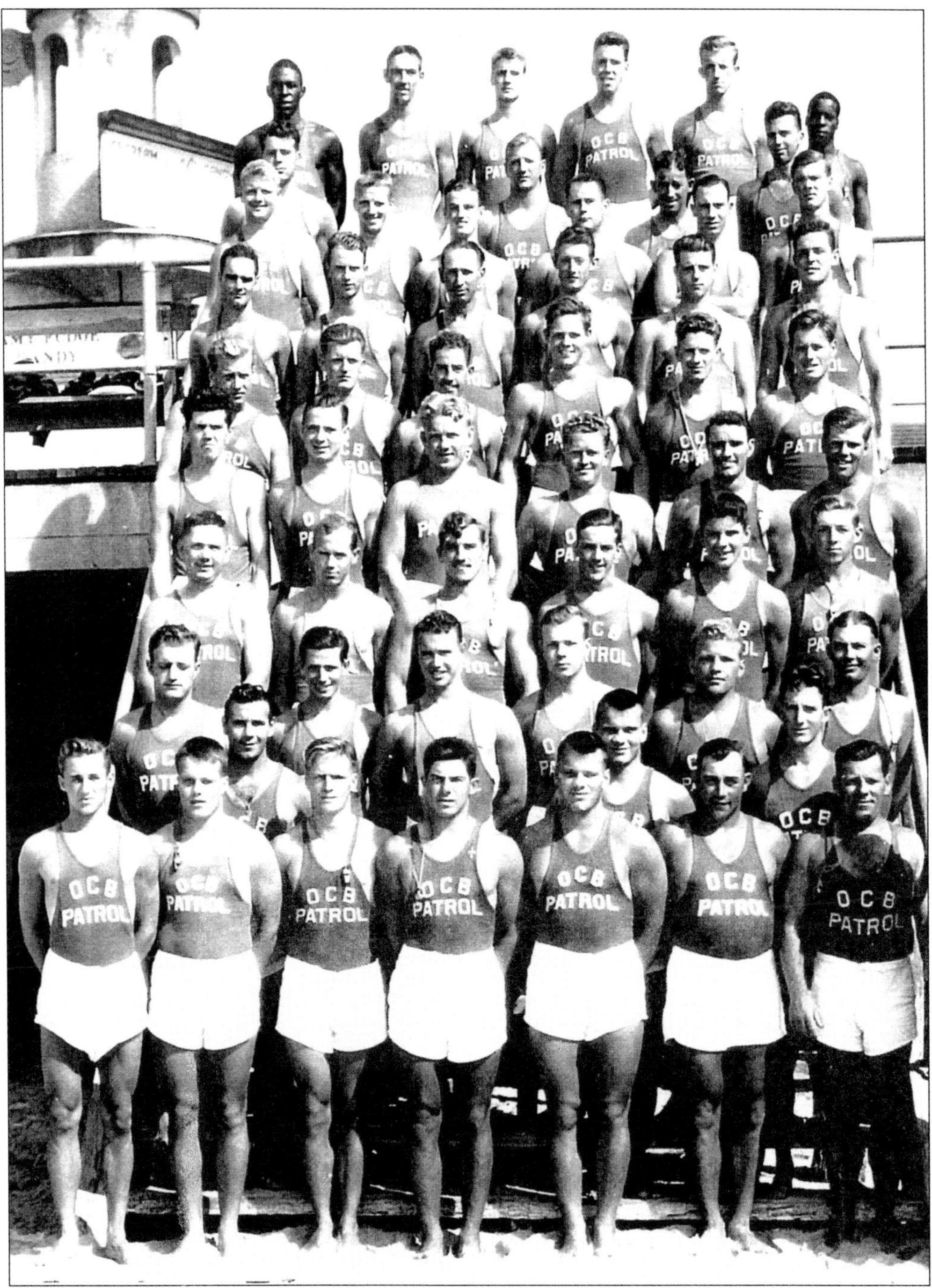

Many of the Ocean City lifeguards who were members of the 1938 squad fought in World War II. Three members, Jack Mintzer, John O'Brien, and Norman Blackman, lost their lives in the war.

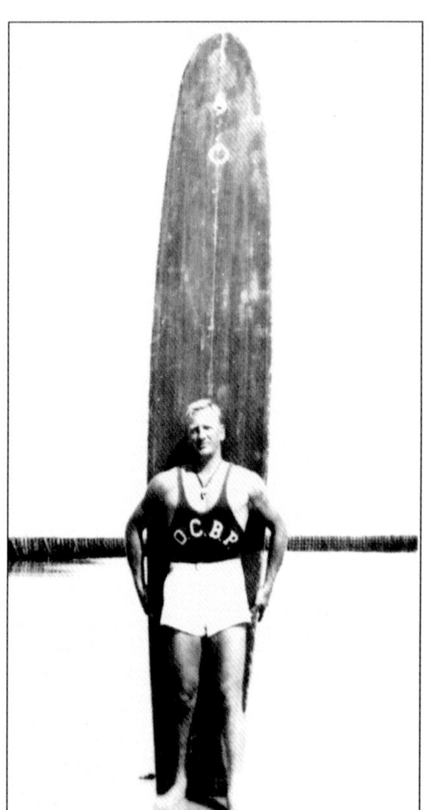

The Ocean City Beach Patrol was the first patrol on the East Coast to use surfboards as rescue equipment. In 1934, John B. Kelly bought the first board for the patrol from Tom Blake, the Hawaiian surfboard champion.

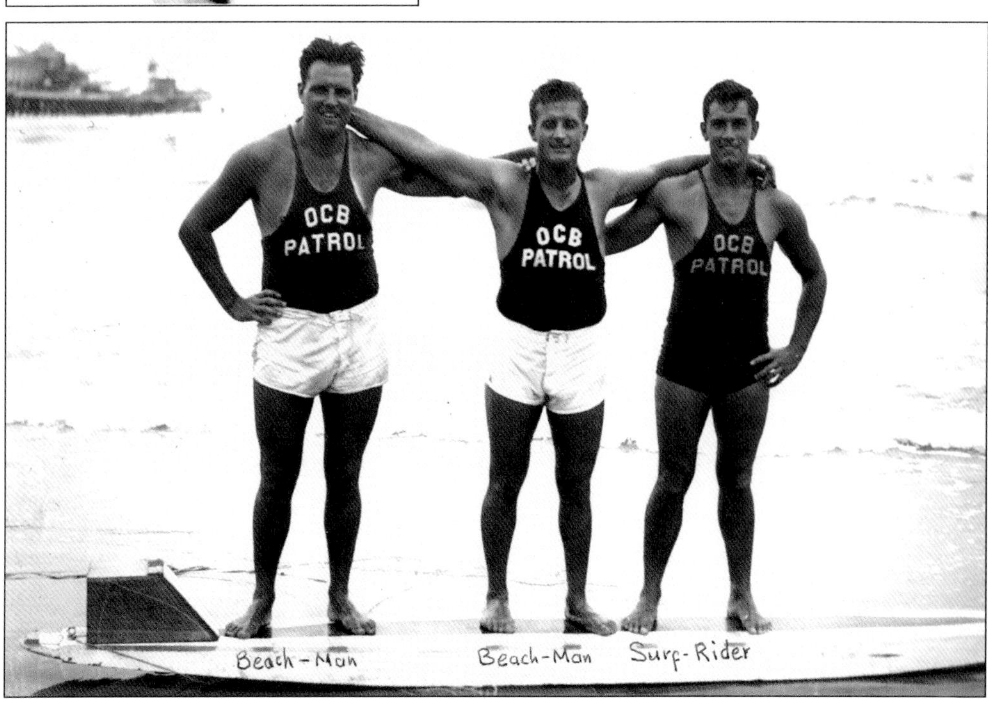

In 1936, George Becker, Al Reichenbach , and T. John Carey (left to right) were national lifeguard champions in surfboard rescue.

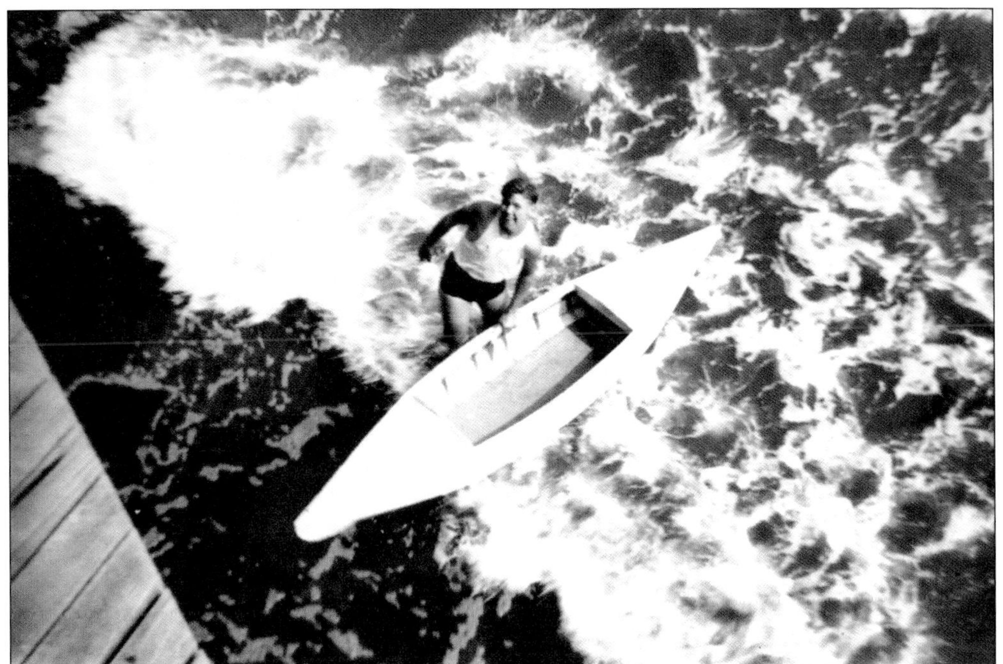

In 1940, Ocean City Beach Patrol member Ben Dungan experiments with using a kayak for ocean rescues.

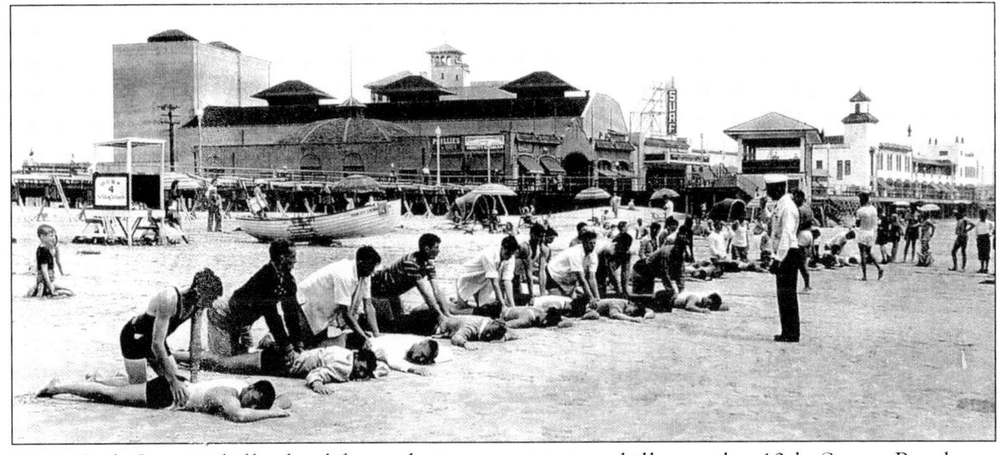

Capt. Jack Jernee drills the lifeguards in resuscitation skills on the 12th Street Beach on June 21, 1939.

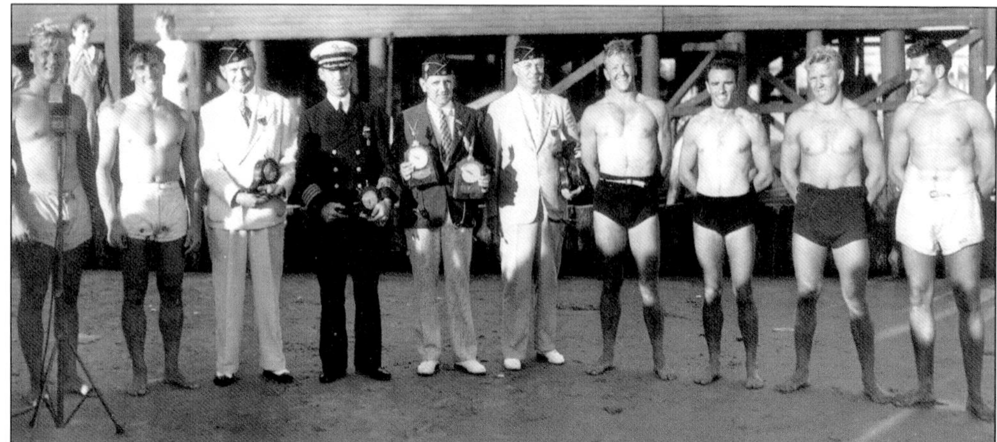

This picture was taken at the award ceremony following the 1937 Ocean City Beach Patrol doubles rowing championship. From left to right are third-place winners Lynn Streeter and Ed Gilbert, American Legionnaire John Fisher, Capt. Jack Jernee, Legionnaire Fred Spicer, public safety director George Richards, champions Bud Humphrey and Fenton Carey, and second-place finishers Stan Kelly and Al Okavage.

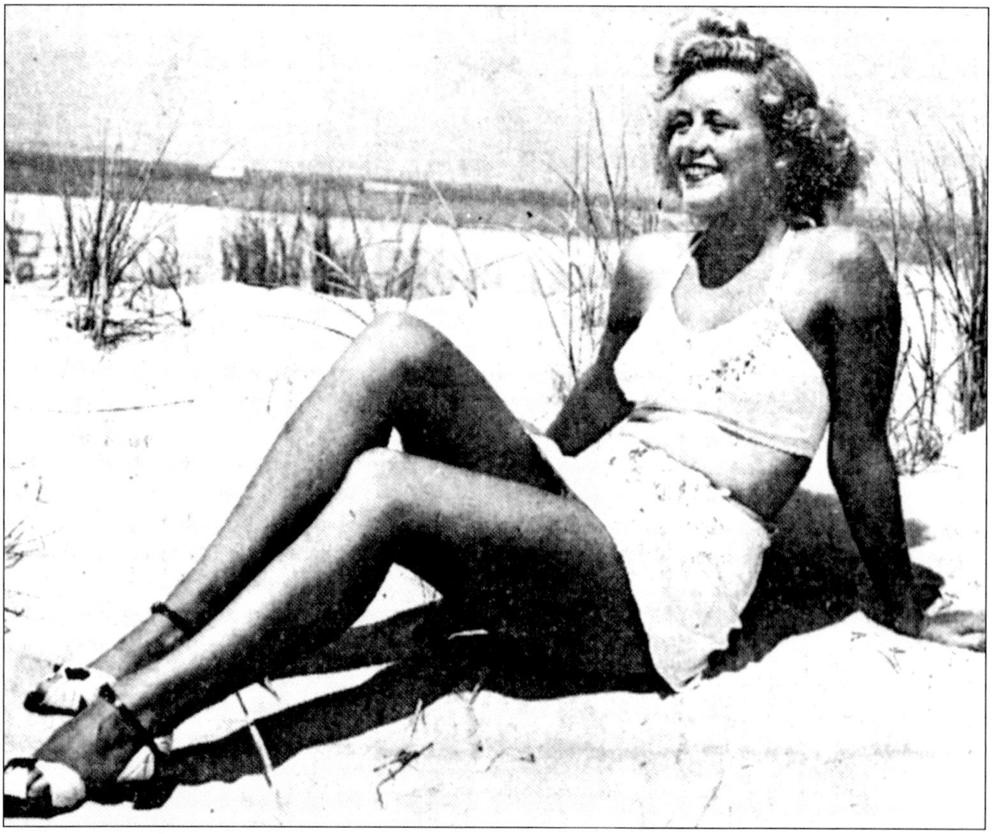

Mary Lou Smith, Miss Ocean City Beach Patrol of 1939, eloped with boxer Billy Conn the day after he lost the heavyweight championship to Joe Louis. Conn vacationed often in Ocean City and admitted that he wanted to be a lifeguard but that his boxing career would not allow it. In 1962, the couple's son, William Conn, became a member of the Ocean City Beach Patrol.

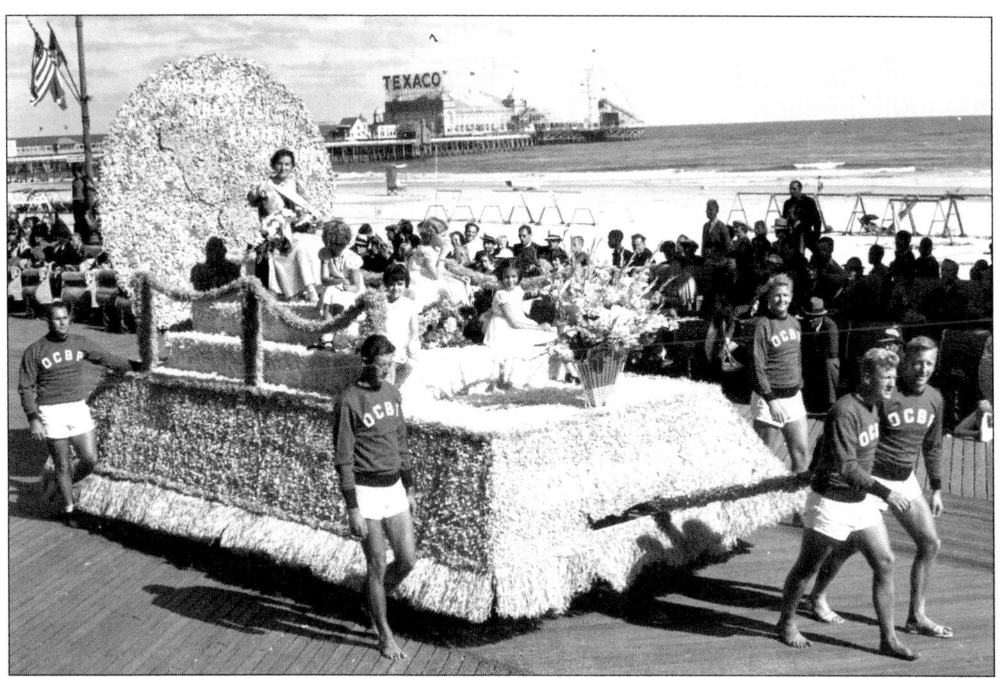

Ocean City Beach Patrol members escort the Ocean City float in the Miss America Pageant in Atlantic City in 1940.

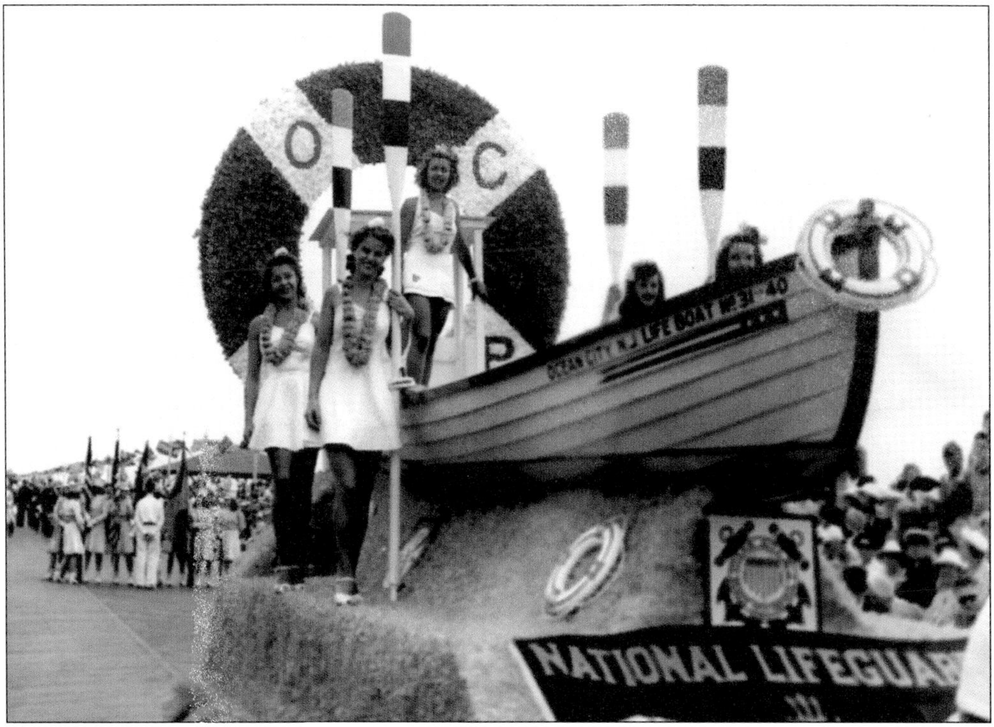

This float, celebrating the Ocean City Beach Patrol's National Lifeguard Championship teams, was in the 1941 Ocean City Baby Parade. Note the U.S. Coast Guard emblem on the front of the float.

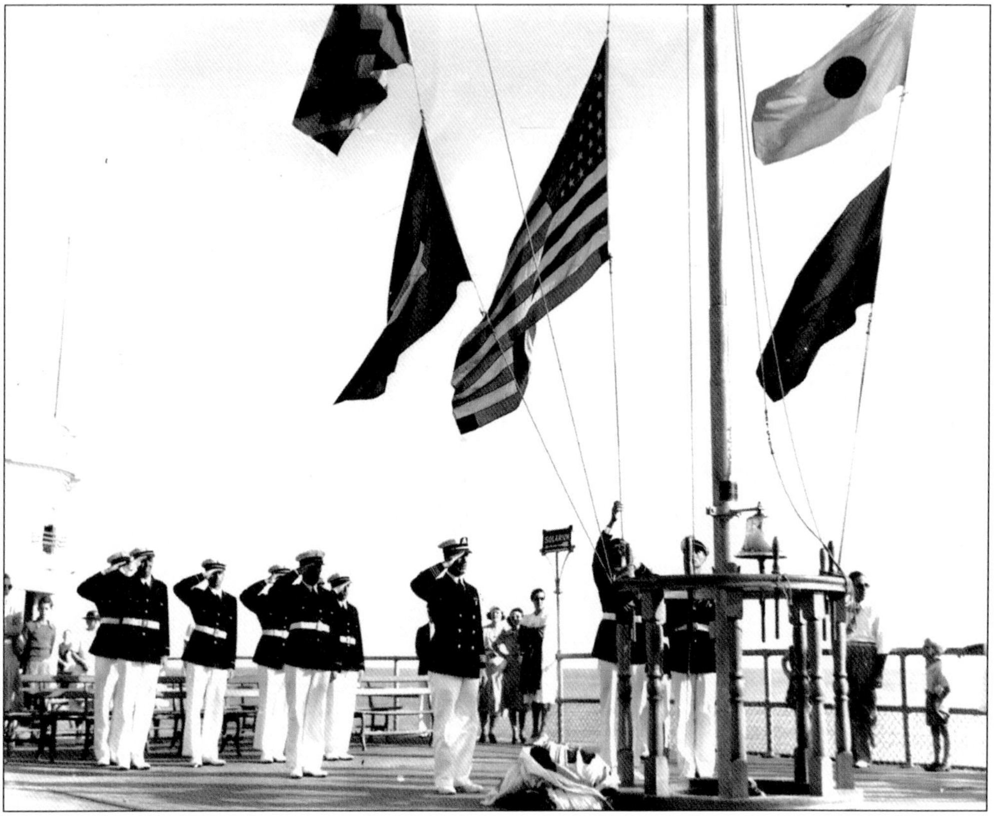

At 9:30 a.m. on July 4, 1940, Ocean City lifeguards, dressed in their ceremonial uniforms, raise the American flag and international signal code flags for the first time to the top of a newly erected 50-foot steel flagpole in front of the Music Pier.

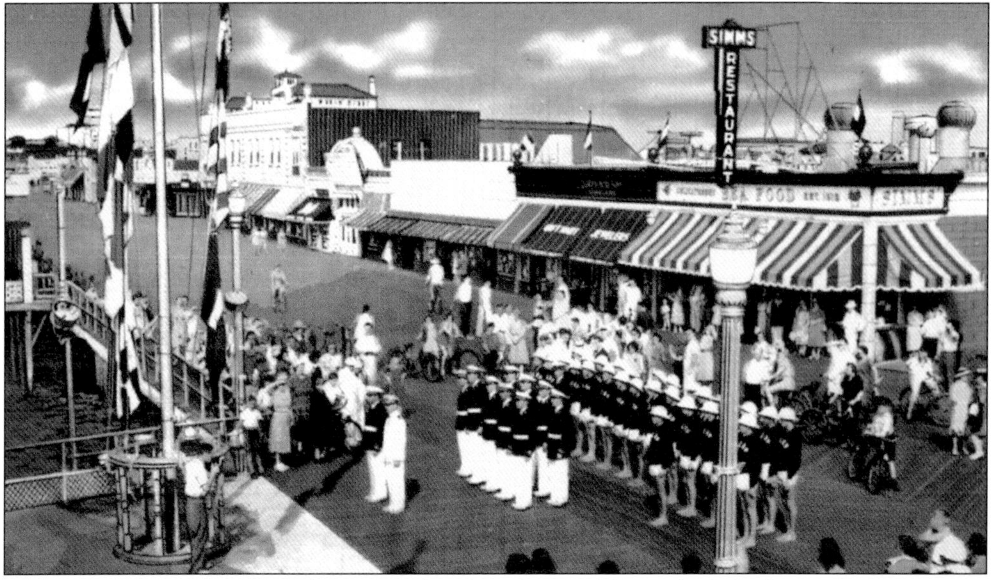

Capt. Jack Jernee salutes as a large crowd gathers for the lifeguards' daily flag-raising ceremony. This scene was popularized on many Ocean City postcards from the 1940s.

Four

The Williams Years

Thomas A. Williams became the fourth captain of the Ocean City Beach Patrol in 1942. He began his career as a lifeguard in 1922. During his tenure, the beach patrol operated under the director of public safety. The beach patrol headquarters was located at 10th Street and the Boardwalk, with other first-aid stations at 1st Street, 14th Street, and 32nd Street. Along with the captain and guards, there were also one or two lieutenants, a physician, two nurses, and two first-aid attendants.

Williams reestablished the South Jersey Lifeguard Championship in 1944, with the help of John B. Kelly Sr. The championship, a one-mile, doubles rowing race between beach patrol teams from 10 seaside resorts, was first held in 1924 and is considered the most prestigious of the lifeguard races. In 1945, a half-mile swim was added, and in 1973, a singles row. Williams also reestablished the South Jersey Lifeguard Swim Meet. He had the beach patrol participate in numerous other rowing and swimming competitions, believing that the skills they practiced for the races were the same skills they needed on the job, and that their prowess in these competitions enhanced the beach patrol's reputation.

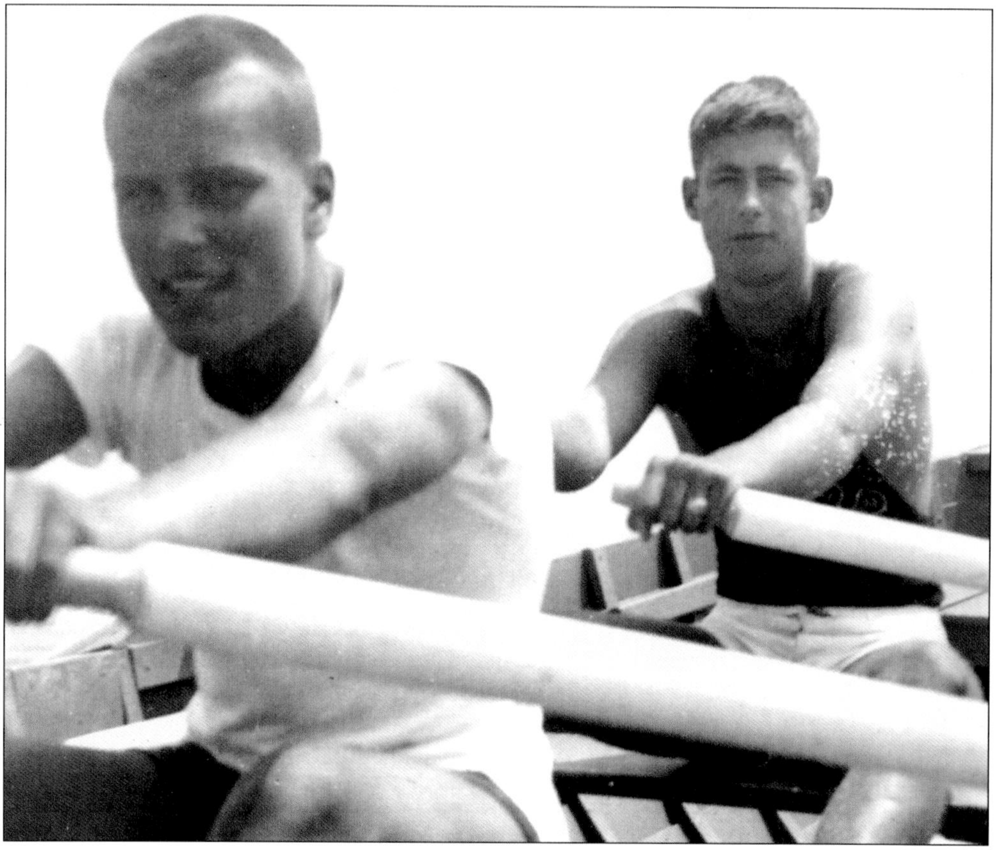

Jack Kelly Jr. (left)and Sims Drain won the Ocean City Beach Patrol doubles rowing championship during the summer of 1943.

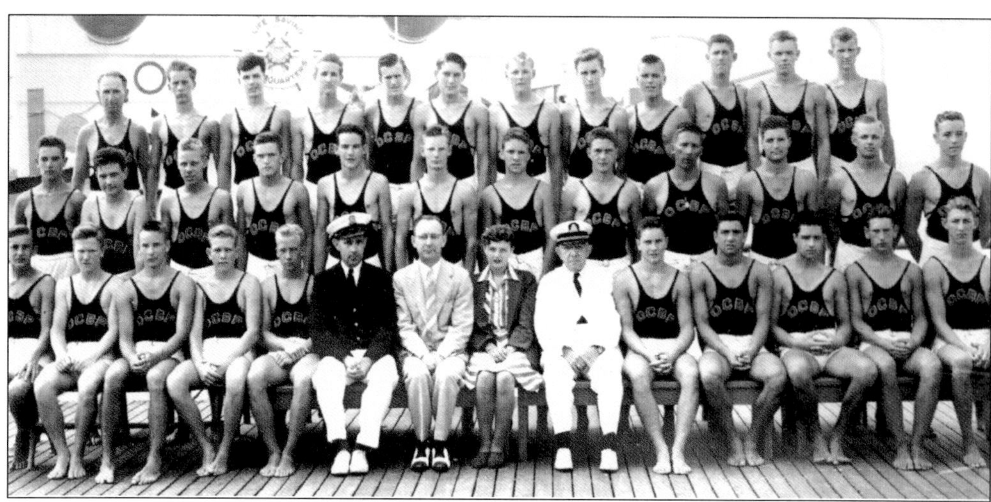

Pictured with the 1943 Ocean City Beach Patrol in the center of the first row are, from left to right, Capt. Tom Williams, Mayor Clyde W. Struble, an unidentified woman, and Dr. Willets Haines. In 1943, many lifeguards were in the military service in World War II and the number of protected beaches was smaller than usual.

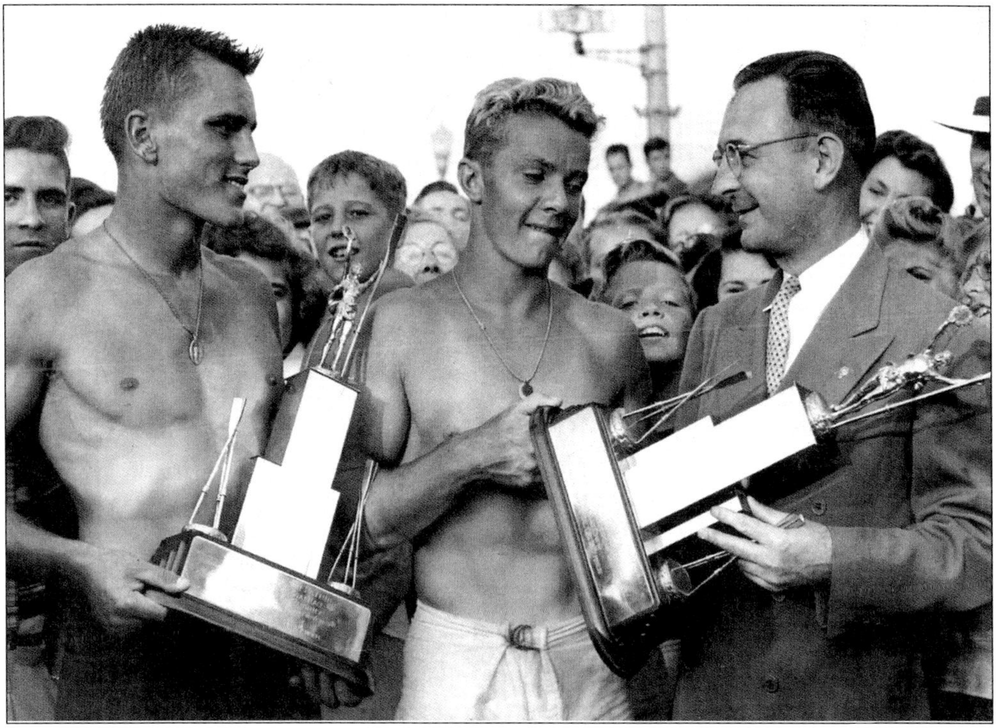

Clyde W. Struble, mayor of Ocean City, presents the Ocean City Beach Patrol doubles rowing championship trophies to Jack Kelly Jr. (left) and Joe Regan on August 18, 1944.

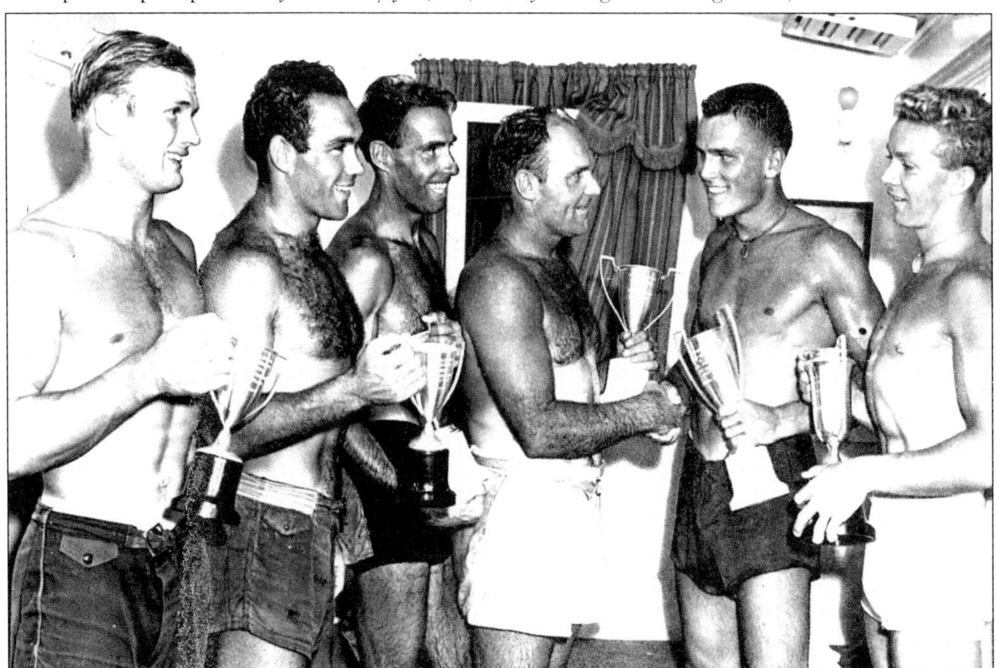

Place winners from Wildwood and Atlantic City congratulate the winners of the 1944 South Jersey Lifeguard Championship, Ocean City's Jack Kelly Jr. (second from the right) and Joe Regan (right).

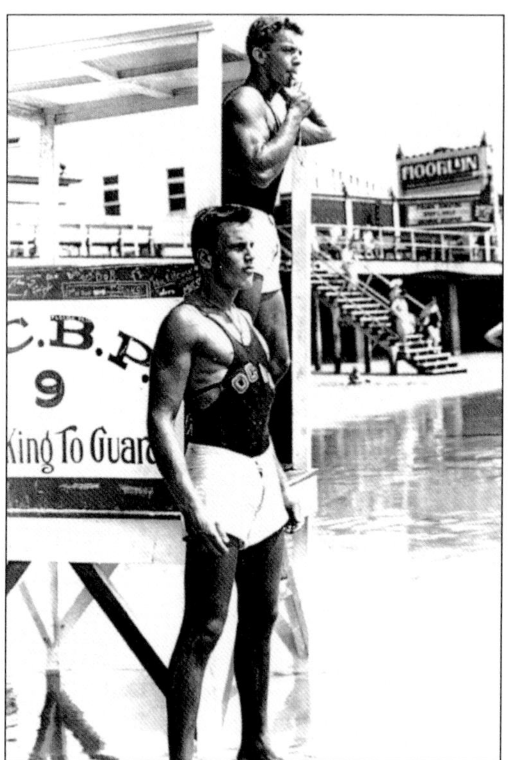

The 1944 spring edition of the *Ocean City Sentinel-Ledger* had this picture of Jack Kelly Jr. (left) and Joe Regan.

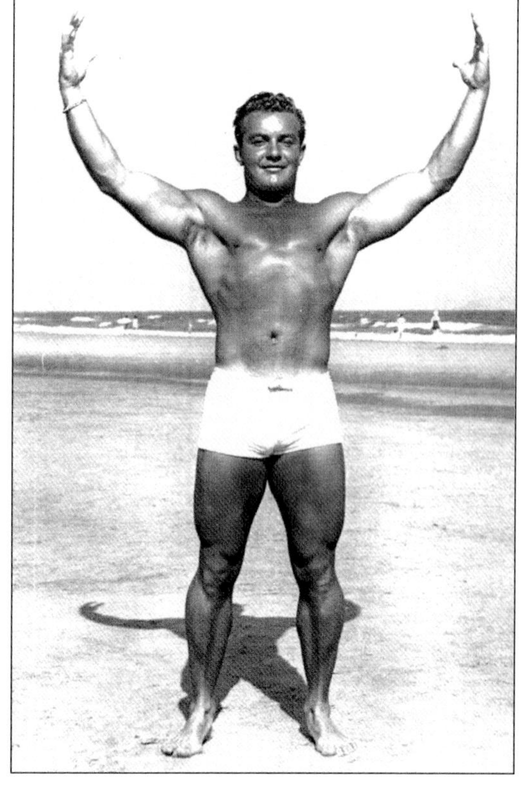

Ocean City Beach Patrol member Joe Regan, who was "Mr. Philadelphia," gained local notoriety in April 1945 when he became the first bather of the season to be arrested for not having a top on his bathing suit. He had already been warned to comply with the city ordinance against exposed torsos and was fined $5 for his transgression. Signs on the lifeguard stands in those days read, "No Ball Playing" and "No Topless Bathing."

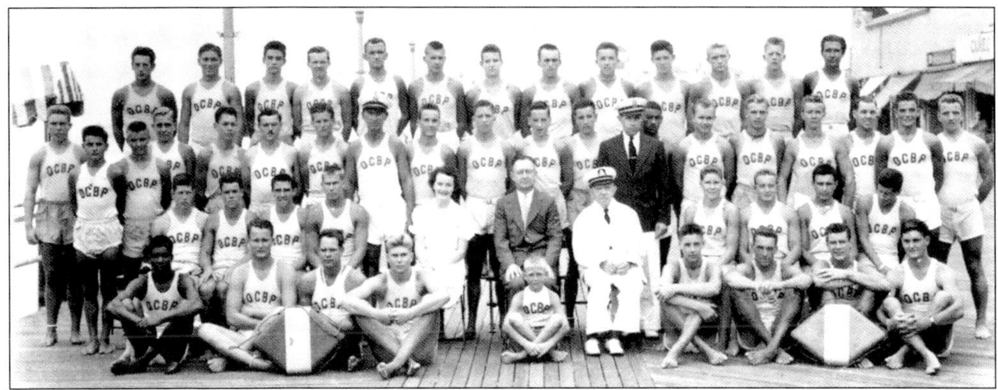

Among those pictured in this 1945 Ocean City Beach Patrol photograph are the following: (second row) Mayor Clyde W. Struble (in a suit) and beach surgeon Dr. Willets P. Haines (next to the mayor); (third row) Lt. Charles "Bake" Schock (in a lifeguard uniform with a hat) and Capt. Tom Williams (in the dark jacket). This was the only year the Ocean City Beach Patrol members were outfitted in white uniforms. They realized how difficult it was to keep the white uniforms clean, and the next year they were back in red and blue.

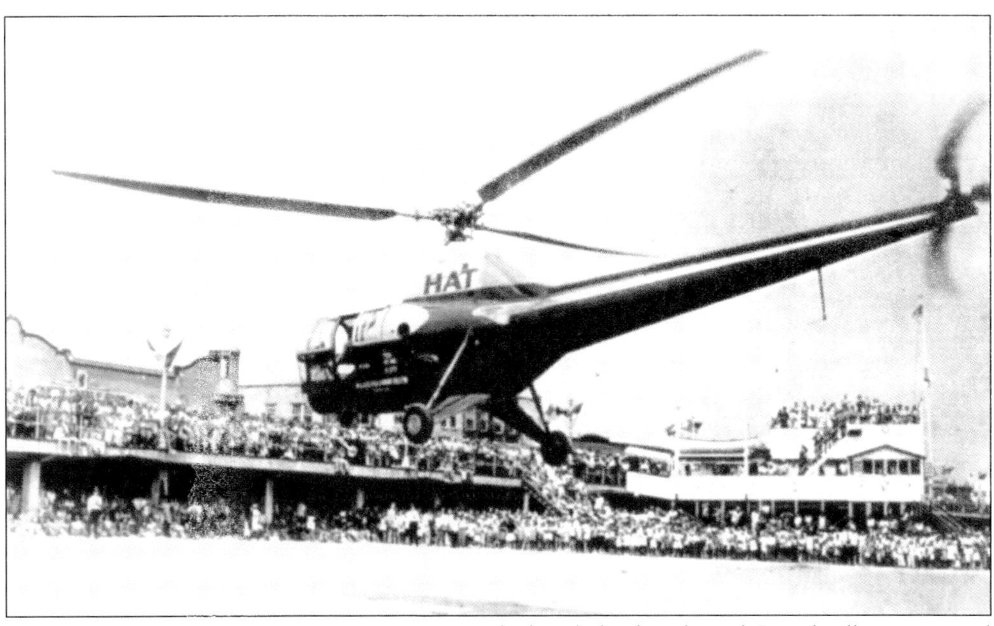

On August 14, 1946, more than 10,000 people lined the beach and Boardwalk near patrol headquarters at the 10th Street Beach to watch the lifeguards perform a simulated rescue using a helicopter. It was the first time in flight history such a feat was attempted.

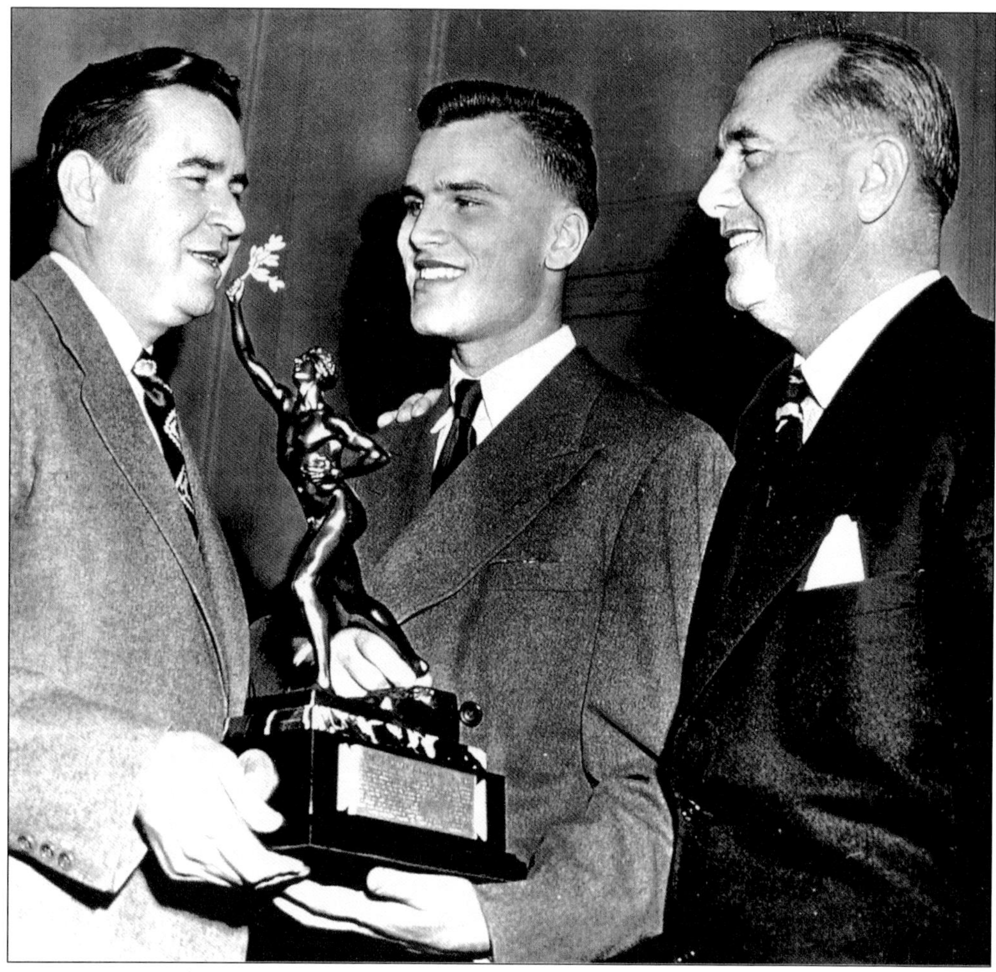

Ocean City Beach Patrol member Jack Kelly Jr. (center) accepts the 1947 James E. Sullivan Award from James A. Rhodes, president of the Amateur Athletic Union. John B. Kelly looks on proudly. The James E. Sullivan Award is given to America's top amateur athlete every year.

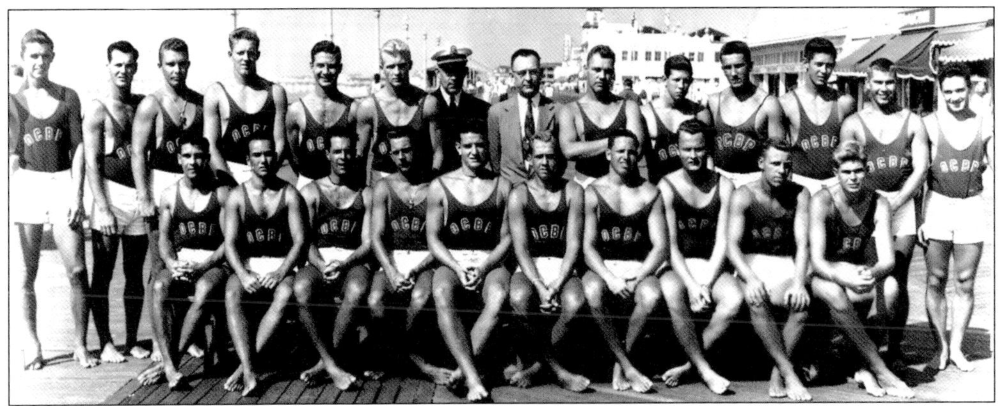

These Ocean City Beach Patrol members competed in the 1947 one-mile doubles rowing championship. From left to right are the following: (first row) Jacques Moore, Dave Lupton, James "Butch" Macallister, Frank Schiesser, Bruce Parker, Bob Harbaugh, Bill Potterton, Jack O'Donnell, George Buchanan, and Charles Turner; (second row) Jay Seibert, Tom Mulhern, Bill Spence, John McCutcheon, Jim Haines, Lou Woyce, Capt. Tom Williams, Mayor Clyde W. Struble, John Doerr, John Taylor, George "Spike" Beitzel, Les Taylor, George Weissberg, and Jim Sunstrom. Beitzel and Taylor won the championship.

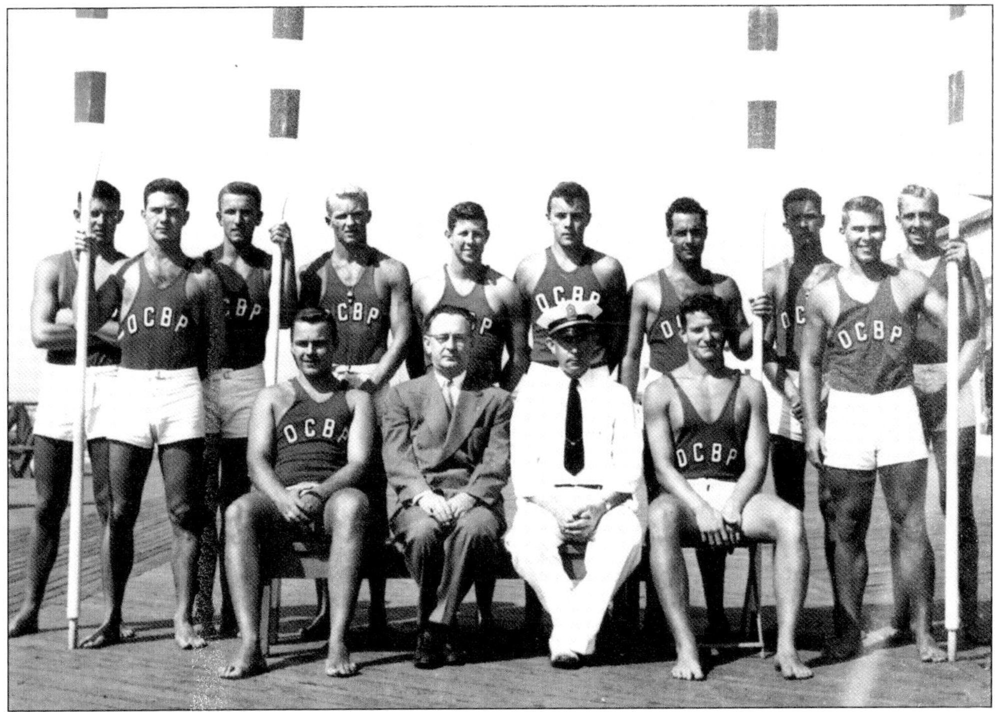

The 1948 Ocean City Beach Patrol competition team placed third in the National Lifeguard Championship and won the Margate Memorial Lifeguard Championship. At Margate, Bob Harbaugh won the singles rowing race, and Jim Macallister and Frank Schiesser took second in the doubles lifeboat race. From left to right are the following: (first row) Dave Lupton, Mayor Clyde W. Struble, Capt. Tom Williams, and Bruce Parker; (second row) Les Taylor, Jim Haines, George Beitzel, Lou Woyce, John Taylor, Joe Myers, Jim Macallister, Frank Schiesser, George Weissberg, and Bob Harbaugh.

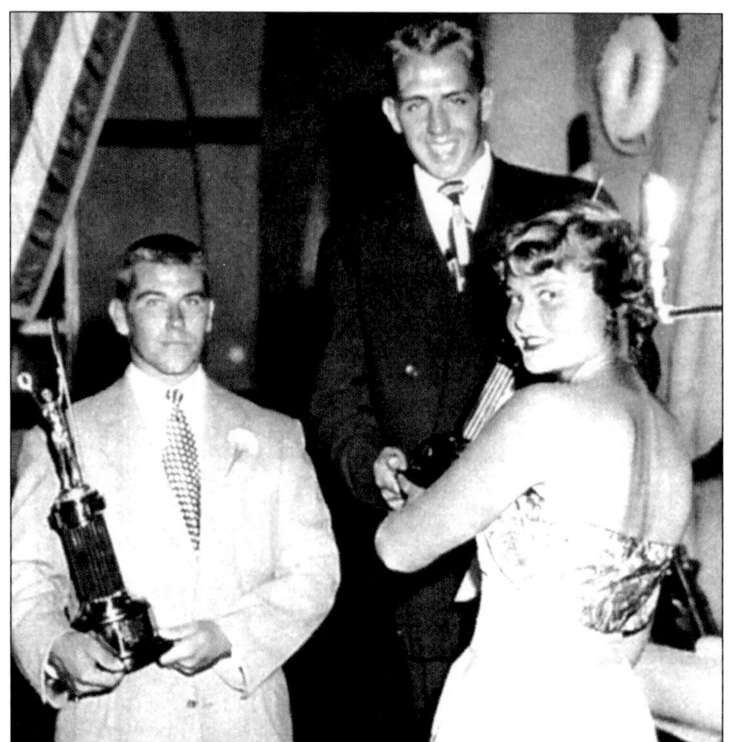

Lizanne Kelly, younger sister of Olympian Jack Kelly and actress Grace Kelly, presented the Kelly awards to George Weissberg (left) and Bob Harbaugh at the 1949 annual Lifeguard Ball.

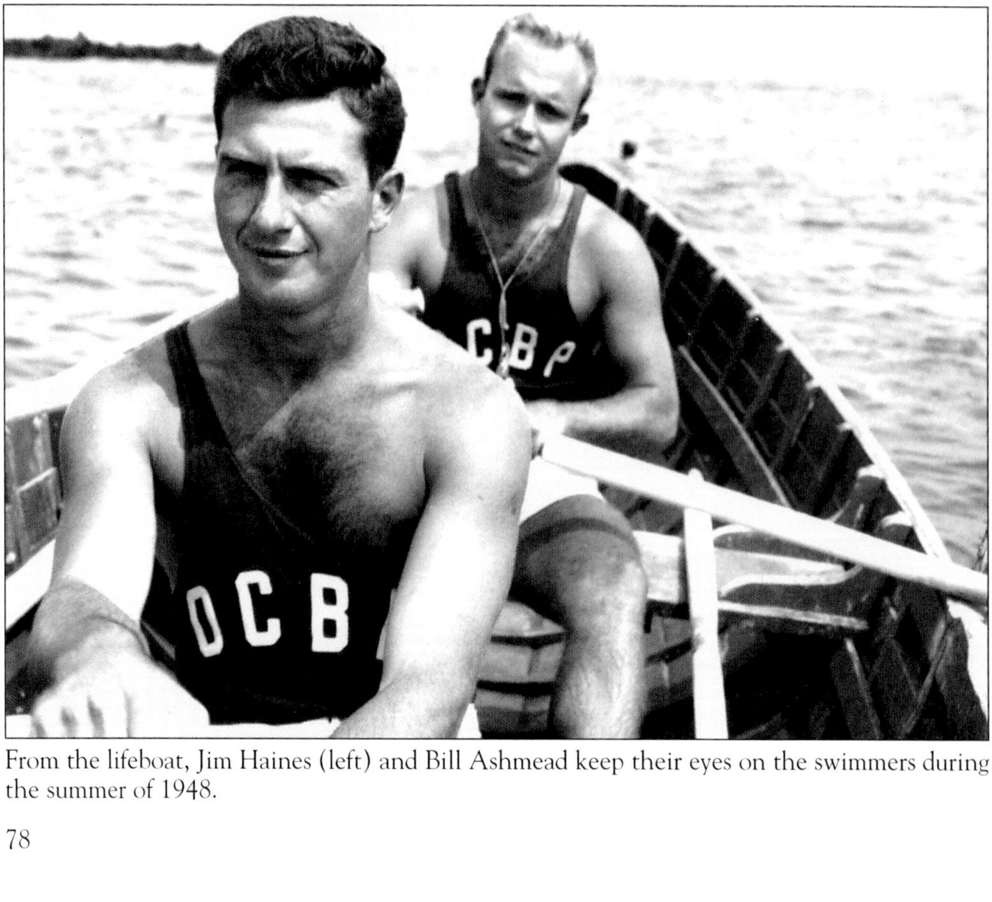

From the lifeboat, Jim Haines (left) and Bill Ashmead keep their eyes on the swimmers during the summer of 1948.

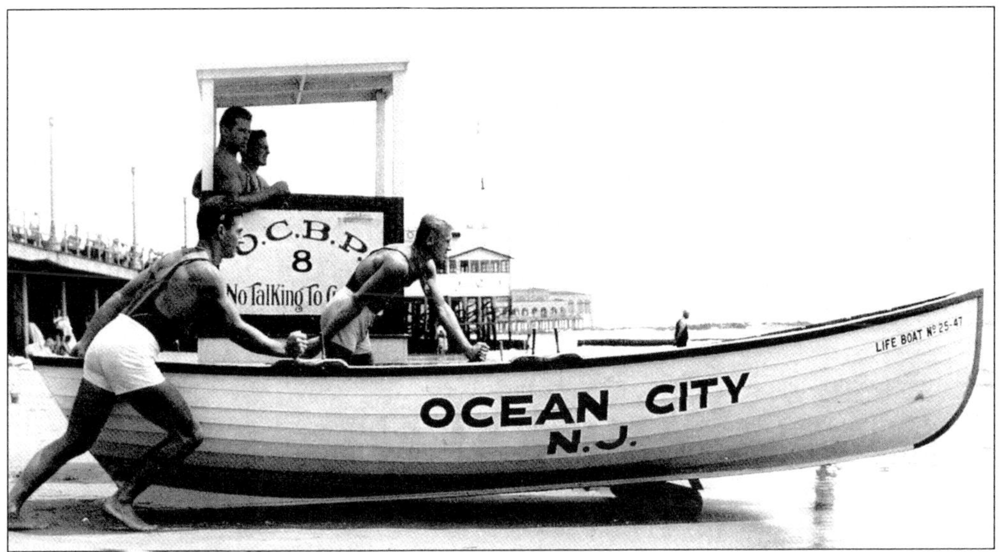

In 1947 on the 10th Street Beach, Jim Haines (left) and Lou Woyce push the lifeboat toward the surf, while Dick Malley (left) and Joe Sweeney watch bathers from the stand.

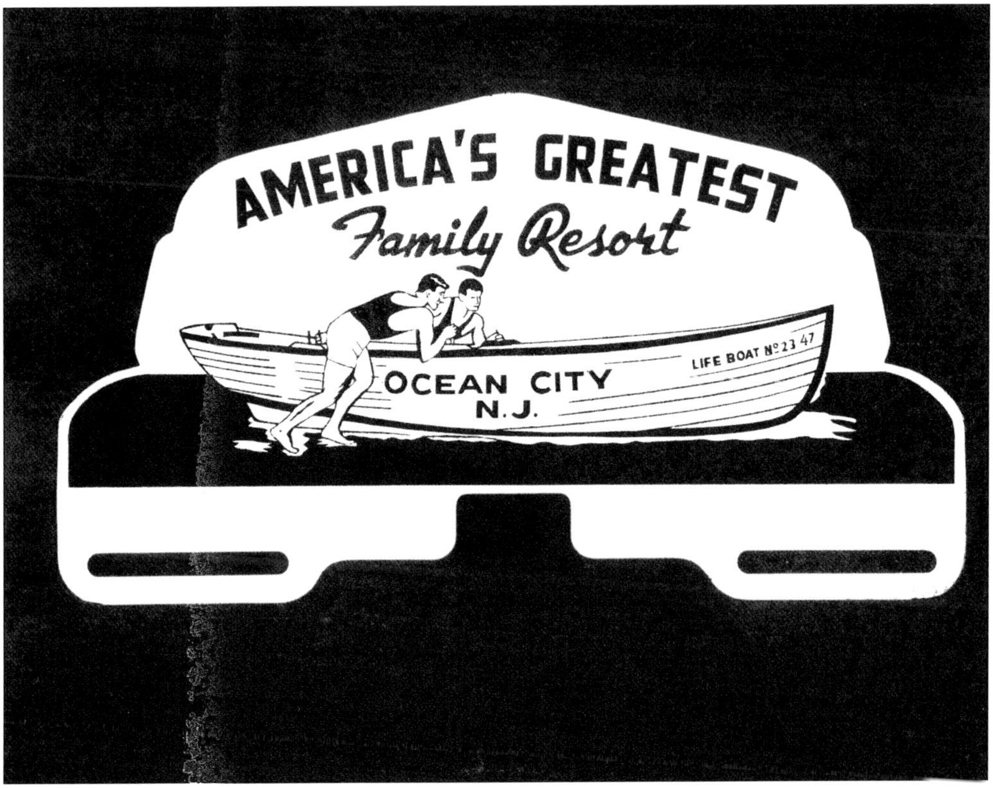

This 1947 license plate attachment bears a lifeboat with a number ending in 47.

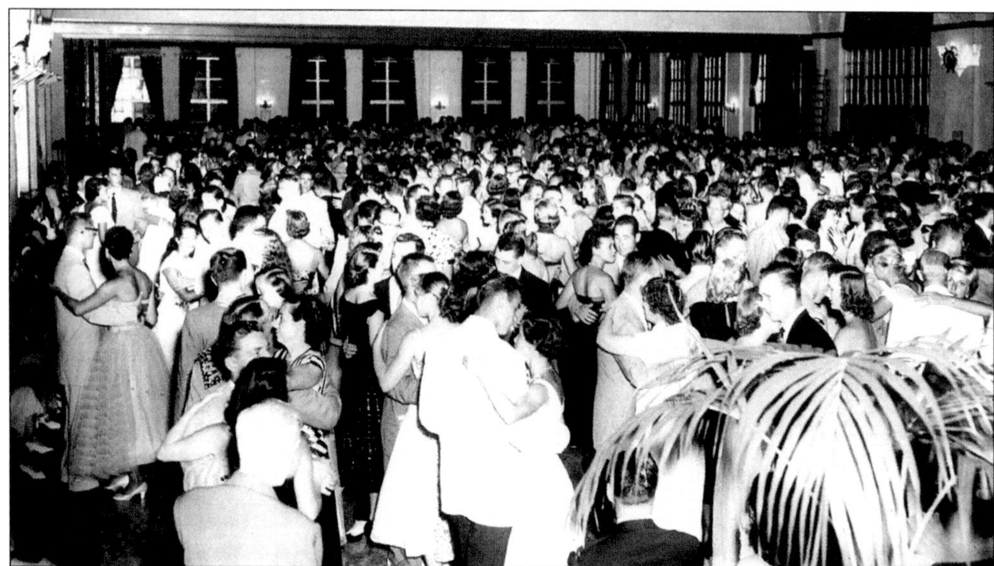

The social event of the summer of 1950 was the annual Lifeguard Ball, held at the Music Pier on August 25. More than 1,000 people danced to the music of Clarence Fuhrman and His Rhythmaires. A highlight of the evening was the presentation of an engraved wristwatch to Lt. Charles "Bake" Schock for his 41 years of dedicated service to the Ocean City Beach Patrol.

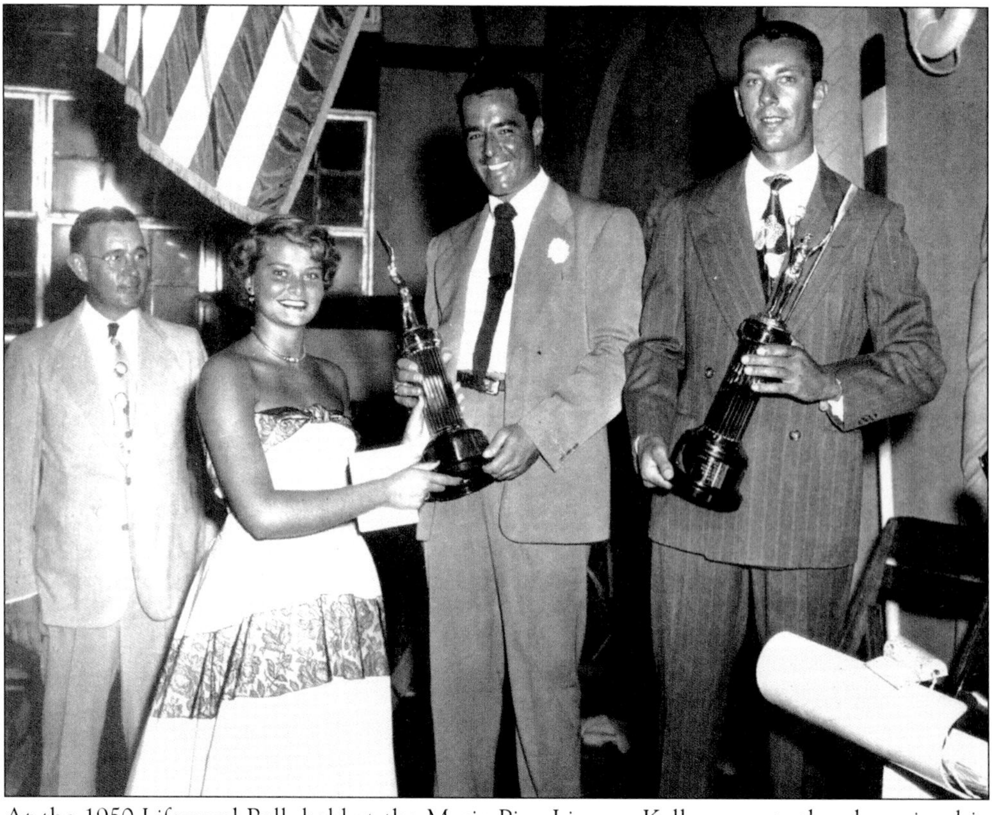

At the 1950 Lifeguard Ball, held at the Music Pier, Lizanne Kelly presents the championship trophies to Jim Macallister (left) and Frank Schiesser, as Capt. Tom Williams looks on.

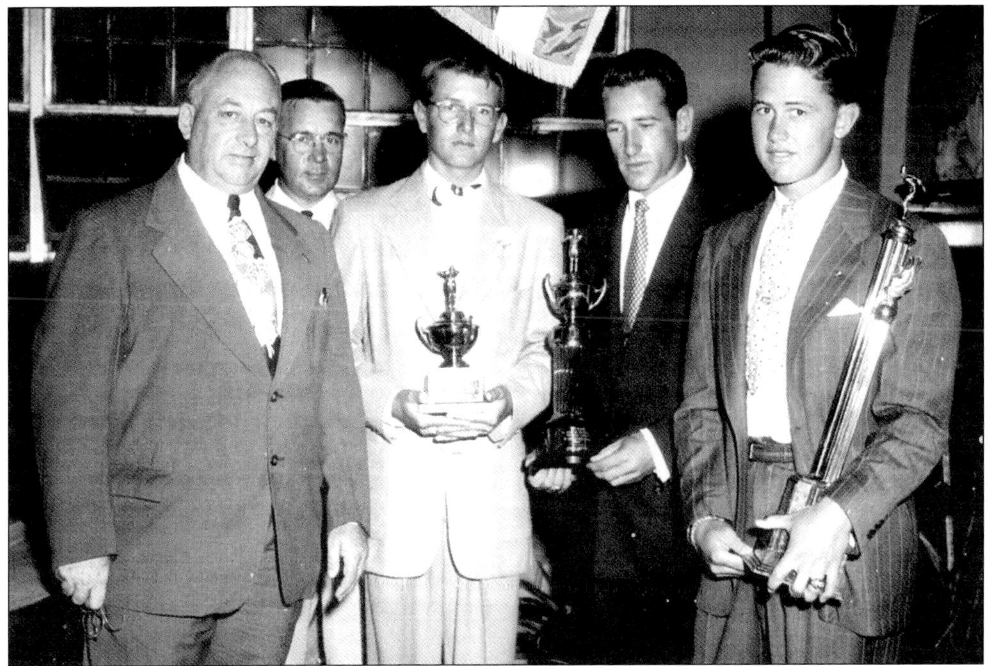

Ocean City Beach Patrol's three fastest swimmers are honored in 1949. From left to right are Mayor Edward B. Bowker, Capt. Tom Williams, and swimmers Barney Hungerford, Joe Sweeney, and Paul Geithner.

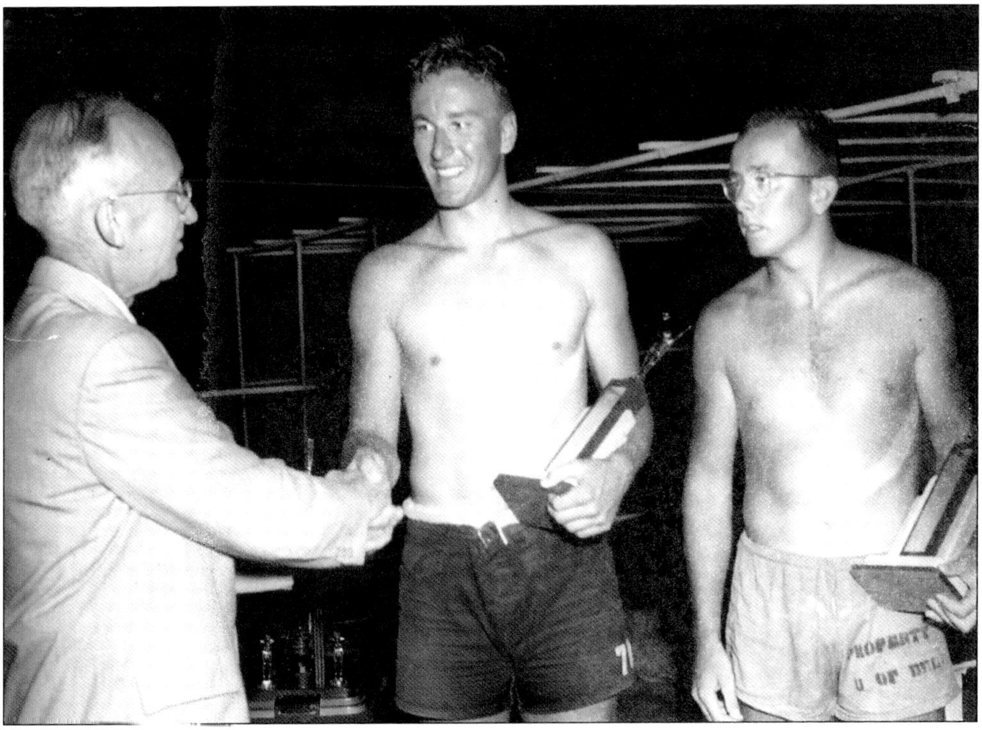

City Commissioner Laurence P. Lunny congratulates Tom Oves (center) and Jerry Angulo after they won the doubles rowing race in the 1952 South Jersey Lifeguard Championship.

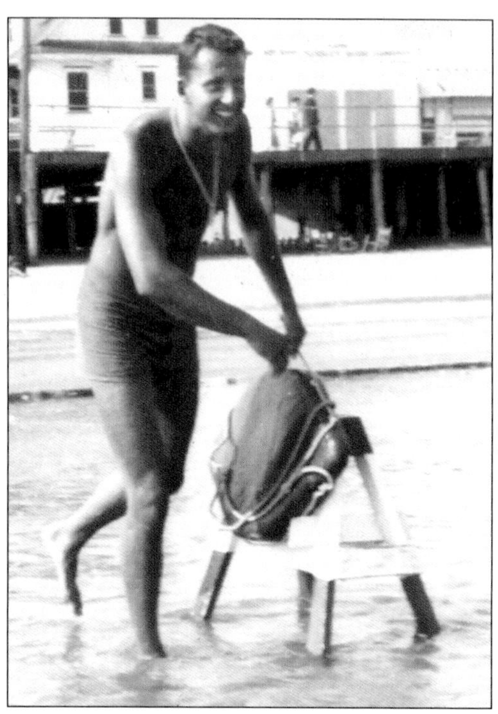

On July 19, 1951, Ocean City Beach Patrol rookie lifeguard George Haggerty performs an ocean rescue drill. Four years later he won the half-mile ocean swim in the South Jersey Lifeguard Championship.

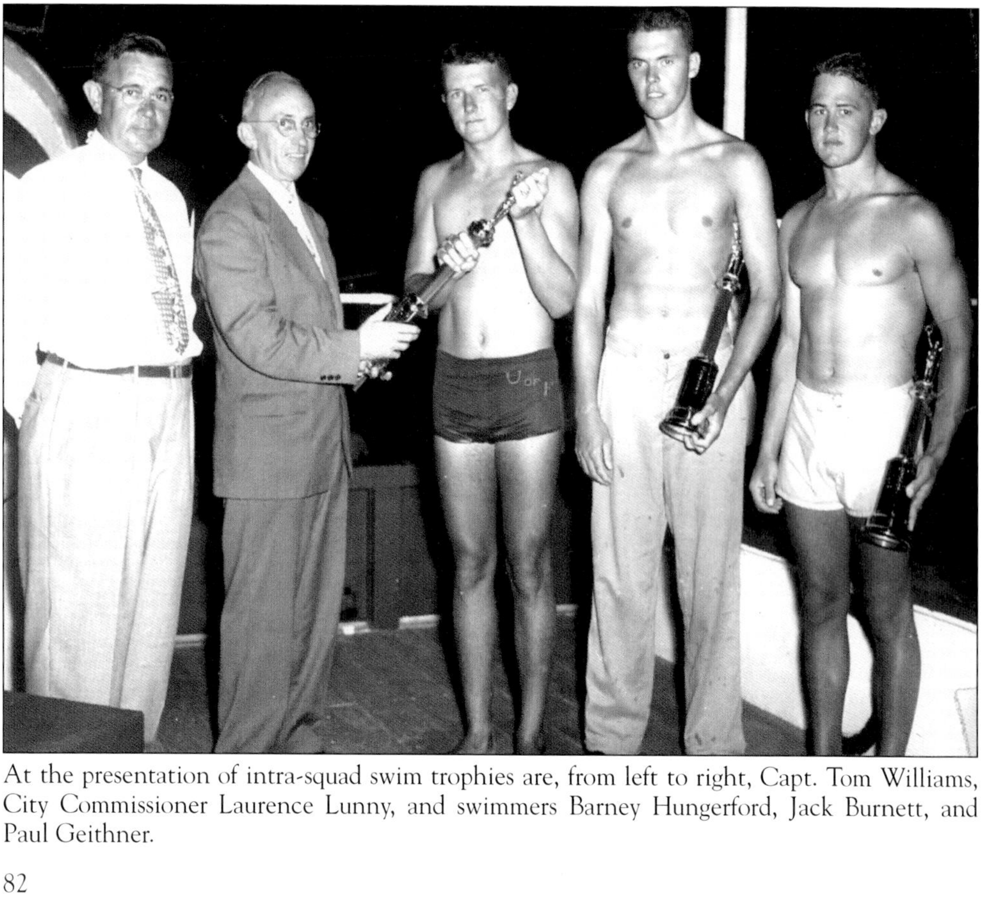

At the presentation of intra-squad swim trophies are, from left to right, Capt. Tom Williams, City Commissioner Laurence Lunny, and swimmers Barney Hungerford, Jack Burnett, and Paul Geithner.

Lt. Warren North (left) and Tom Heist show off their rowing trophies at the 1956 Lifeguard Ball. Later that summer, North and Heist rowed a lifeboat completely around the island in 5 hours and 10 minutes. They were the first Ocean City crew to attempt this feat.

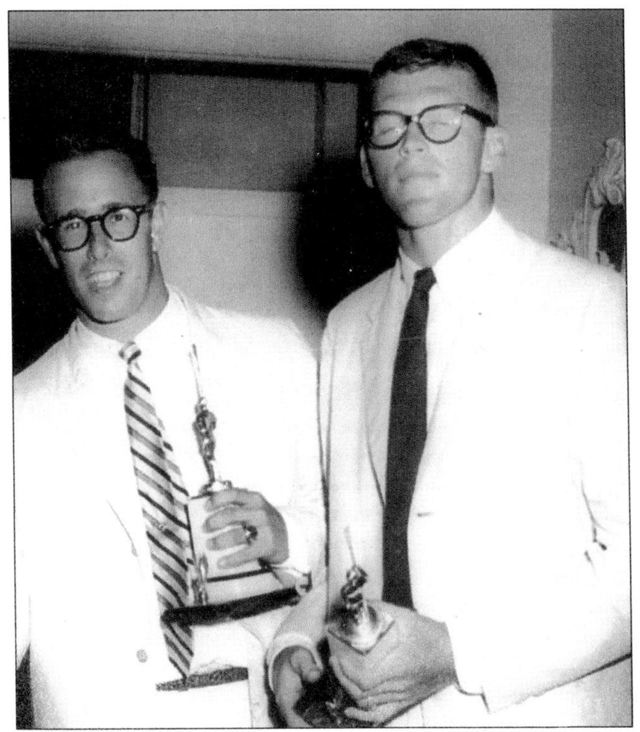

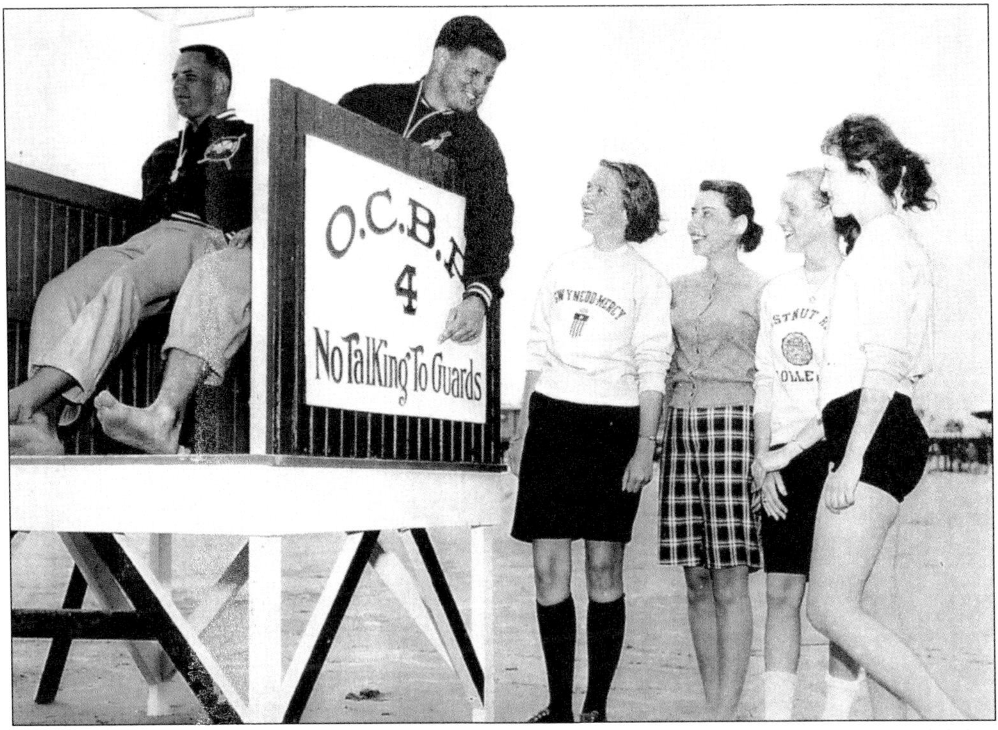

Ocean City lifeguard Nelson Baker points out the "No Talking To Guards" sign to Philadelphia visitors, from left to right, Claire Boyle, Barry Doloway, Nancy Egan, and Clair Watson. Lifeguard Doug Fogg keeps his eyes on the water.

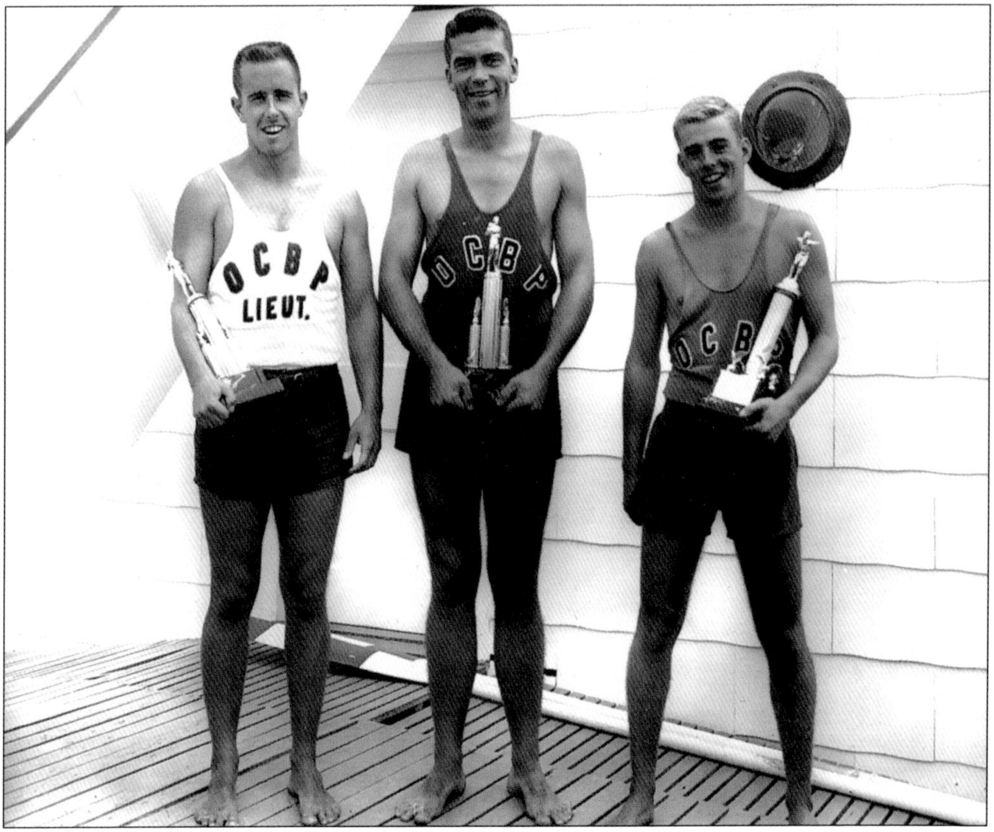

The Ocean City Beach Patrol won the 1957 South Jersey Championship. From left to right are Lt. Warren North and Bob Schwab, who placed second in the doubles rowing race, and Lou Schoener, who won the swim race.

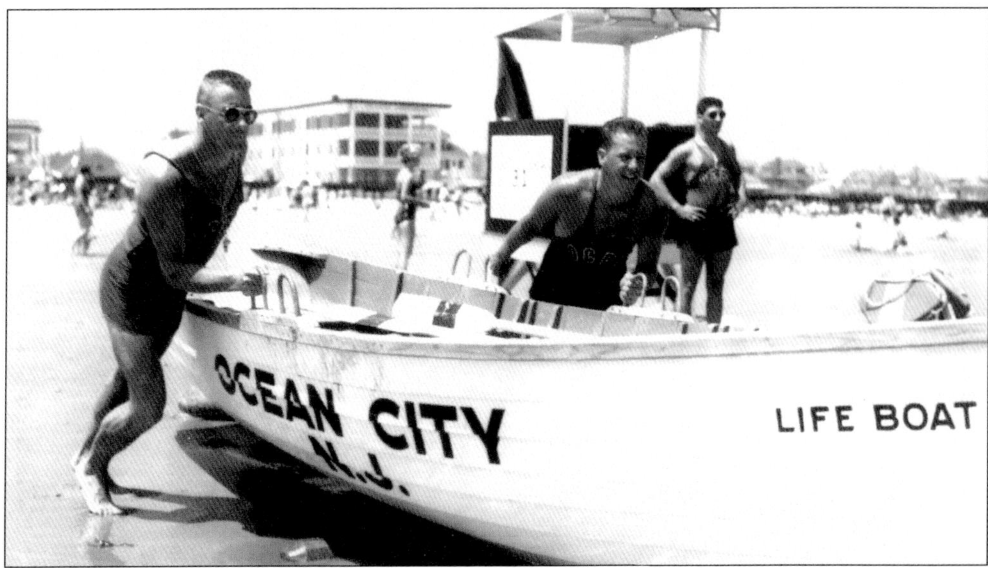

Guarding the 14th Street Beach in 1955 are, from left to right, Bill Patterson, Ed Keenan, and rookie Lee Spampinato.

Five

THE LAFFERTY YEARS

George T. Lafferty was appointed captain of the Ocean City Beach Patrol in 1962. He was a member of the patrol beginning in 1939 but left after two years to join the navy. On his retirement from the navy, he took over the lifeguard post. Lafferty was credited with making the Ocean City Beach Patrol into an athletic powerhouse, a legacy that continues today. Under his command, the Ocean City Beach Patrol won 15 South Jersey Lifeguard Championships, including a record 11 straight; 17 South Jersey Lifeguard Swim Championships, including a record 13 straight; 8 Margate Memorial race titles; and 7 Dutch Hoffman race titles.

Lafferty was the first captain to encourage women to try out for the beach patrol, and in 1976, he hired the first female member, Judith Lichtner. He made sure that his lifeguards had the newest equipment, bringing in two-way walkie-talkie radios so that the lifeguards no longer had to rely on hand gestures and whistles to communicate with each other. This allowed the beach patrol headquarters to monitor problems and enabled them to get immediate emergency help where it was needed. Lafferty also began to replace old wooden boats with fiberglass ones, which are lighter, faster, and easier to maintain.

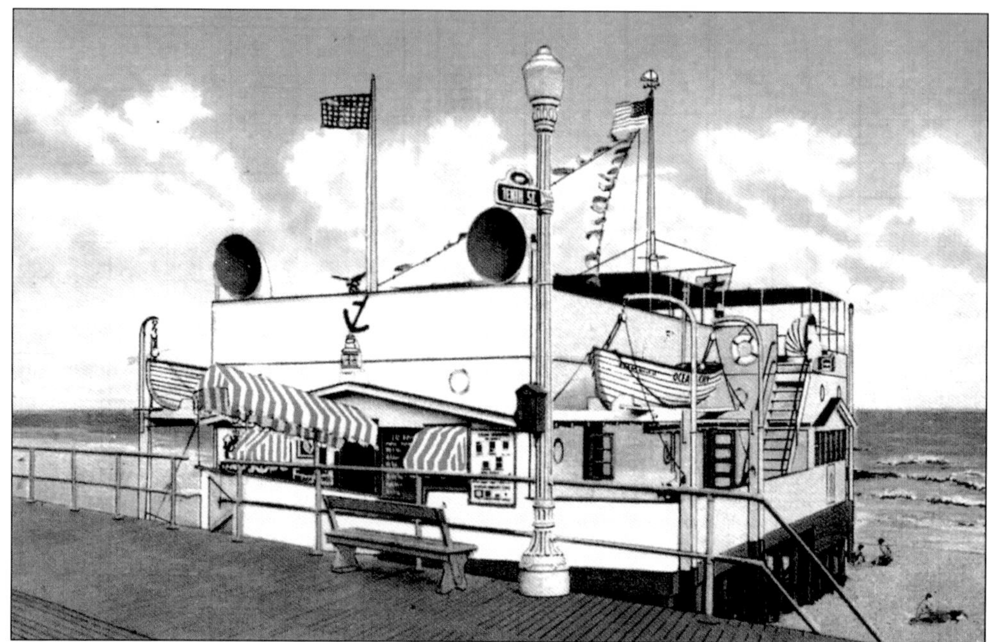

The 10th Street patrol headquarters, designed and built under the supervision of Capt. Jack Jernee in the late 1920s to resemble the bridge of an ocean liner, was the most unique building of its kind. It was a favorite of photographers and visitors.

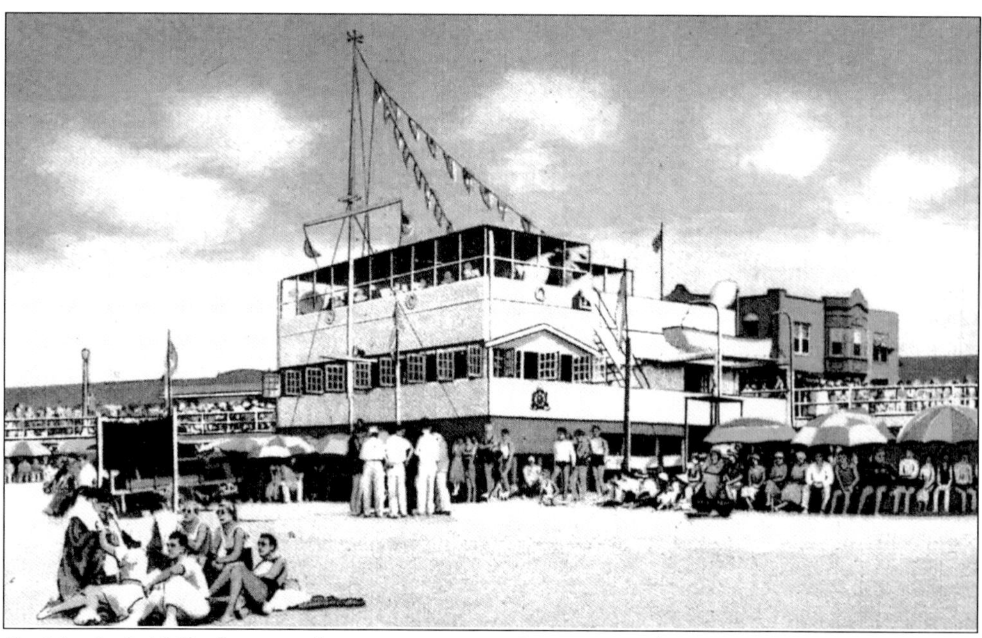

On March 6, 1962, the most disastrous storm in Ocean City's history struck. The 10th Street patrol headquarters was completely lost, taking with it trophies, pictures, and other lifeguard memorabilia dating back to 1920.

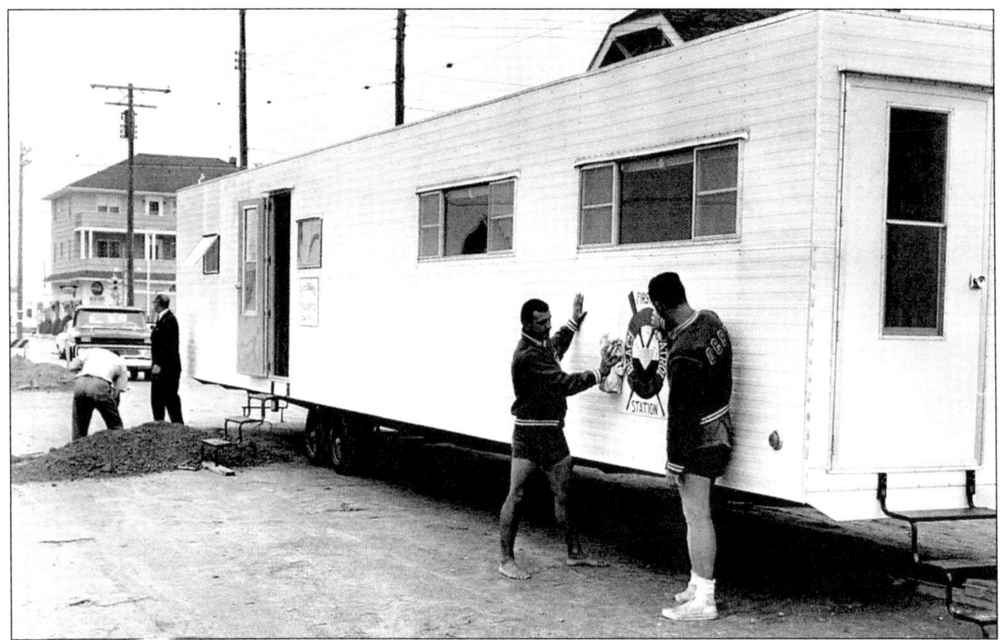

Lifeguards Angelo Psaltis (left) and Gene Platt shine the Ocean City Beach Patrol emblem on the side of the new south end beach patrol headquarters. The 50-foot trailer, which was parked at 34th Street and the beach, replaced a building destroyed in the March 1962 storm.

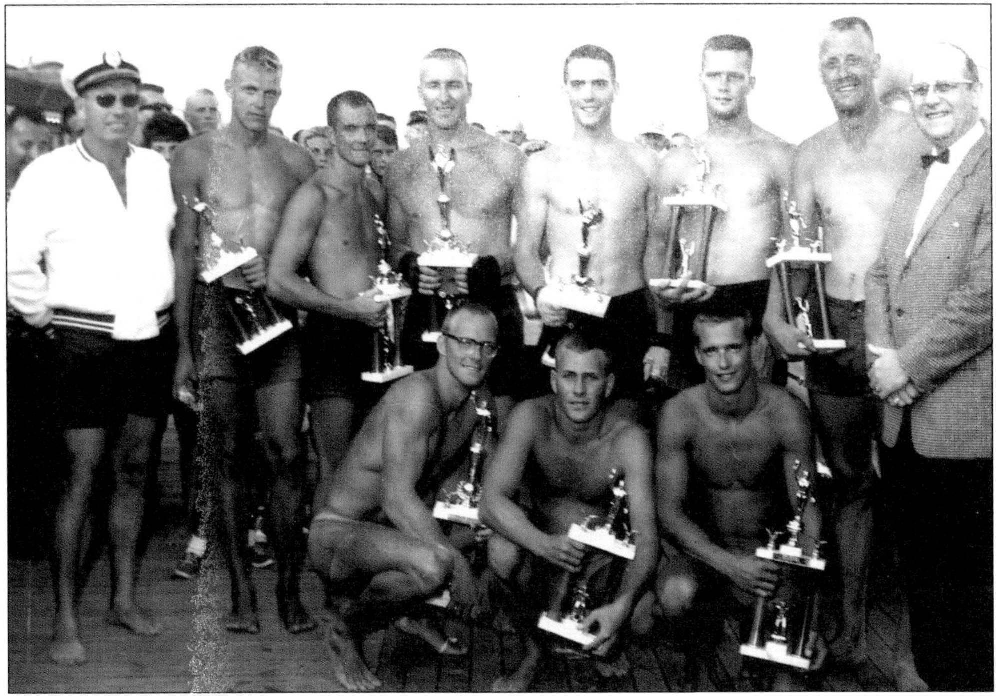

Pictured are the 1962 intra-squad trophy winners. From left to right are the following: (first row) lifeguards Dick Thieler, Bob Bennett, George Thieler, and City Commissioner D. Allen Stretch; (second row) Capt. George T. Lafferty, Hans Giesecke, Bud McKinley, Tom Oves, Ed Field, Charlie Cox, and Tom Swenk.

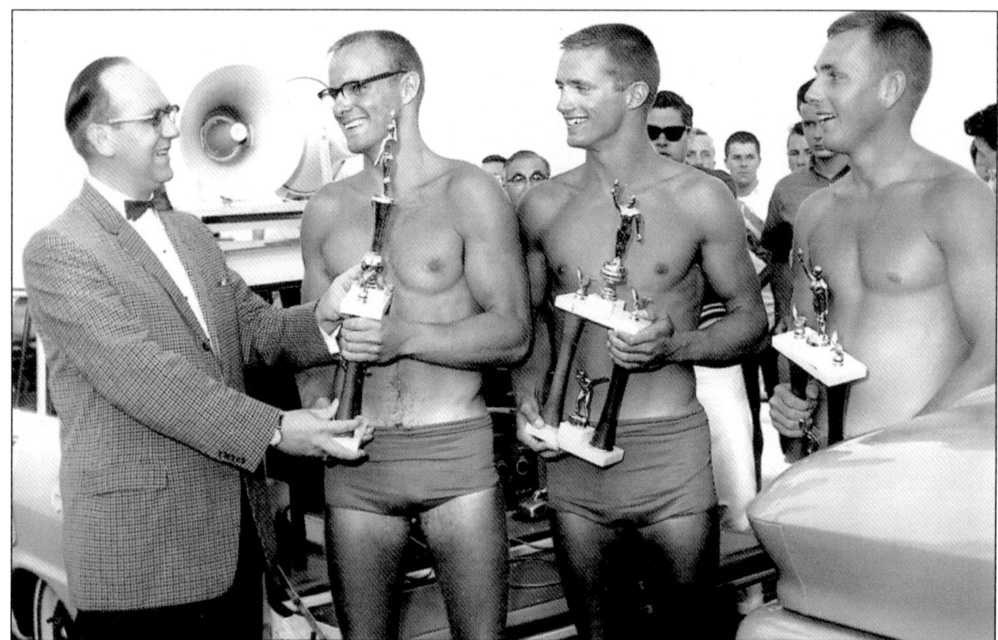

City Commissioner D. Allen Stretch presents trophies to 1962 Ocean City Beach Patrol swimmers, from left to right, first-place winner Dick Thieler, second-place winner George Thieler, and third-place winner Bob Bennett.

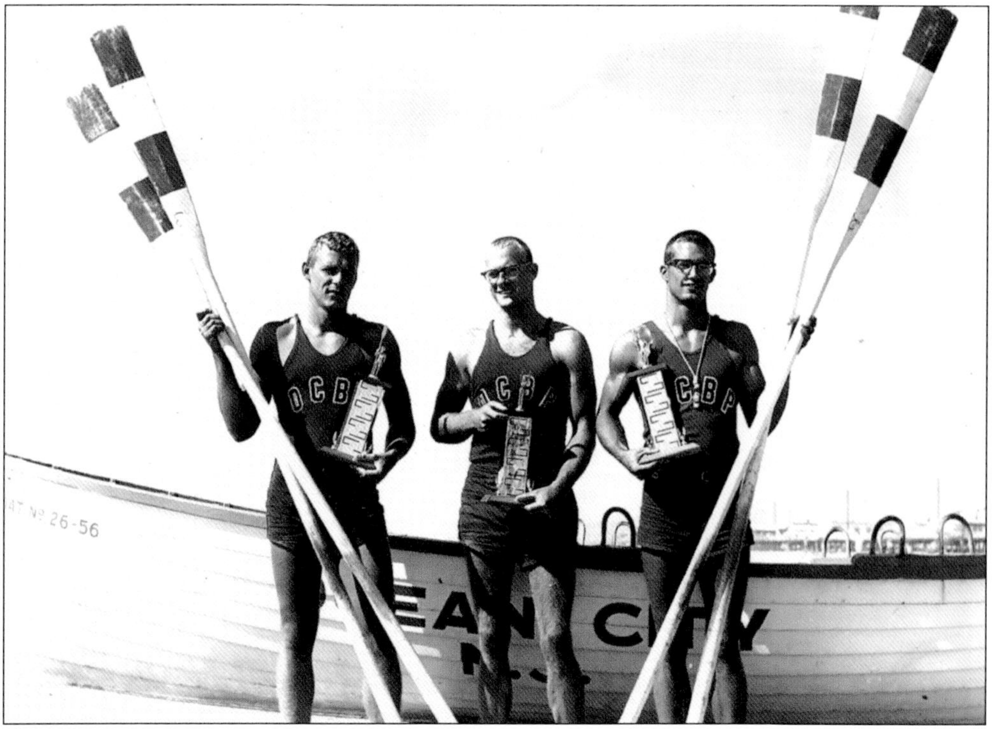

In 1963, the Ocean City Beach Patrol won both events in the South Jersey Lifeguard Championship to capture its third straight title. Swim champion Dick Thieler is flanked by doubles rowing champions Hans Giesecke (left) and George Thieler.

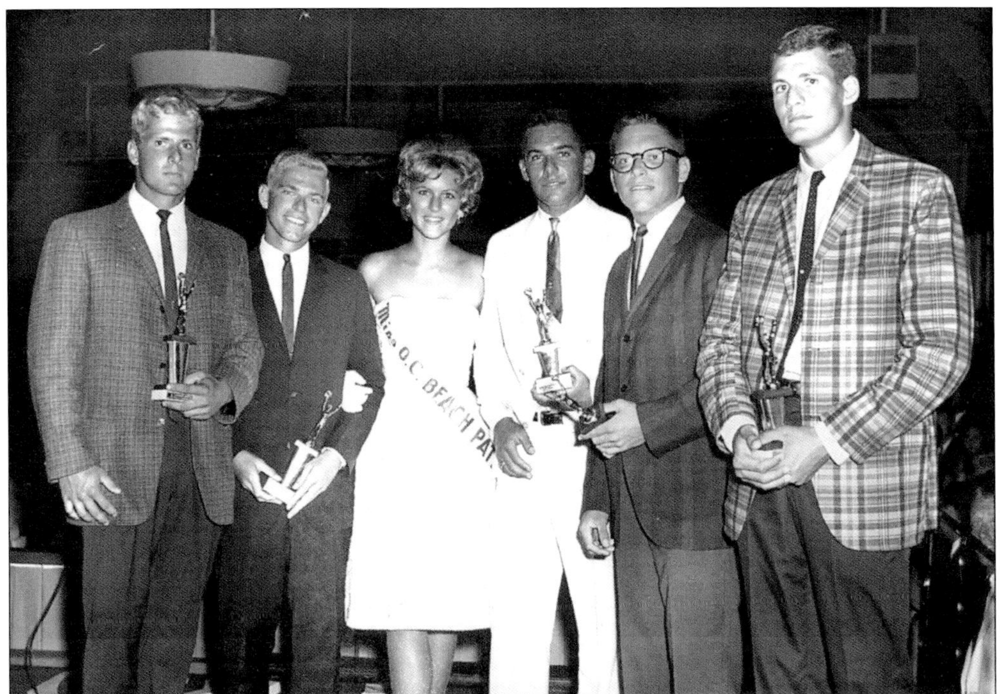

The 1963 top rookie rowers receive their trophies at the annual Lifeguard Ball and pose with Carol Yeasley, Miss Ocean City Beach Patrol. The rowers are, from left to right, William Haug, John Schmidt, Perry White, Dan McGarrigan, and Rick Adams.

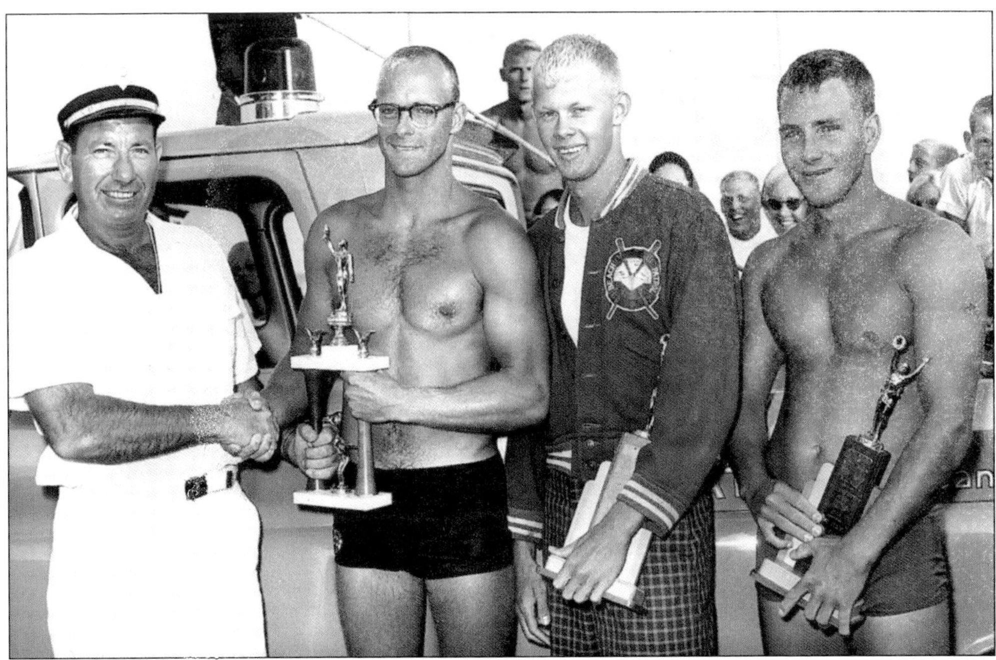

Capt. George Lafferty presents the 1963 intra-squad trophies to the Ocean City Beach Patrol's fastest swimmers. From left to right, they are Dick Thieler, Charles Wigo, and Dick Bennett.

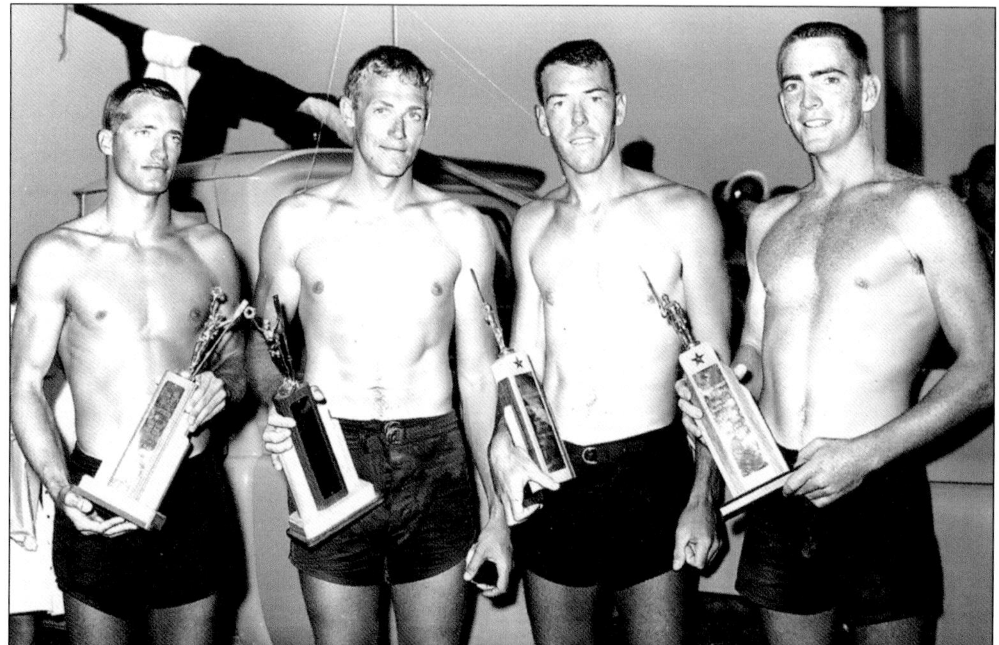

The 1963 Ocean City Beach Patrol top rowers are, from left to right, George Thieler, Hans Giesecke, James Kane, and Ed Field. Thieler and Giesecke went on to win the South Jersey Lifeguard Championship doubles rowing race later that summer.

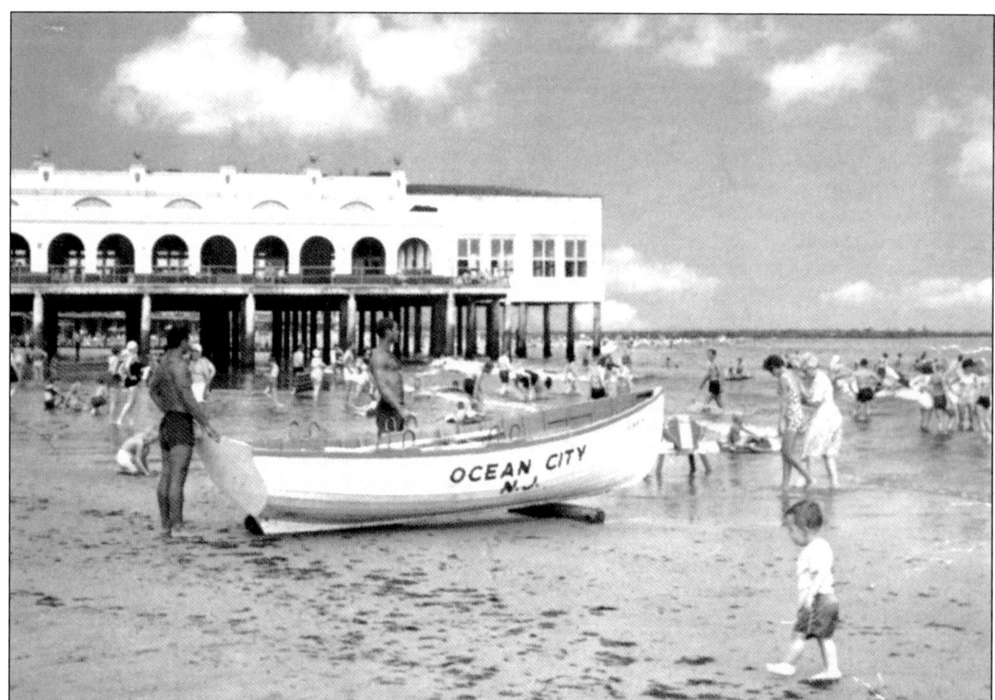

The 9th Street Beach was the most popular beach in New Jersey for the collegiate crowd in 1963. It was nicknamed "Little Fort Lauderdale." Angelo Psaltis (left) and Jim DiSabatino were the lifeguards on that beach.

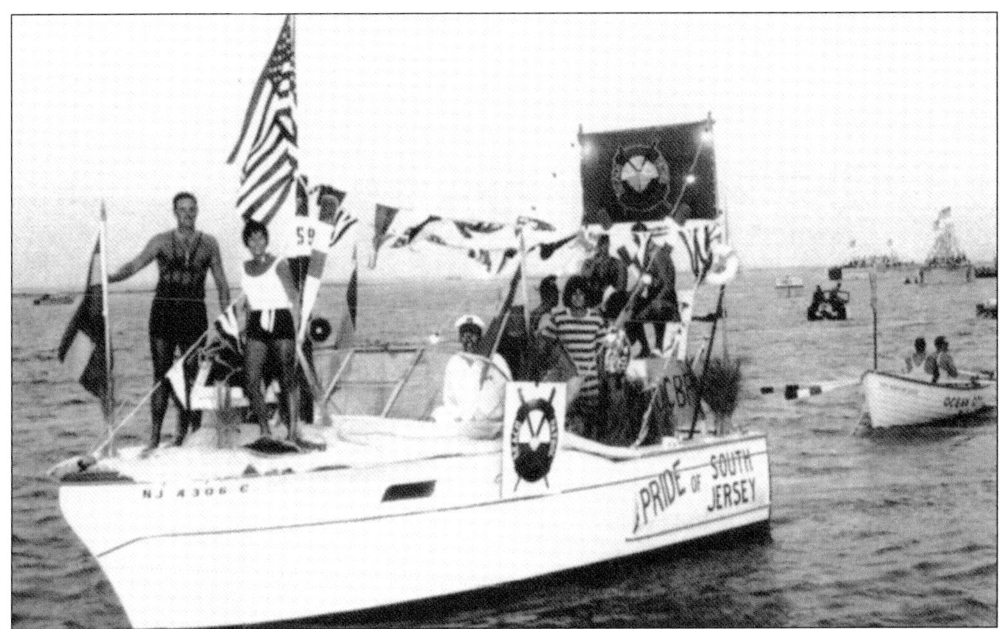

On July 25, 1964, Chester Derr's boat *Patchet III*, with its Ocean City Beach Patrol-Pride of South Jersey theme, was a prizewinner in the annual Night in Venice Boat Parade. Aboard are lifeguards Chet Derr Jr., Jack McCreesh, John Dodds, Bob Schneider, and George Sonneborn; following in the lifeboat are Lts. Tom Oves and Charles Bowman, South Jersey champions.

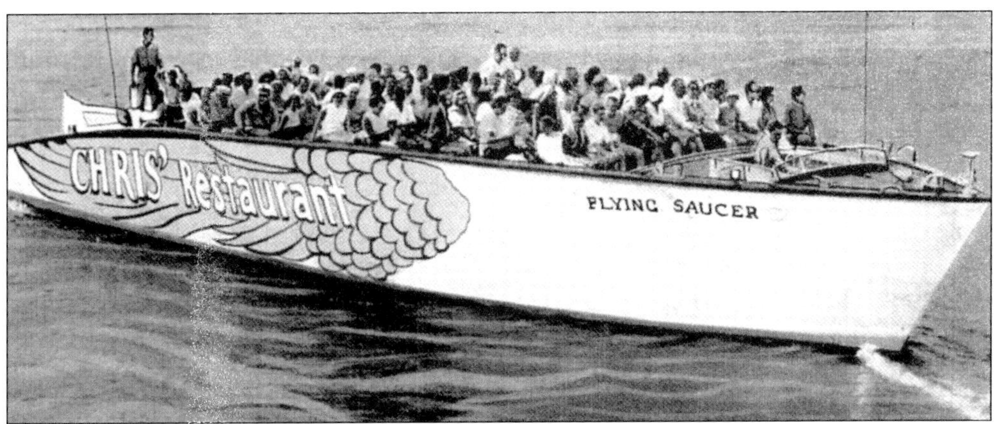

On August 5, 1964, the 75-foot tourist boat the *Flying Saucer* hit a submerged object while doing 60 miles per hour in the ocean. With the boat taking on water, Capt. Chris Montagna turned it towards the beach and ran it aground at 31st Street. Lifeguards quickly arrived on the scene and formed a human chain to get all the passengers safely ashore through the breakers.

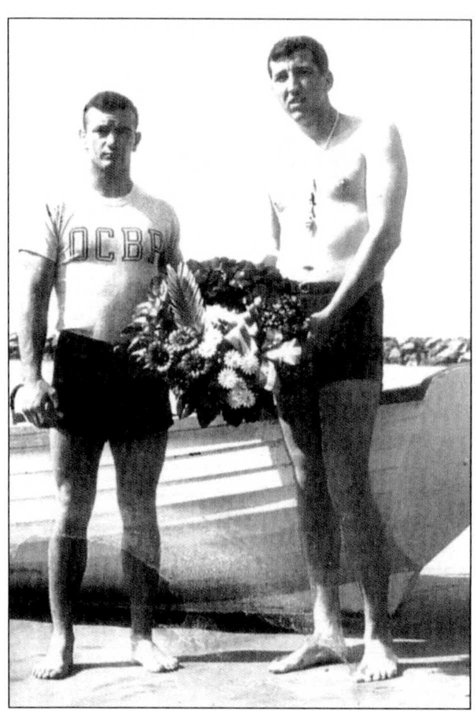

On Memorial Day 1964, Ocean City lifeguards Angelo Psaltis (left) and James Witchko pose with a memorial wreath. The lifeguards later rowed their lifeboat a short distance away from the 9th Street Beach and placed the wreath in the ocean to honor the military men and women who sacrificed their lives to maintain the country's freedom.

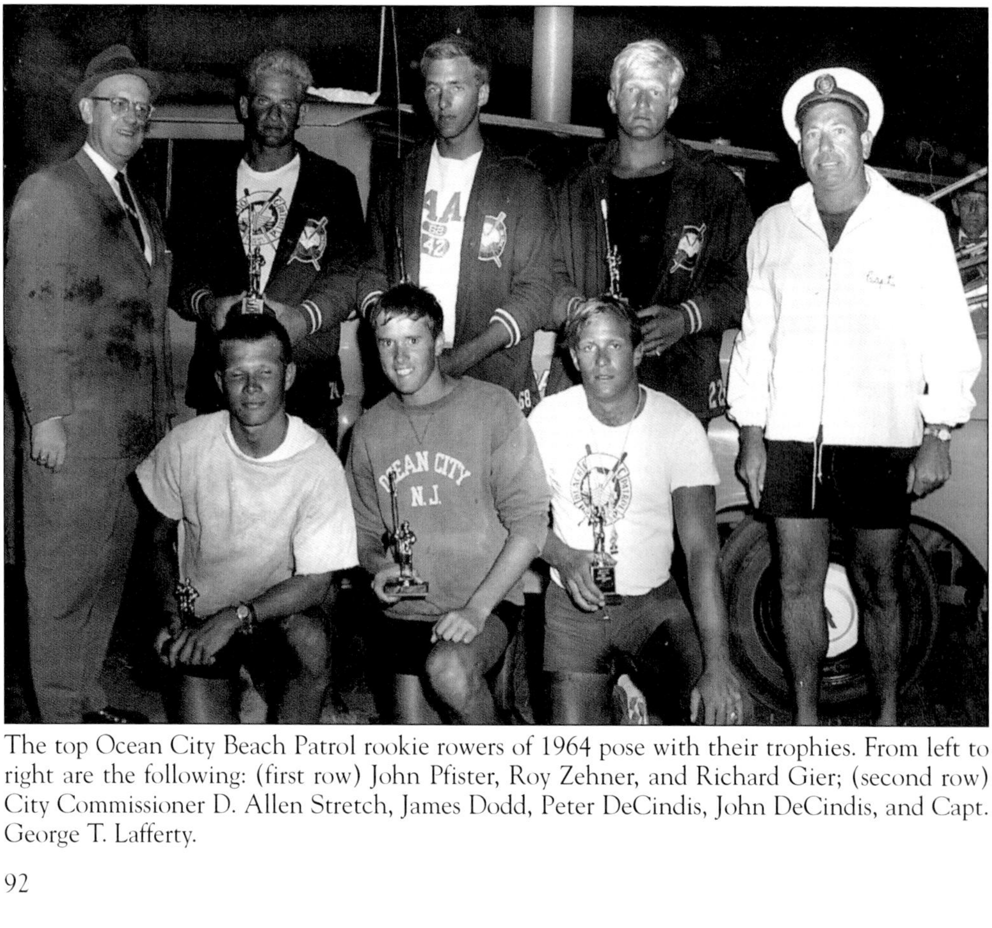

The top Ocean City Beach Patrol rookie rowers of 1964 pose with their trophies. From left to right are the following: (first row) John Pfister, Roy Zehner, and Richard Gier; (second row) City Commissioner D. Allen Stretch, James Dodd, Peter DeCindis, John DeCindis, and Capt. George T. Lafferty.

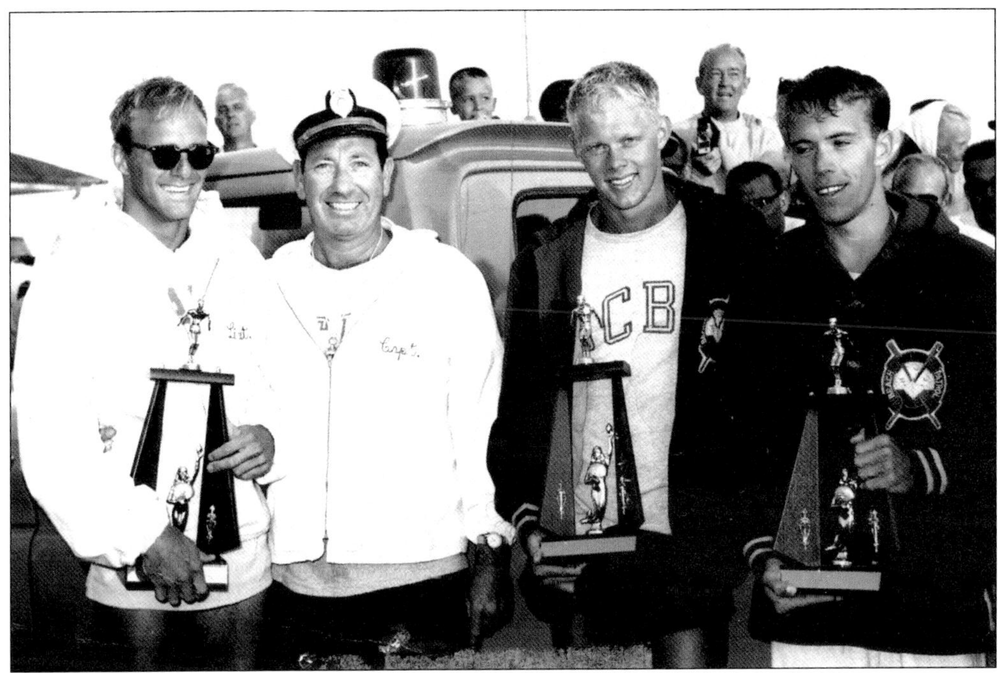

Dick Thieler (left) proudly displays the trophy for the Ocean City Beach Patrol swimming championship, which he won for the fifth consecutive year in 1965. With him are, from left to right, Capt. George Lafferty, second-place finisher Charles Wigo, and third-place winner Mike Hamilton.

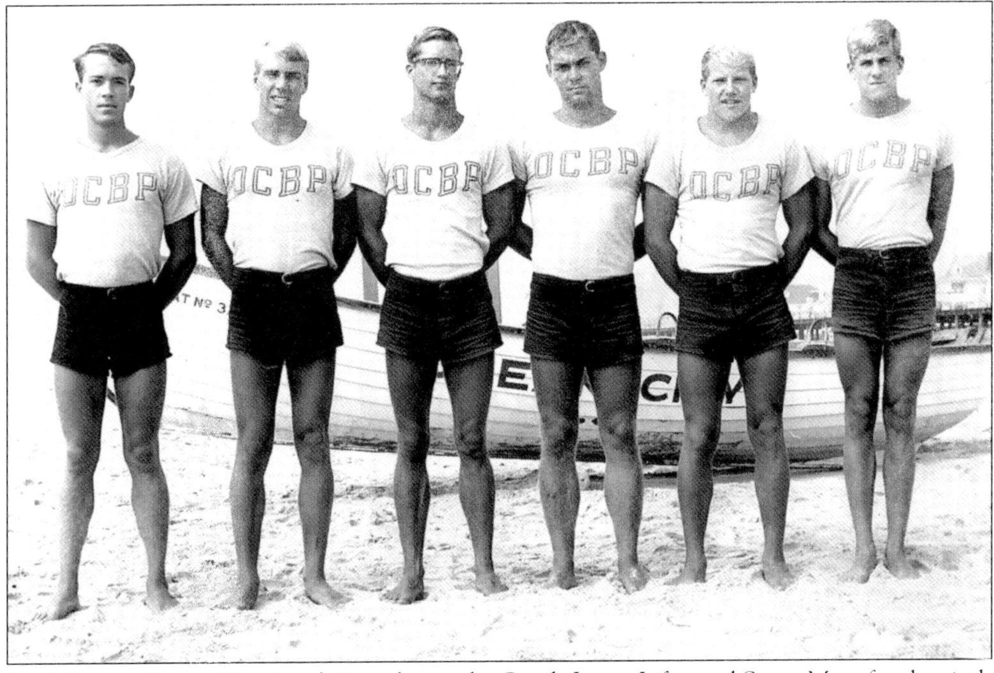

In 1965, the Ocean City Beach Patrol won the South Jersey Lifeguard Swim Meet for the sixth consecutive year. From left to right are champions Mike Hamilton, Jim Abel, George Thieler, Andy Deane, Jim Beglinger, and Bill Lafferty.

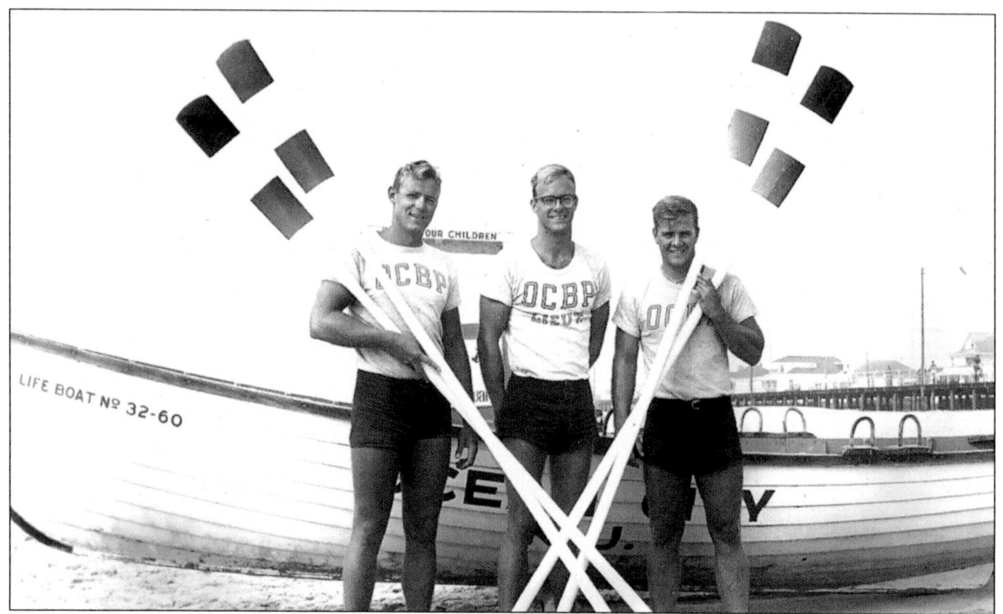

The Ocean City Beach Patrol won the South Jersey Lifeguard Championship in 1965 by winning both events. Dick Thieler, swim champion, is flanked by champion rowers Hans Giesecke (left) and Bob Schneider.

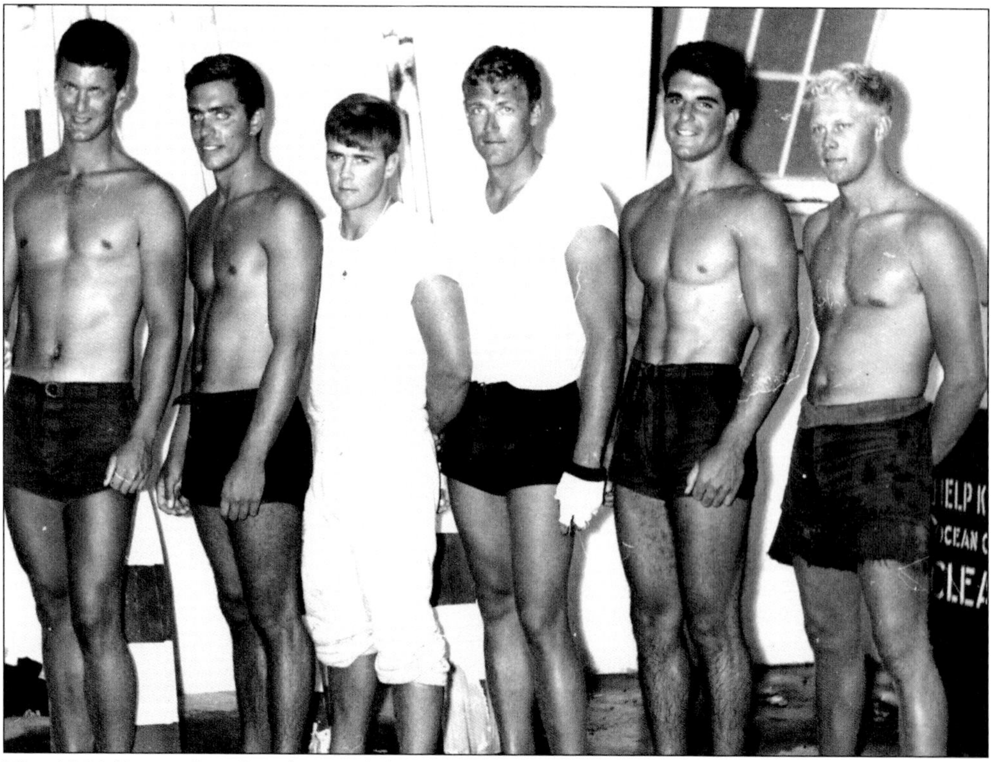

The 1966 Ocean City Beach Patrol doubles rowing trophy winners are, from left to right, Bob Thompson and Dave Townsend, Bob Schneider and Hans Giesecke, and Charles Duffy and Charles Wigo.

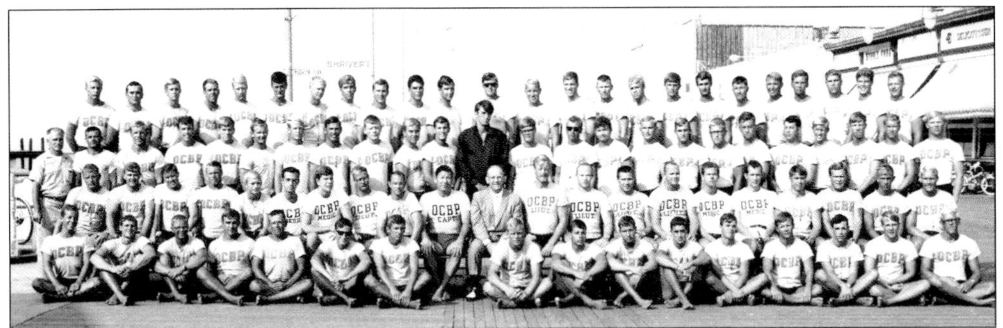

In 1966, the Ocean City Beach Patrol won both the South Jersey Lifeguard Championship and the South Jersey Swim Meet.

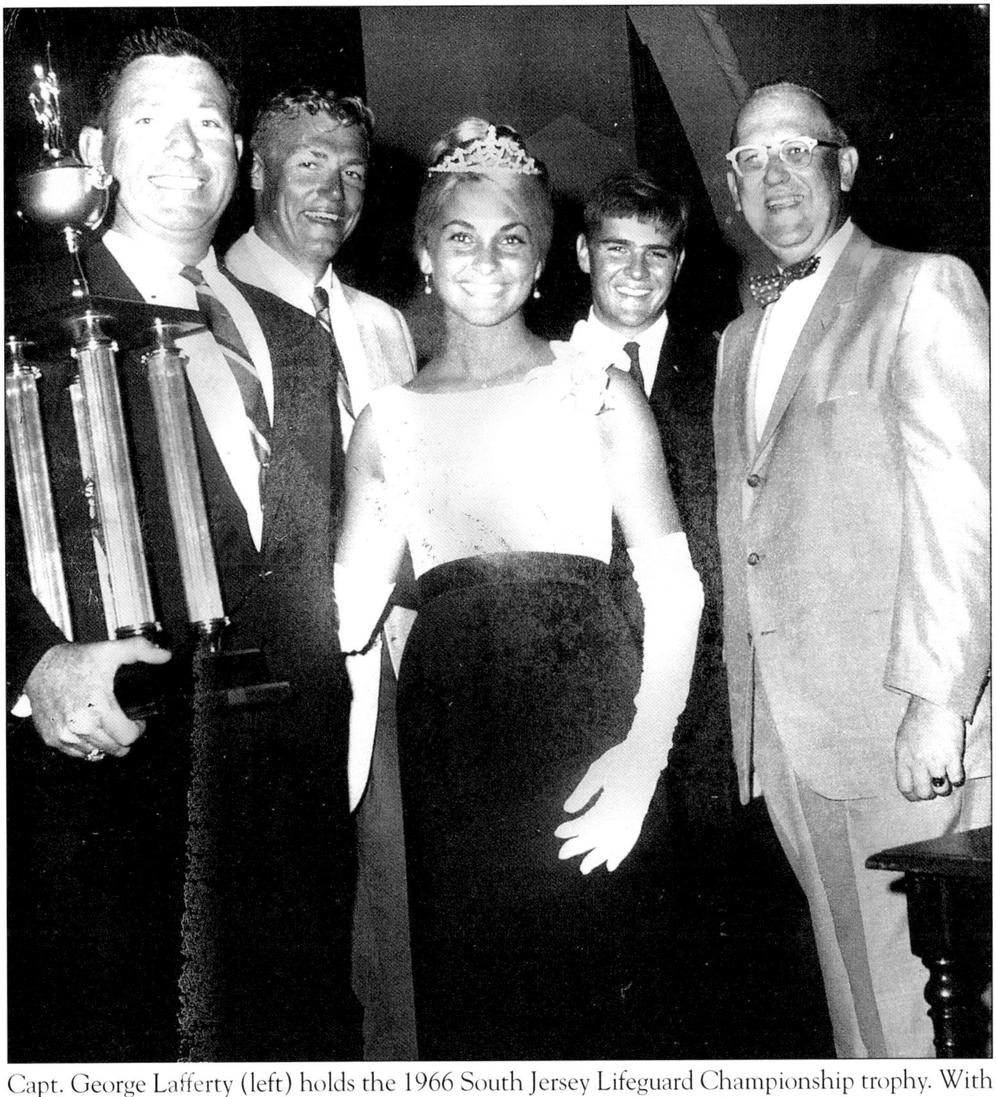

Capt. George Lafferty (left) holds the 1966 South Jersey Lifeguard Championship trophy. With him are, from left to right, Hans Giesecke, beach patrol queen Marie Mercaldo, Bob Schneider, and City Commissioner D. Allen Stretch.

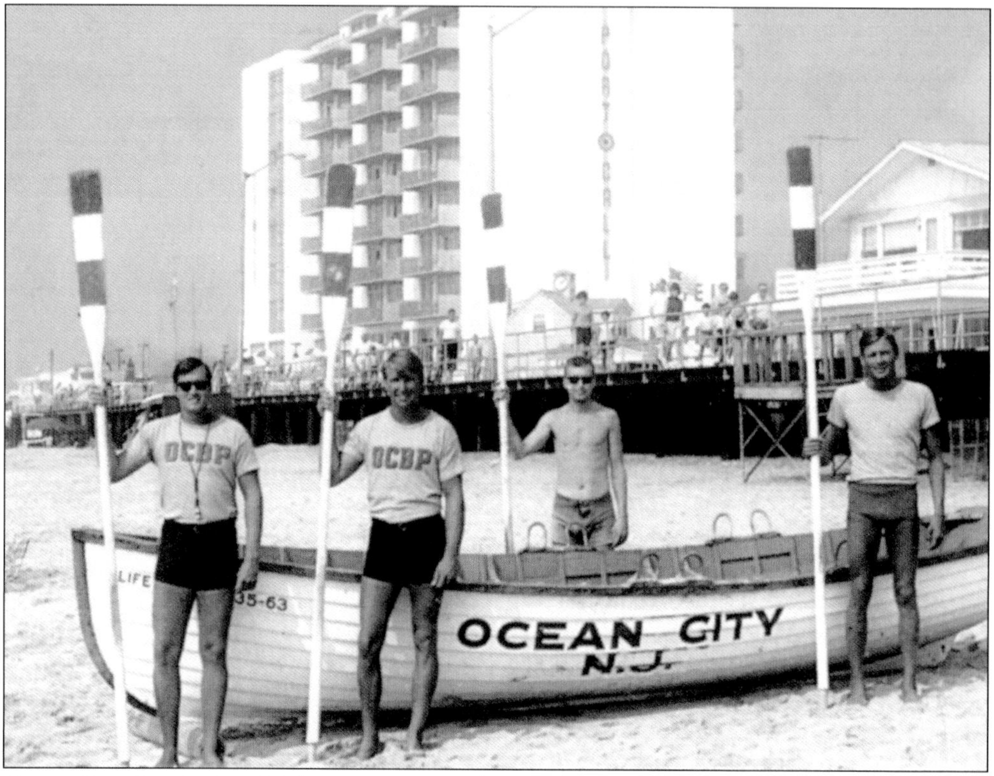

Ocean City Beach Patrol lifeguards pose in front of the newly opened Port-O-Call Hotel in the summer of 1966. From left to right are Lyle Alverson, John Palmer, Richard Buggeln, and Frank Callahan.

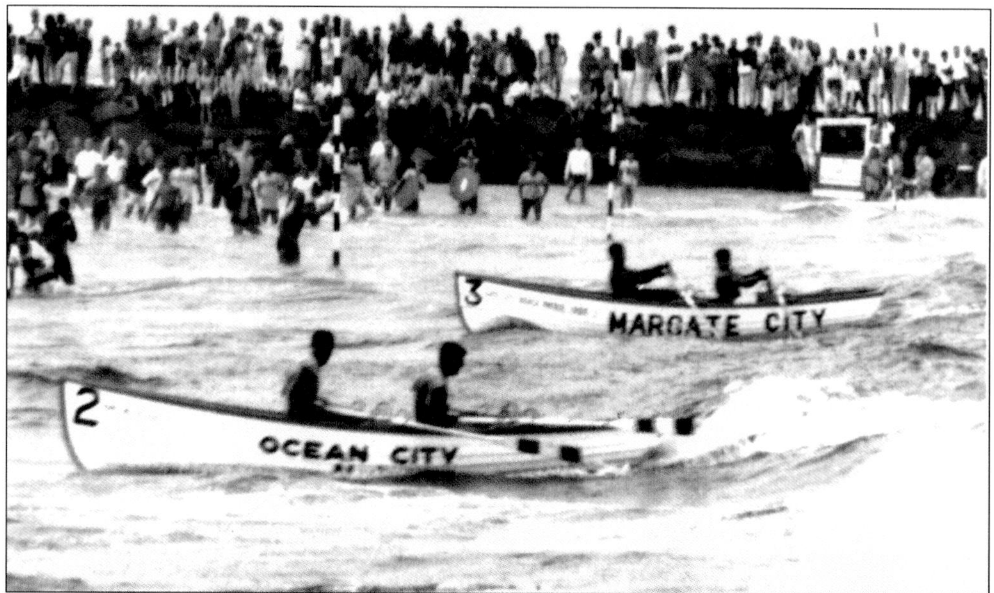

The Ocean City Beach Patrol hosted the South Jersey Lifeguard Championship on the 1st Street Beach in 1966. Ocean City won for the sixth straight year. At the finish line in the doubles race are Hans Giesecke and Bob Schneider, ahead of the second-place Margate boat.

Ocean City Mayor Robert L. Sharp presents the 1967 South Jersey Lifeguard Swim Meet trophy to Bruce Wigo. Wigo won three gold medals, and Ocean City Beach Patrol swimmers won seven of the nine events.

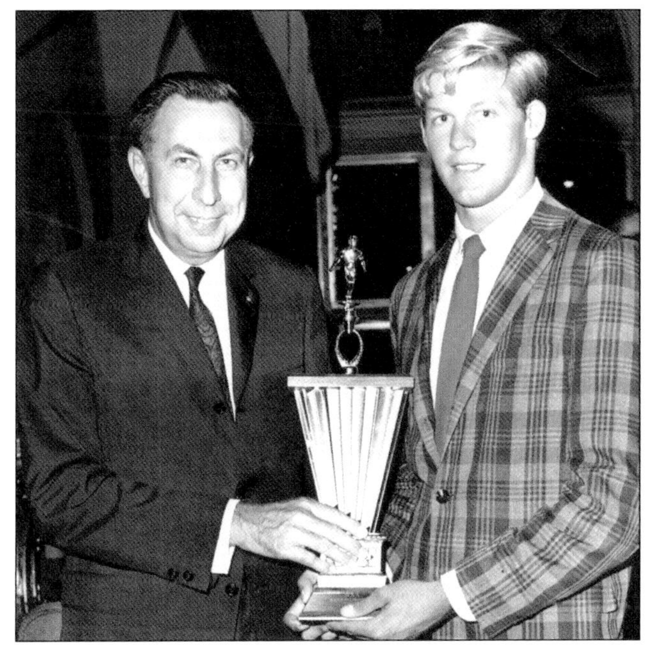

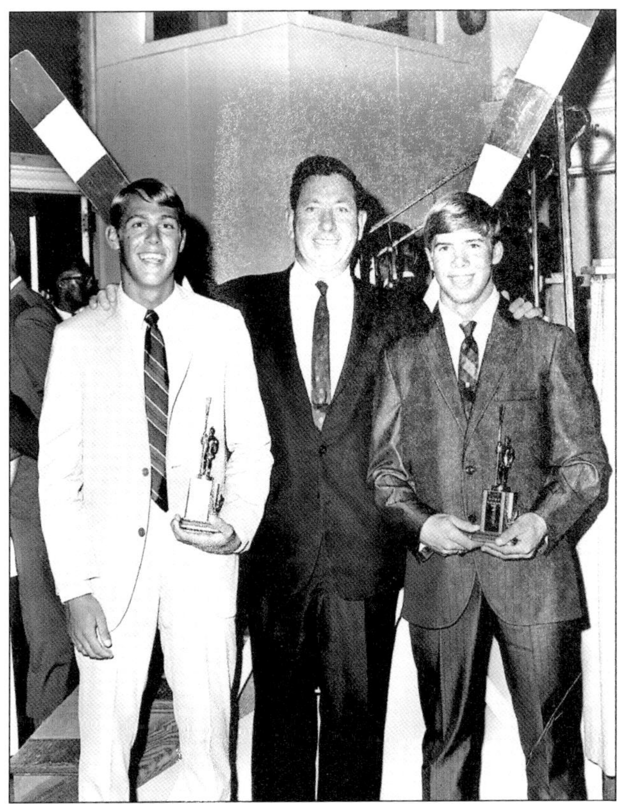

Capt. George Lafferty is flanked by Hank Adams (left) and Gary Blizzard, the winners of the 1967 rookie rowing race.

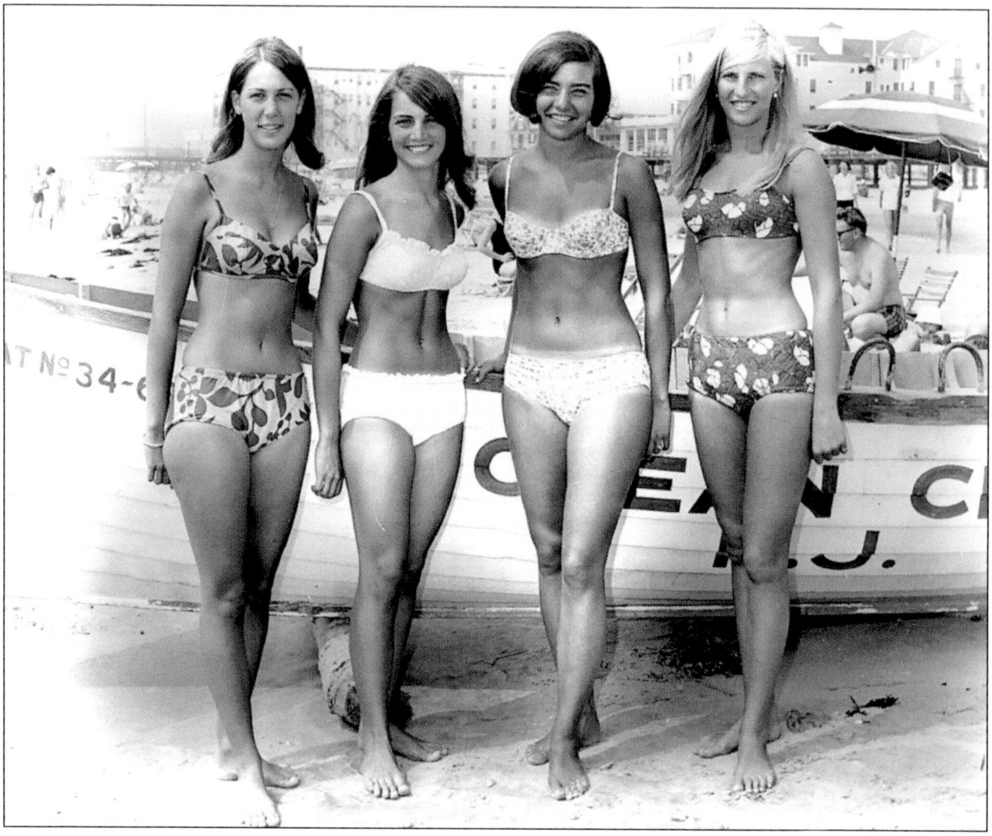

The 1967 Ocean City Beach Patrol zone queens pose on the 1st Street Beach. From left to right are Pat Behrle, Pam Meyer, Stephanie Hyde, and Linda Hemmenway.

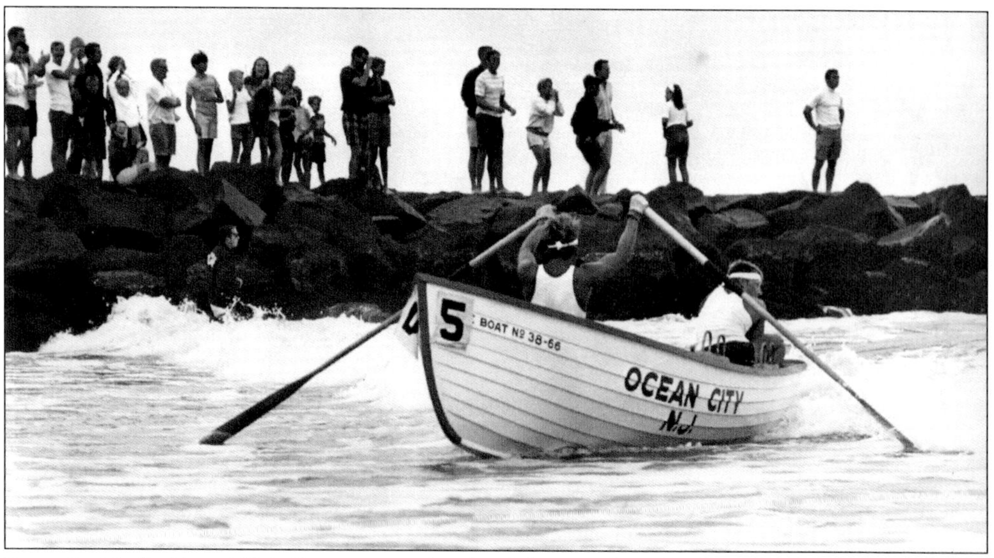

Dave Smith (left) and Bob Young cross the finish line in first place to win the doubles rowing race at the 1968 South Jersey Lifeguard Championship.

St. Charles Place lifeguards Bob Schneider (left) and Greg McKiernan look cold after a long day on the beach.

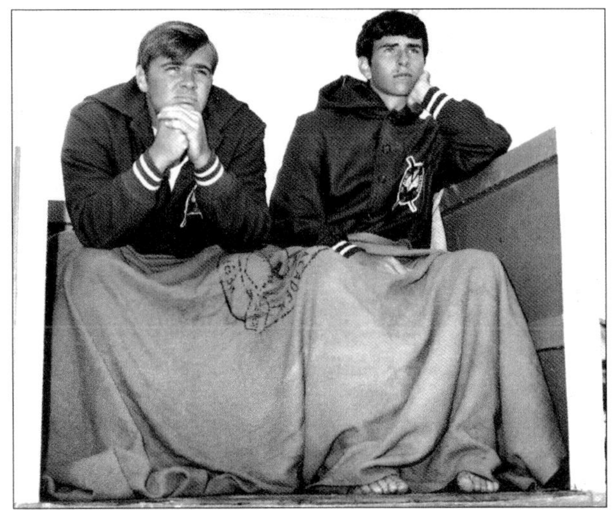

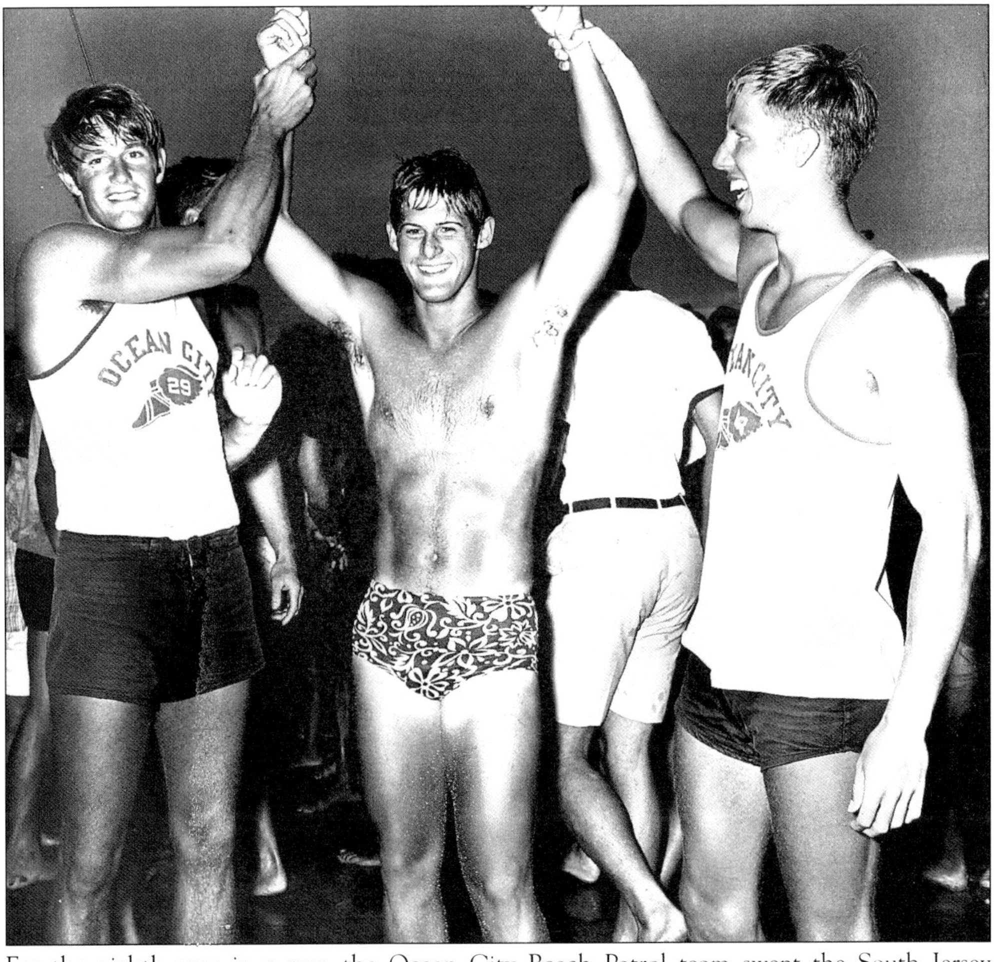

For the eighth year in a row, the Ocean City Beach Patrol team swept the South Jersey Lifeguard Championship in 1968. Swimmer Dave Kelly is flanked by rowers Dave Smith (left) and Bob Young.

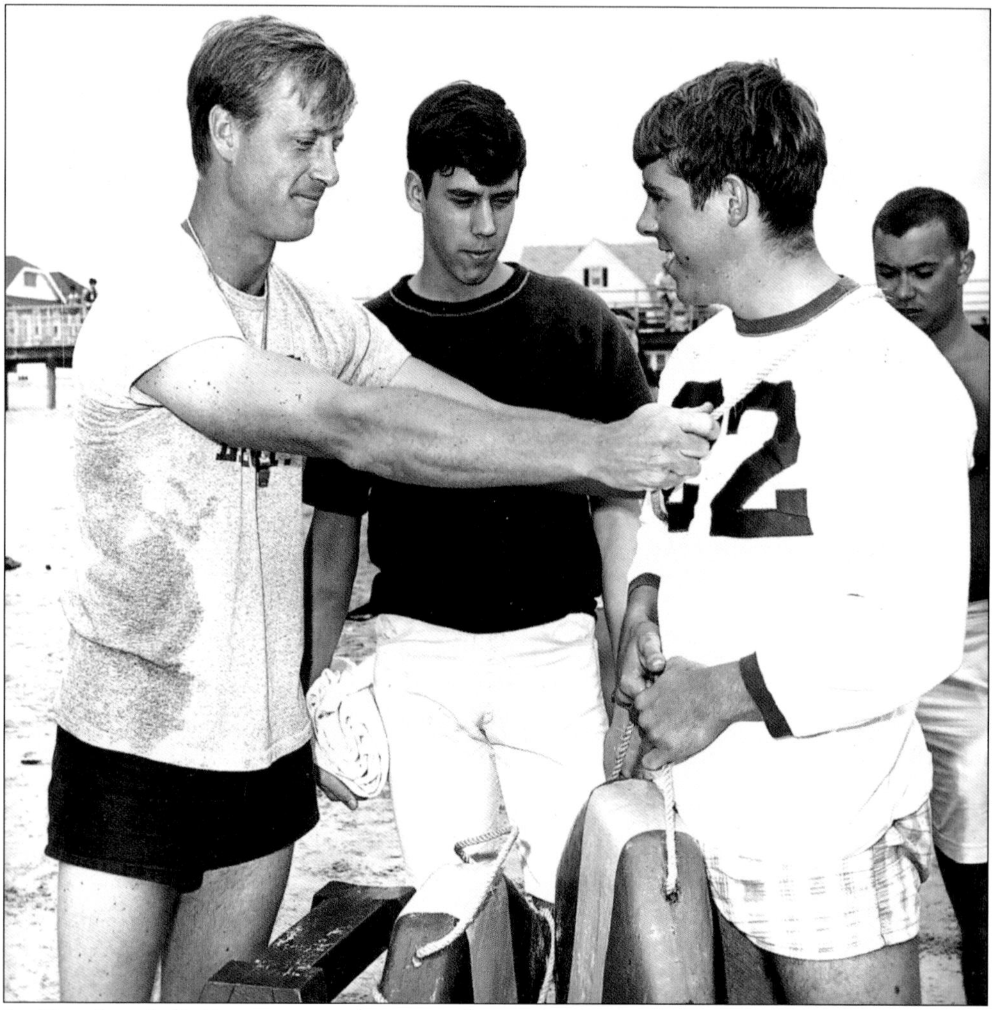

Lt. Tom Swenk (left) gives some directions during the 1968 rookie tryouts.

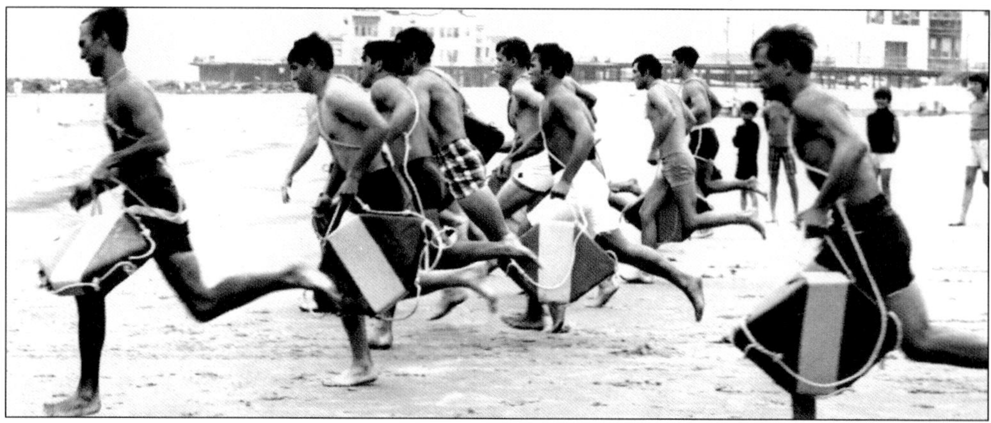

Candidates for the Ocean City Beach Patrol take off with their can buoys for the half-mile ocean swim. Finishing this swim is required to qualify for a position on the patrol. A total of 88 young men tried out for the 1968 patrol.

Fred Miller shows off his award-winning rowing technique in the summer of 1969.

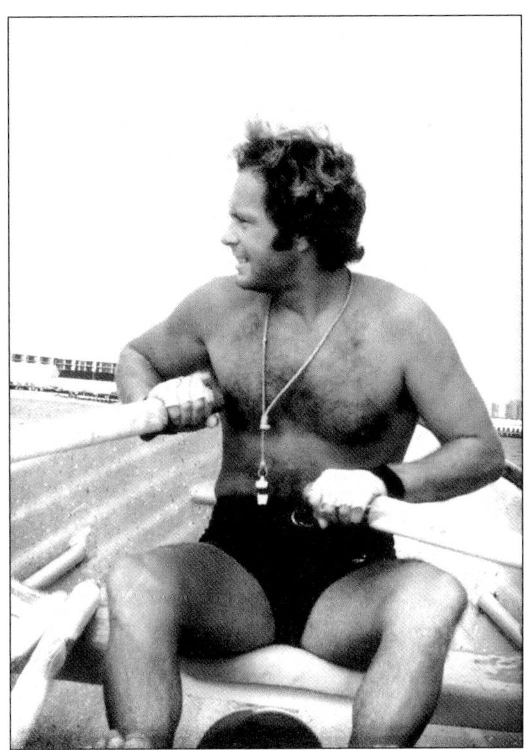

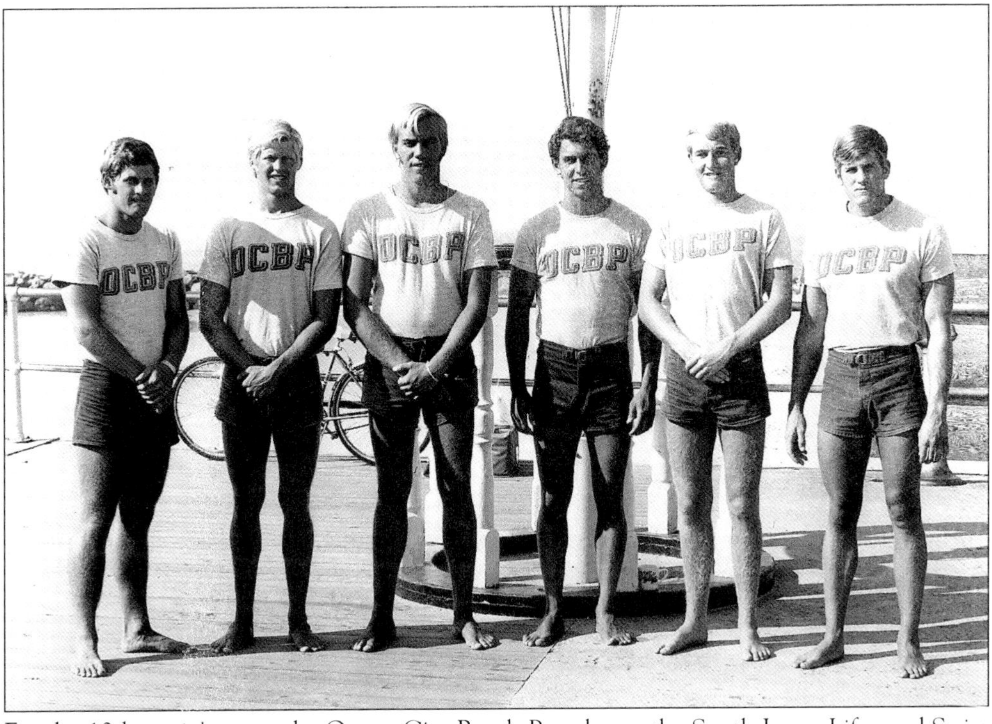

For the 10th straight year, the Ocean City Beach Patrol won the South Jersey Lifeguard Swim Meet. Members of the winning 1969 team are, from left to right, Dave Kelly, Bruce Wigo, Dave Gleason, Steve Kennedy, Dennis Carey, and Bill Lafferty.

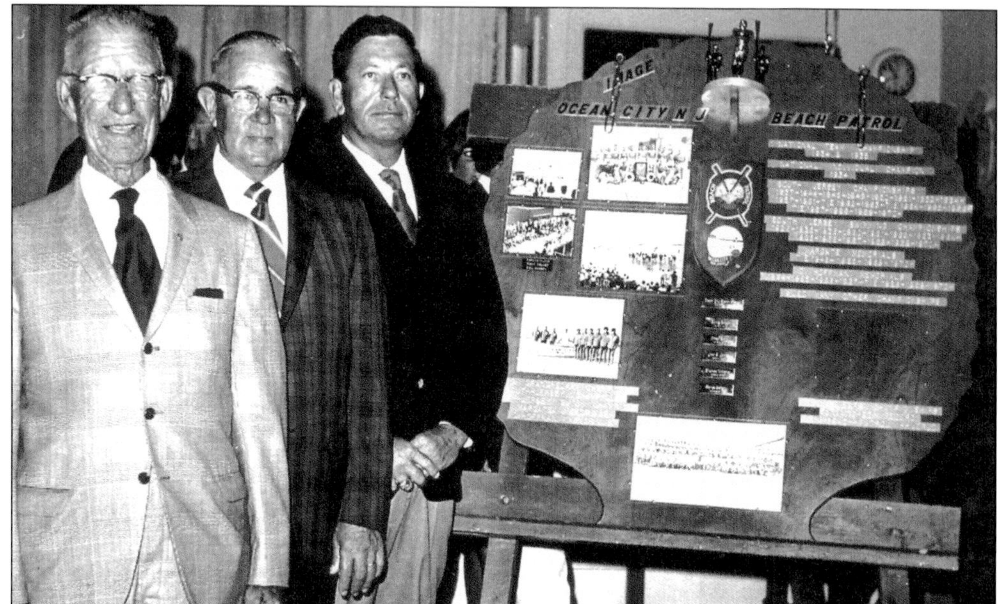

A highlight of the 1970 Lifeguard Ball, held on the Music Pier, was the presentation of an image board constructed by Ocean City Beach Patrol legend T. John Carey. Mounted on the board were photographs and statistics recounting some of the accomplishments of the beach patrol. From left to right are Jack Jernee and Thomas Williams, both former beach patrol captains, and Capt. George T. Lafferty.

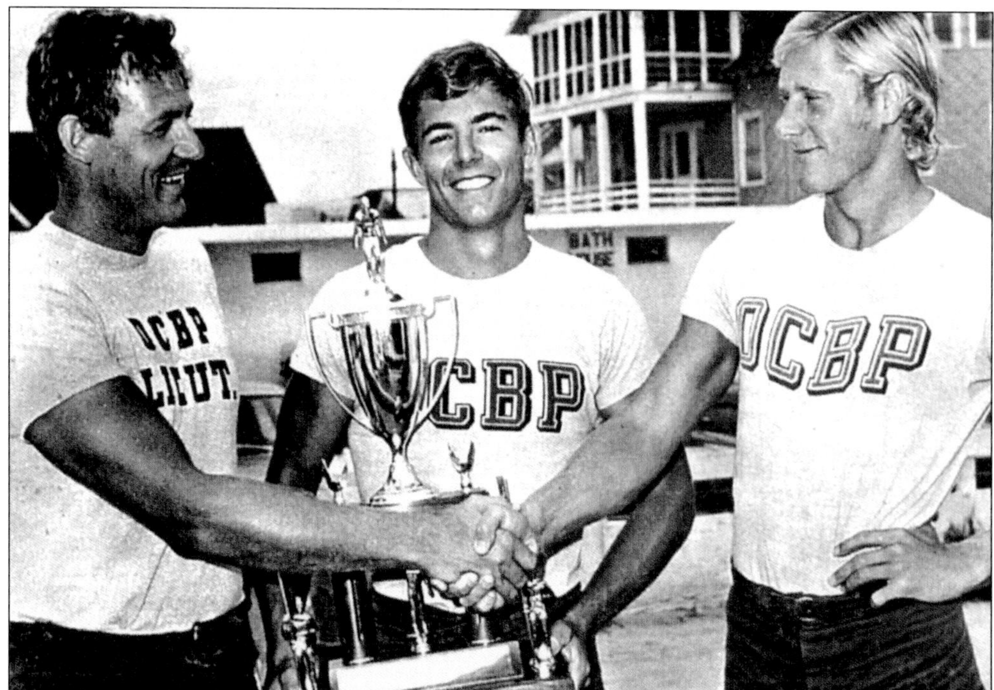

The 1971 winners of the South Jersey Lifeguard Championship congratulate each other. From left to right are doubles rowers Hans Giesecke and Karsten Giesecke and swimmer Bill Dorney. It was the 11th year in a row that the Ocean City Beach Patrol had won the championship.

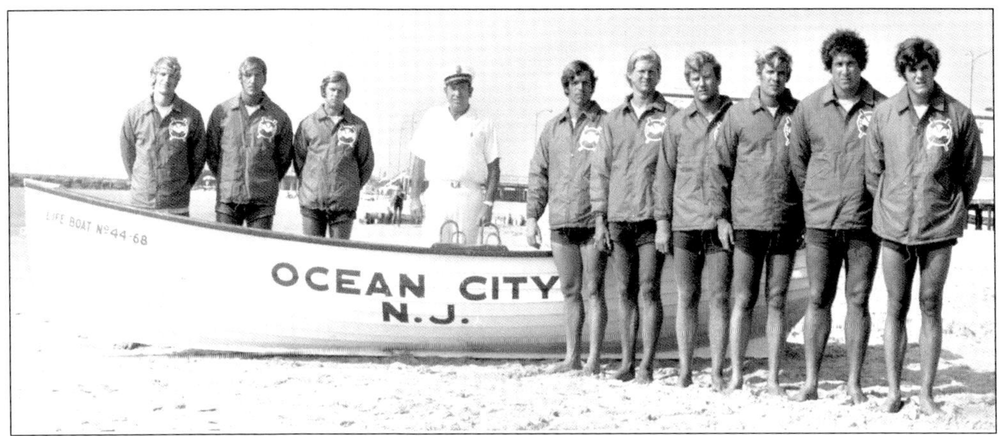

The 1970 Ocean City Beach Patrol competition team won the South Jersey Lifeguard Championship, the South Jersey Swimming Competition, the Hoffman Memorial Championship, and the Margate Memorial Championship. From left to right are Kevin Daly, Mark Nichols, Mike Bradley, Capt. George T. Lafferty, Paul Sweeney, Bruce Wigo, Ernie Wakeman, Jack McDermott, John Hellabush, and Bill Lafferty.

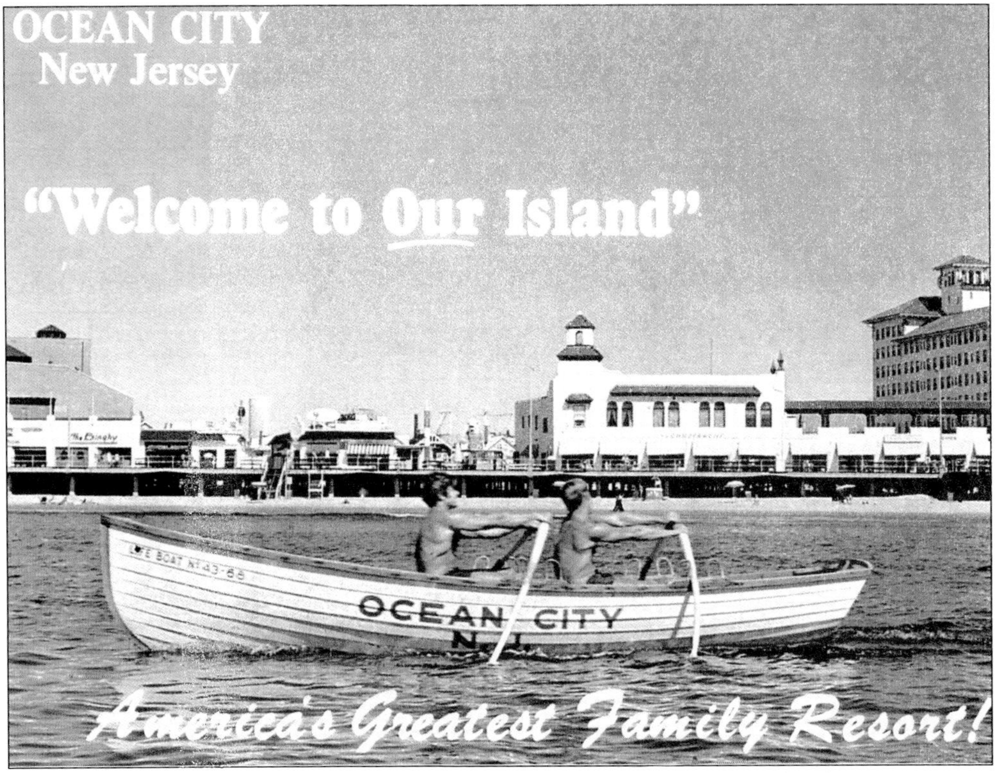

OCEAN CITY
New Jersey

"Welcome to Our Island"

OCEAN CITY
N.J.

America's Greatest Family Resort!

An image of Ocean City Beach Patrol lifeguards Bill Lafferty (left) and Bob Young rowing off the 12th Street Beach was featured on the cover of the 1970 Ocean City promotional brochure.

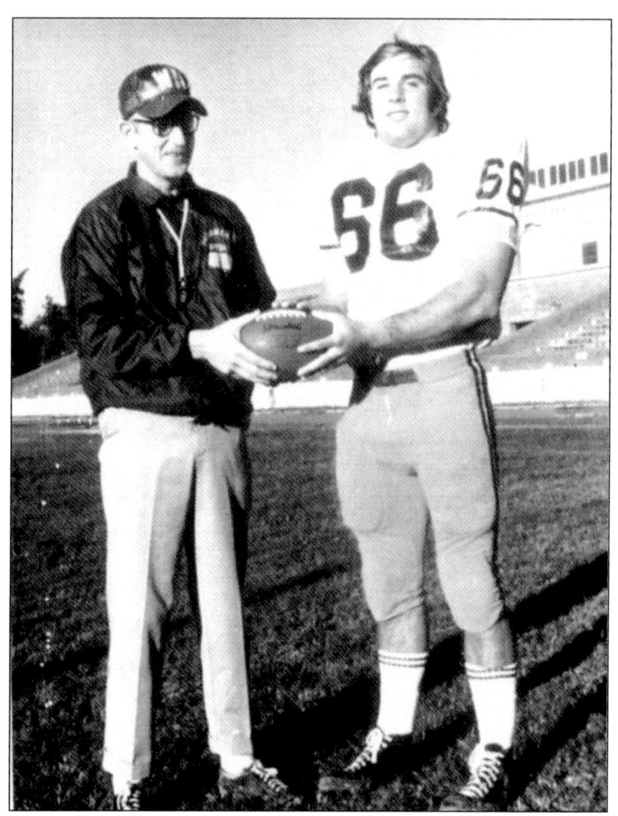

Ocean City Beach Patrol's Jack Neall (right) was named 1971 Ocean City Sportsman of the Year. Lou Holtz, head football coach at William and Mary College, presents a football to Neall, as a symbol of his being elected co-captain of the football squad.

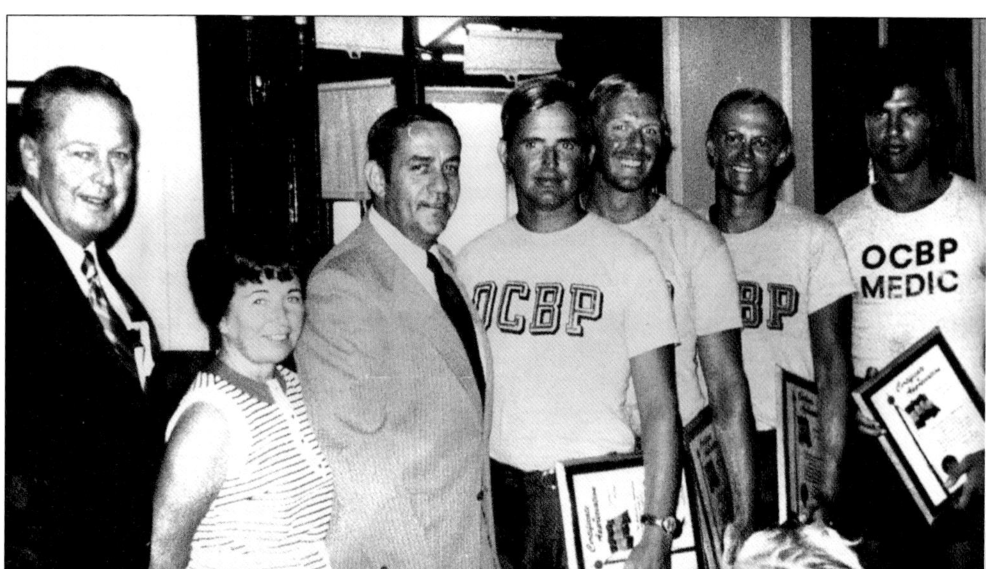

On July 21, 1972, four members of the Ocean City Beach Patrol are honored for making exceptional rescues. From left to right are City Commissioners Luther L. Wallace III, Marilyn K. Moore, and Mayor B. Thomas Waldman, lifeguards Edward Roberts, Paul Painten, and John Pifer, and medic Robert Loeffler.

Joe Grimes was named the best rookie rower in 1972.

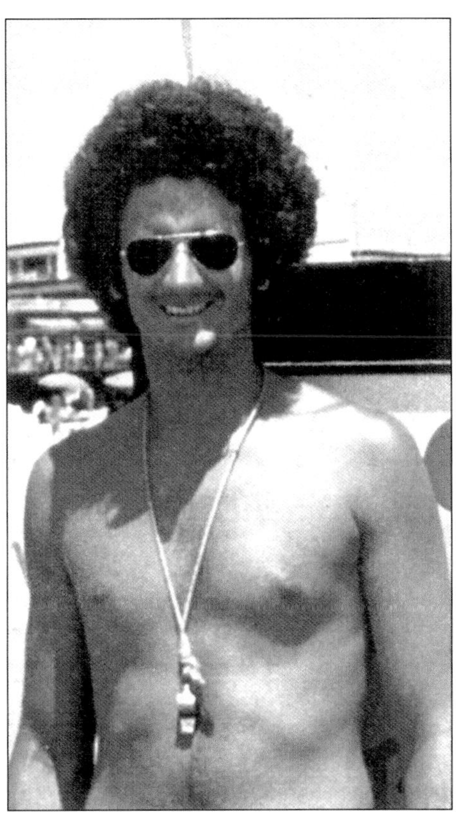

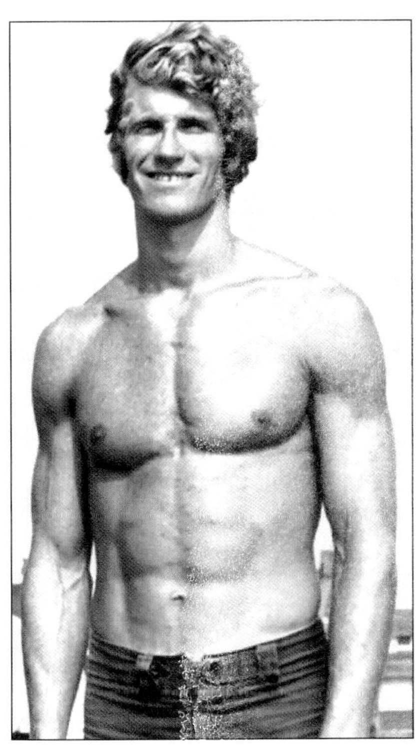

Kevin Daly was named the best singles rower in South Jersey in 1970.

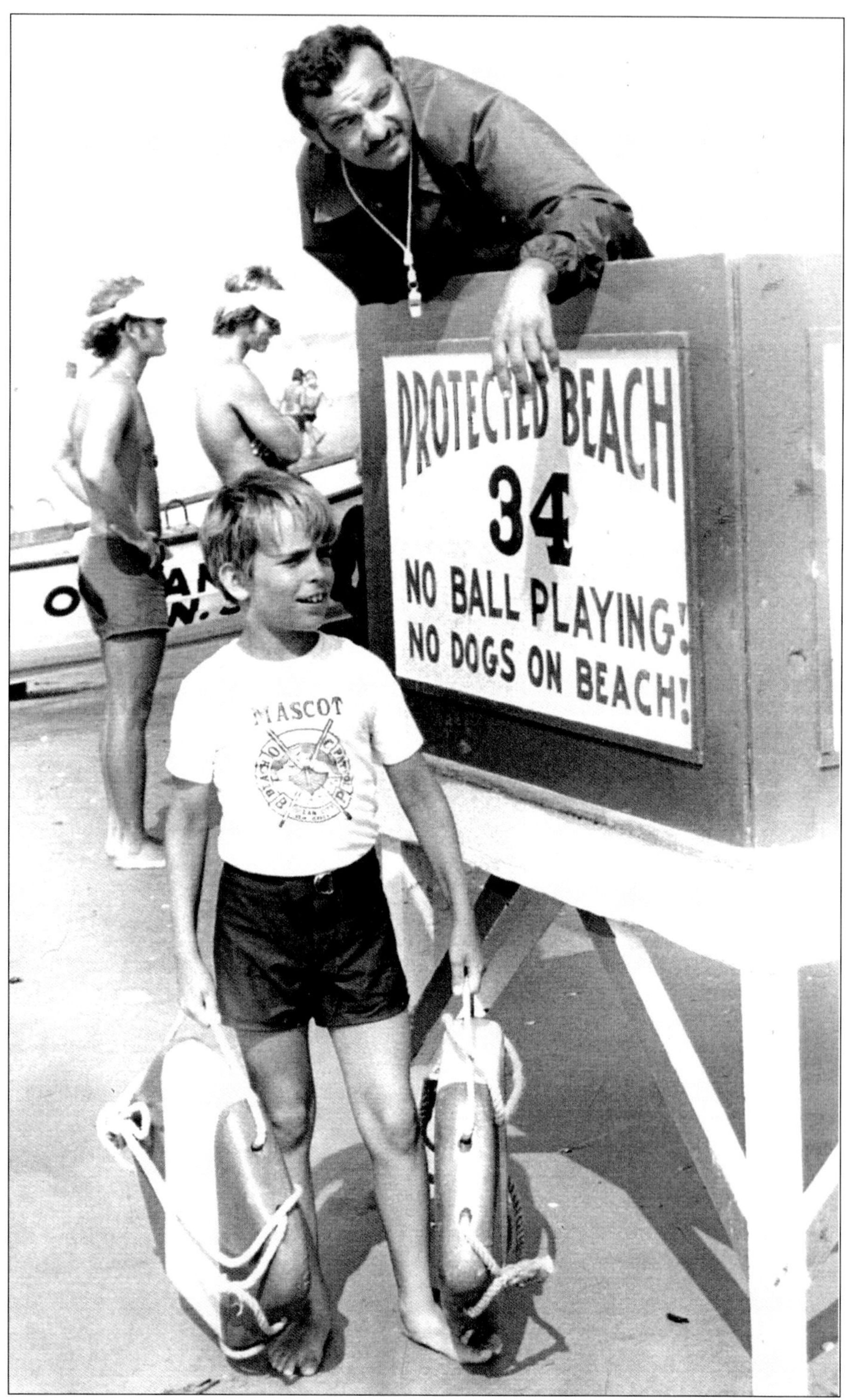

This photograph appeared in the July 13, 1975, *Philadelphia Bulletin* with the caption, "Gus Egnor of Ambler, Pa., mascot for the Ocean City Beach Patrol, gets his orders from Lt. Angelo Psaltis."

As the summer of 1975 began, the terrifying movie *Jaws* was playing at the Village Theatre on the Boardwalk. The movie set off a tidal wave of shark hysteria that kept the bathers close to shore.

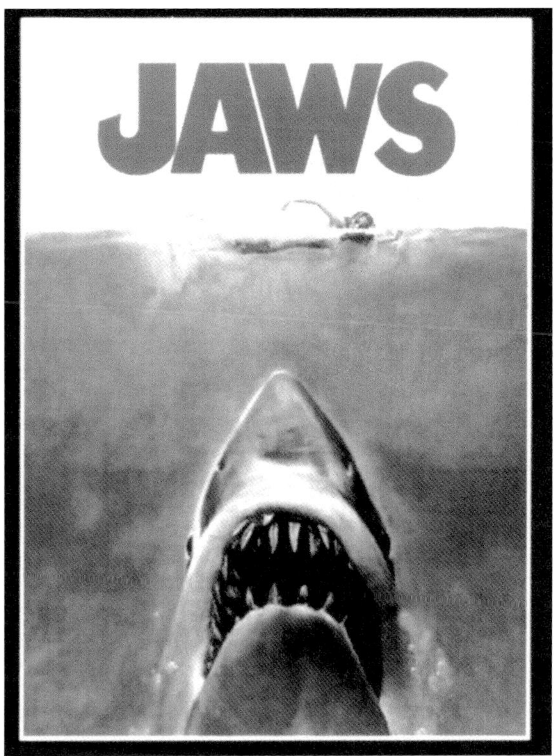

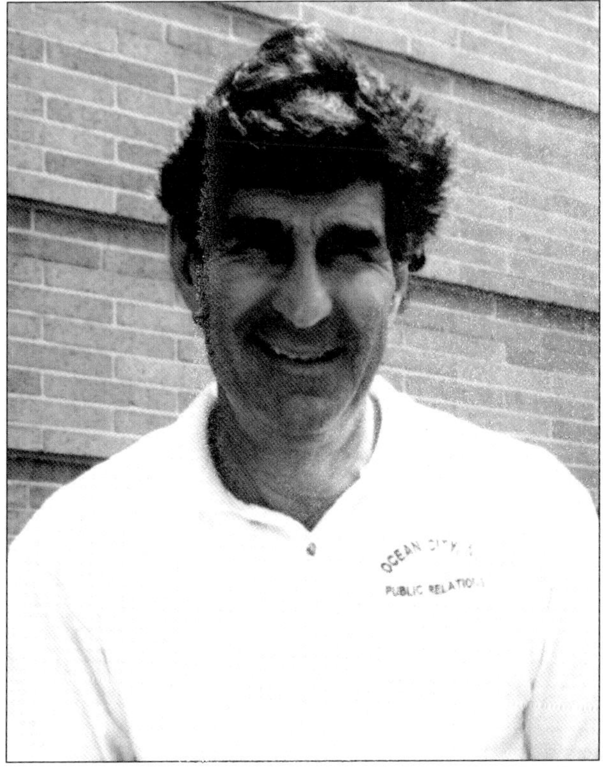

People from all over the region called the city asking if it was safe to come to the shore. Mark Soifer, Ocean City's public relations director, gave the following advice: "Come to Ocean City, enjoy the beach and water. The best way to avoid trouble in the ocean, whether from sharks, strong currents, or man-made objects, is to follow the directions of the lifeguards."

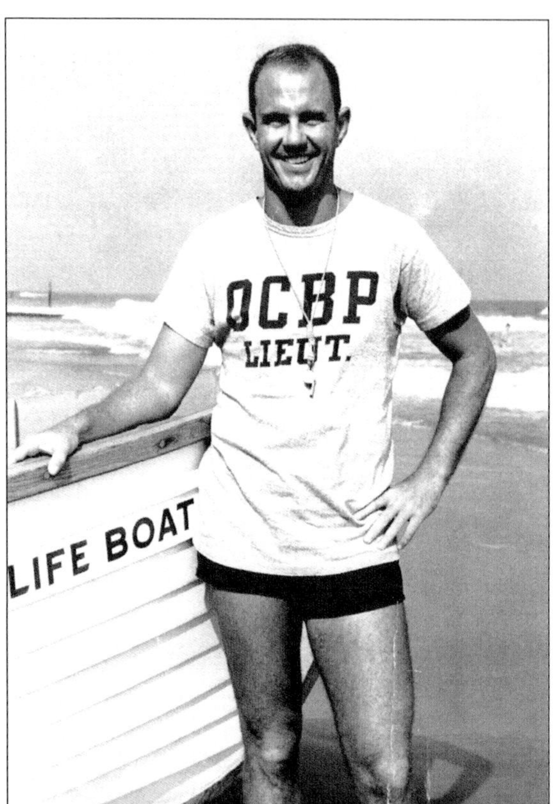

For many years, Lt. Bud McKinley was in charge of training the rookie lifeguards.

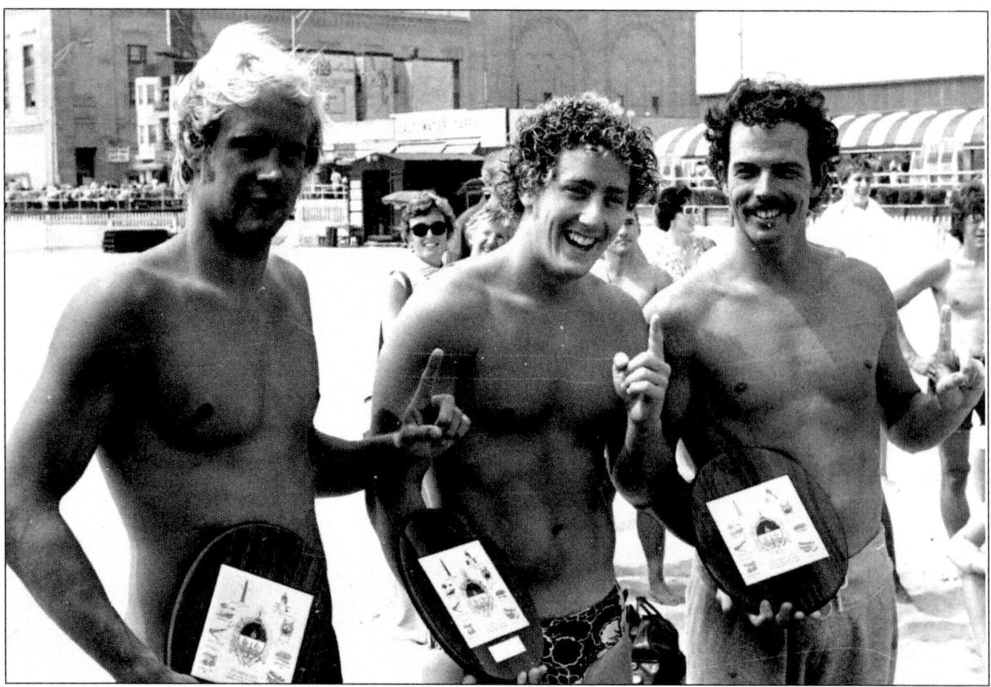

The fastest swimmers in South Jersey during the summer of 1976 are, from left to right, Curt Sulzer, Sid Cassidy, and Paul Sweeney.

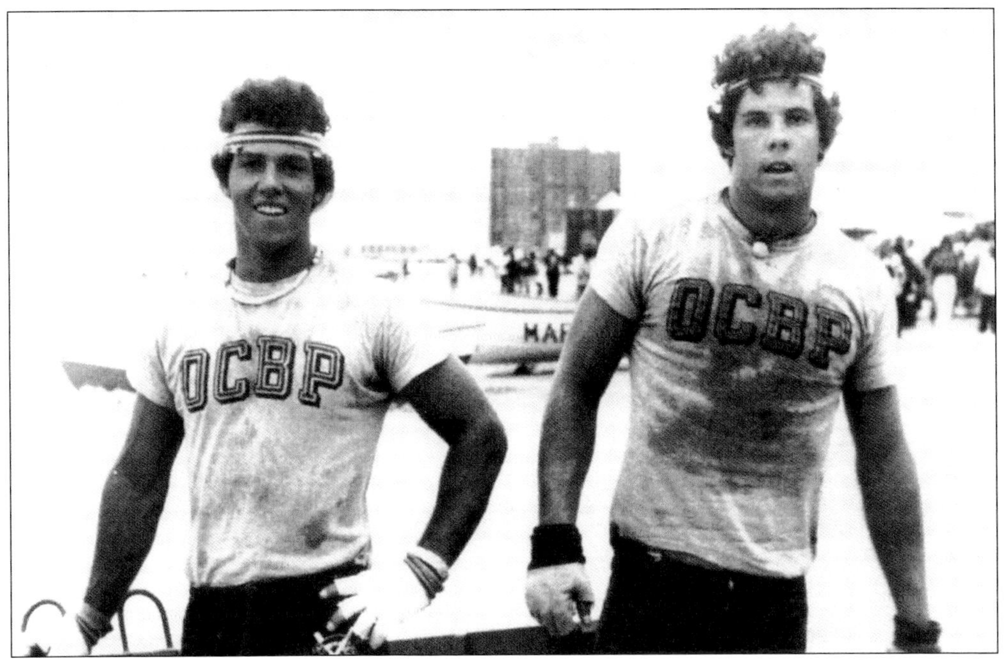

The Jackson brothers, Tom (left) and Marty, were on the Ocean City Beach Patrol competition teams in 1975, 1976, and 1977. Thanks to their rowing, the Ocean City Beach Patrol won three straight South Jersey Lifeguard Championships.

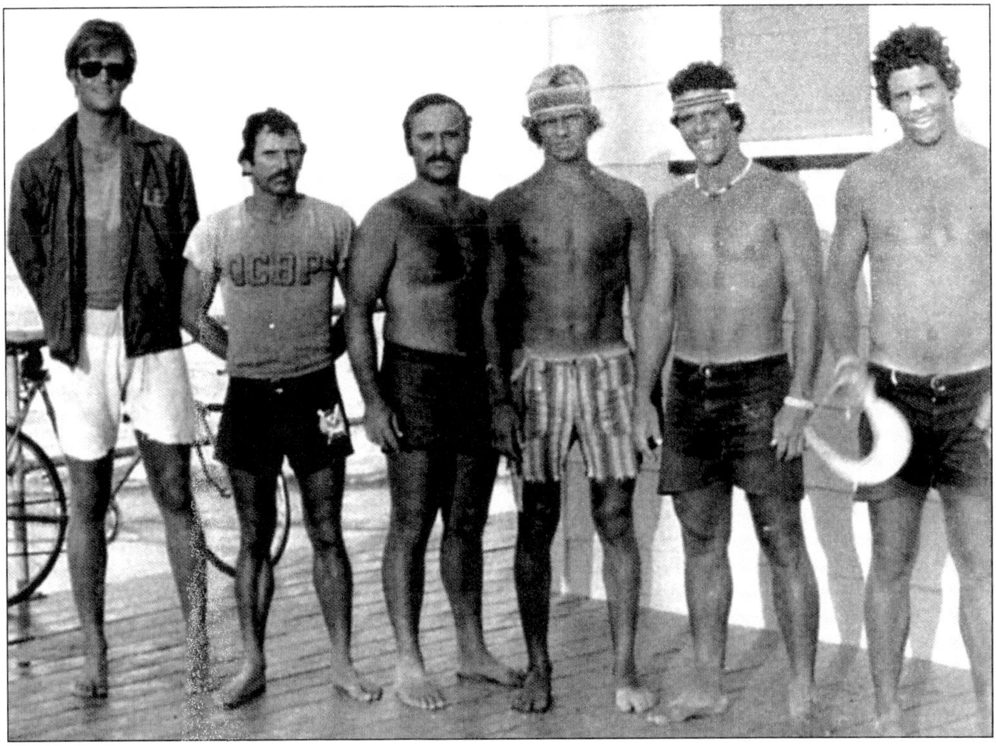

The best Ocean City Beach Patrol rowers in 1975 are, from left to right, Tom Rutherford, Mark Baum, Vince Hink, Tom Stephanik, Tom Jackson, and Marty Jackson.

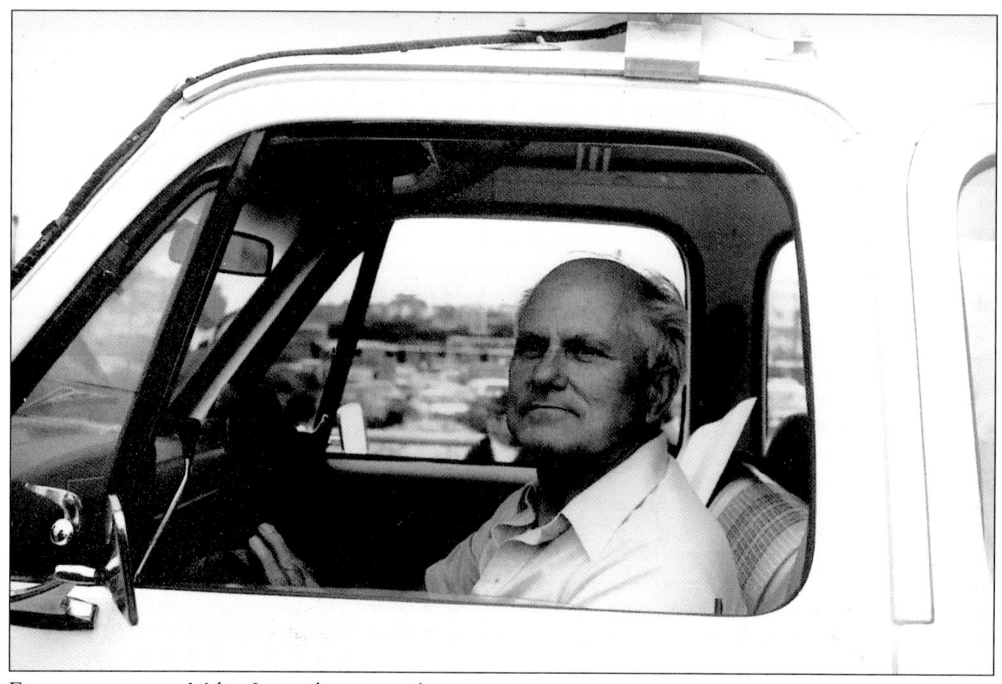

For many years, Mike Impaglizo was the equipment manager and ambulance driver for the Ocean City Beach Patrol.

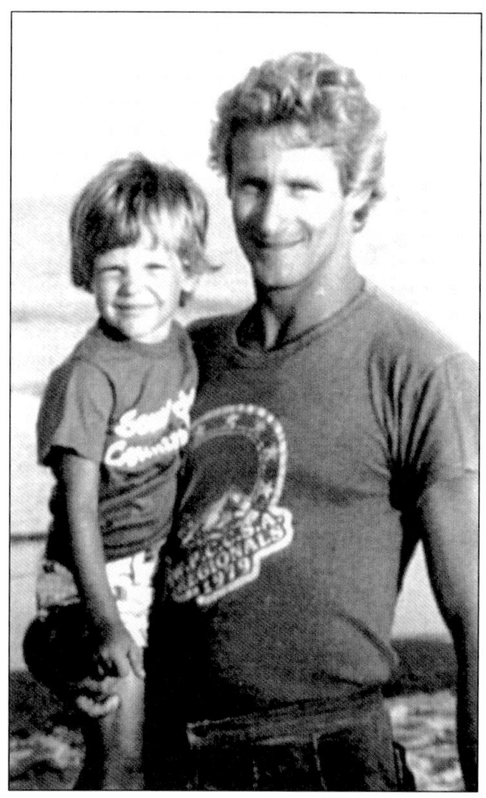

Ocean City Beach Patrol lifeguard Steve Green holds his son, Steve Jr., in 1981. In 1993, Steve Green Jr. became an Ocean City Beach Patrol lifeguard, and he took over his father's stand on the 24th Street Beach after his father retired from the beach patrol at the end of the summer of 1996.

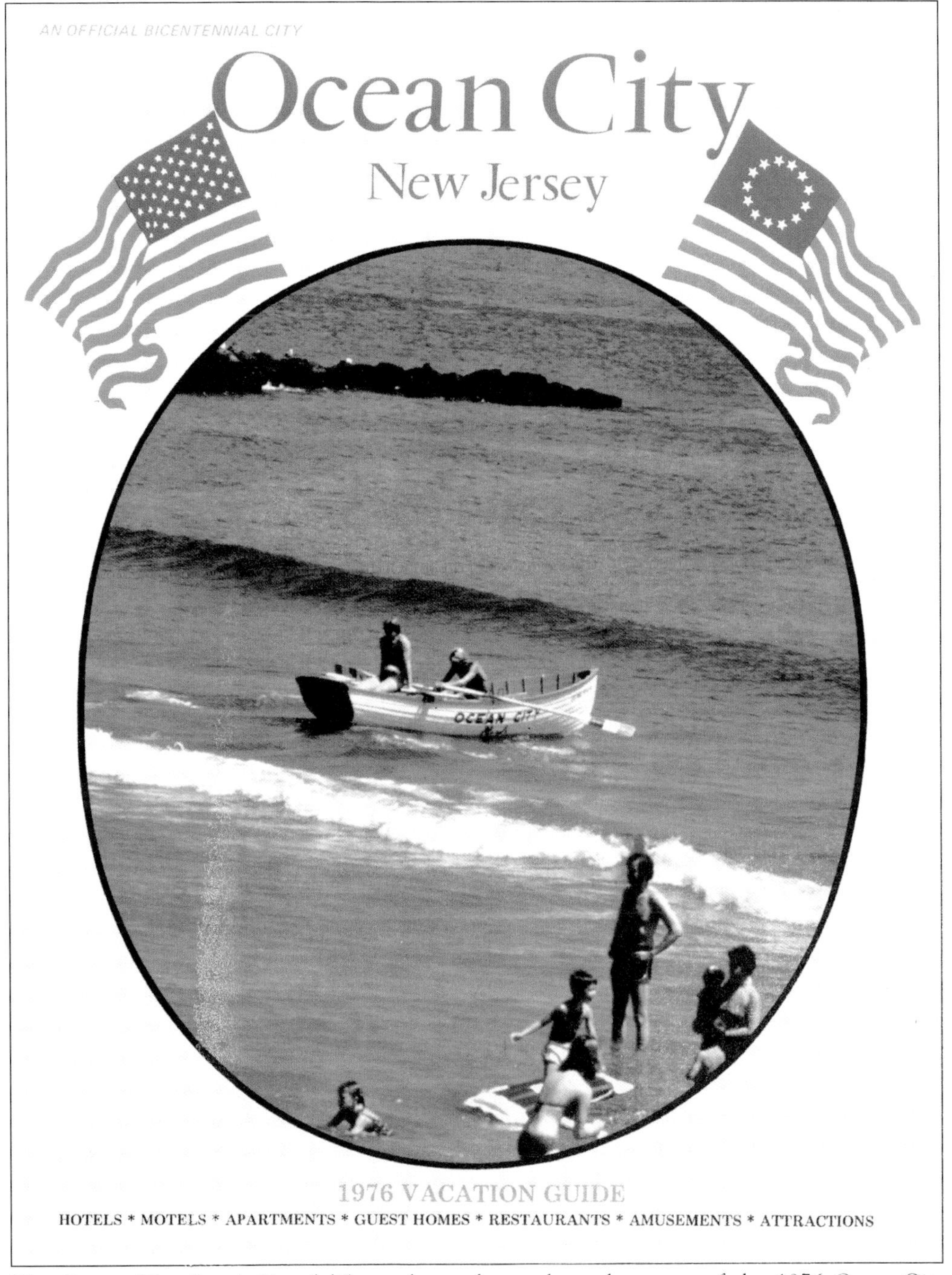

The Ocean City Beach Patrol lifeguards are featured on the cover of the 1976 *Ocean City Vacation Guide*.

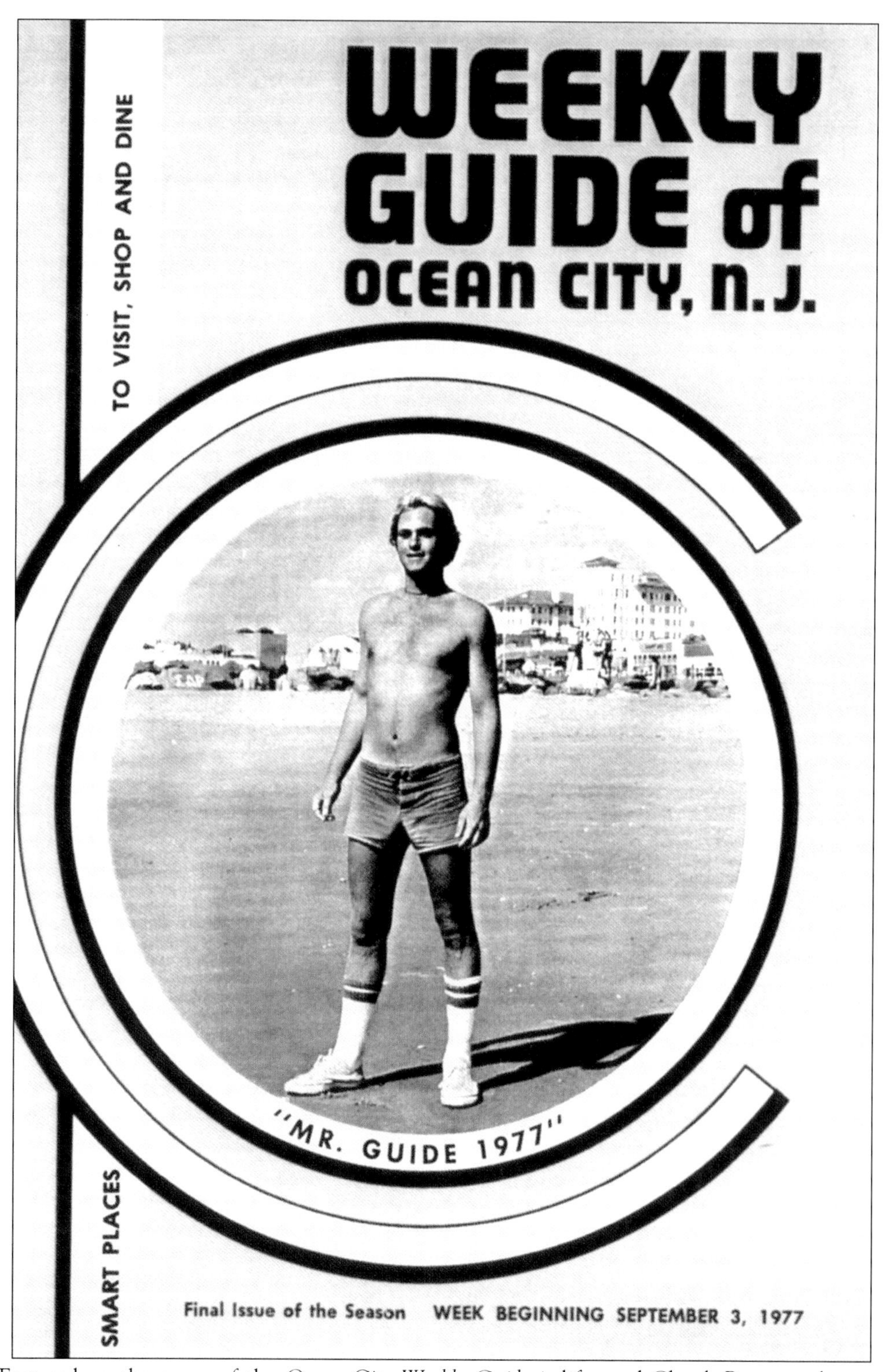

Featured on the cover of the *Ocean City Weekly Guide is* lifeguard Chuck Betson, who was named "Mr. Guide 1977."

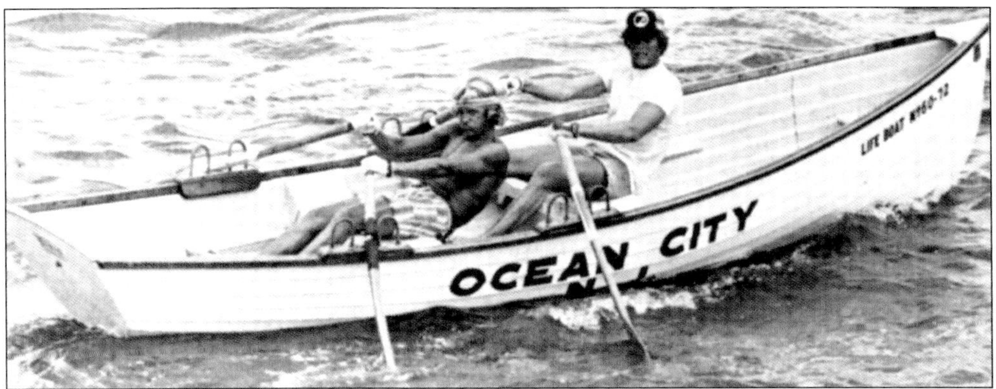

In 1977, Tom Stephanik (left) and Dave Lill were considered the best doubles crew in South Jersey after they won the South Jersey Lifeguard Championship and the Margate Memorial Championship doubles races.

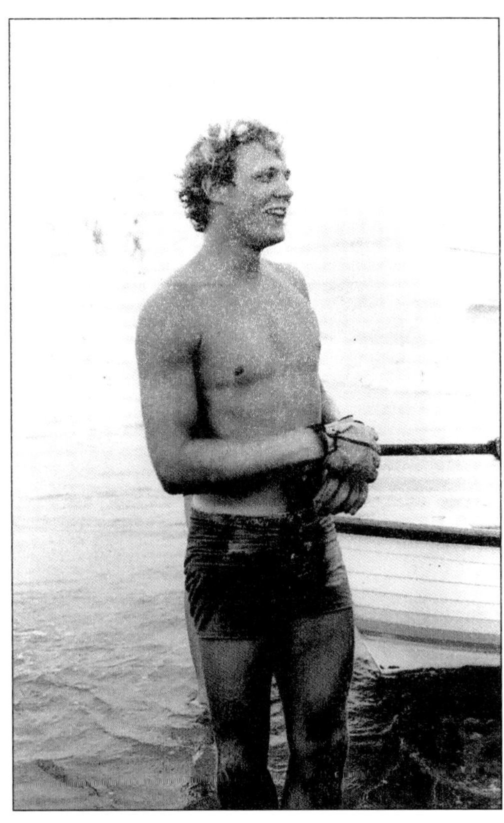

Jack Brook's award-winning performance in the singles rowing race gave the Ocean City Beach Patrol the 1982 Margate Memorial Championship.

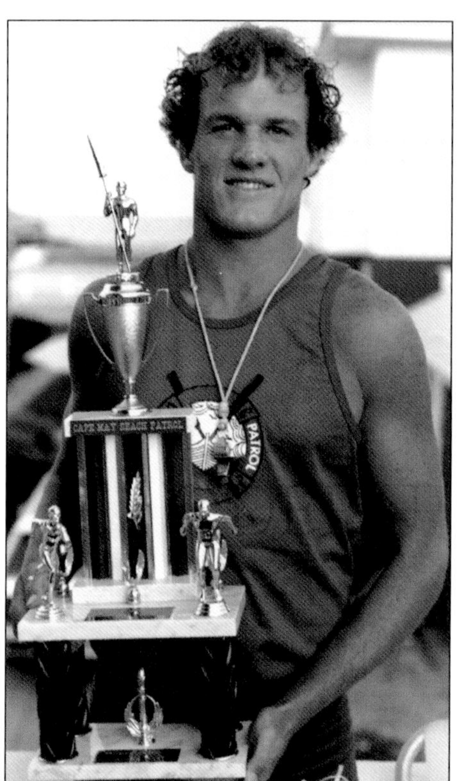

On July 19, 1982, Ocean City Beach Patrol member Bernie Farley won the first Superathlon. Held in Cape May, this event is a lifeguard's triathlon with a two-mile run, a one-and-a-quarter-mile rowing race, and a quarter-mile swim.

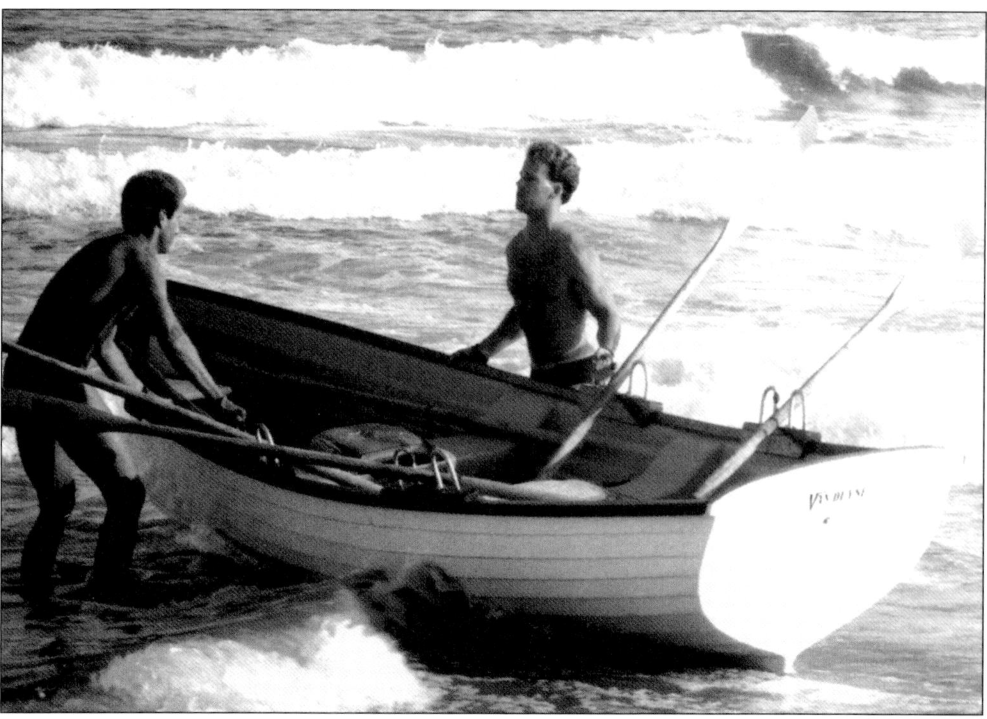

Ron Kirk (left) and John Herron won the South Jersey Lifeguard Championship doubles rowing race in 1981 and 1983.

Six

Modern Lifeguards

The Ocean City Beach Patrol has changed significantly since Capt. George Lafferty retired in 1983. The chain of command is different: the patrol is now a branch of the city's fire department, and it is led by a chief of operations rather than a captain. Senior guards work closely with each year's group of rookies, following guidelines from the U.S. Lifesaving Association for the training of new guards and for the emergency techniques each guard must learn. Today, women make up about 20 percent of the patrol's members, and several women lifeguard tournaments are held. The women of the Ocean City Beach Patrol dominate the South Jersey races, having won every competition in 2003.

The men and women of the Ocean City Beach Patrol continue their mission of protecting the thousands of bathers here each season, while also building on their reputation as ardent swimming and rowing competitors. This tradition of excellence is built on the experience, skill, and dedication of its members.

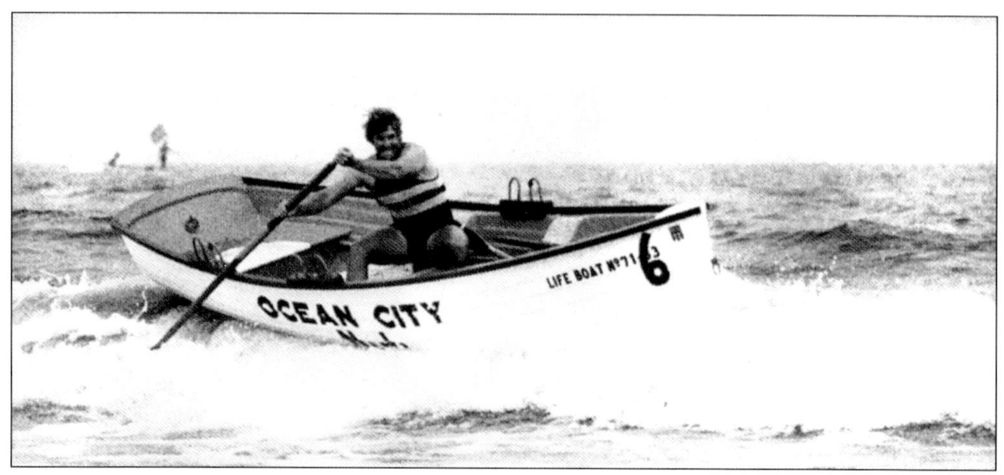

Ocean City Beach Patrol's Tom Morrison guides his lifeboat across the finish line to complete the sweep of the 1983 South Jersey Lifeguard Championship. Earlier that evening, in Avalon, Ron Kirk and John Herron won the doubles lifeboat race and Bill Fallon won the swim.

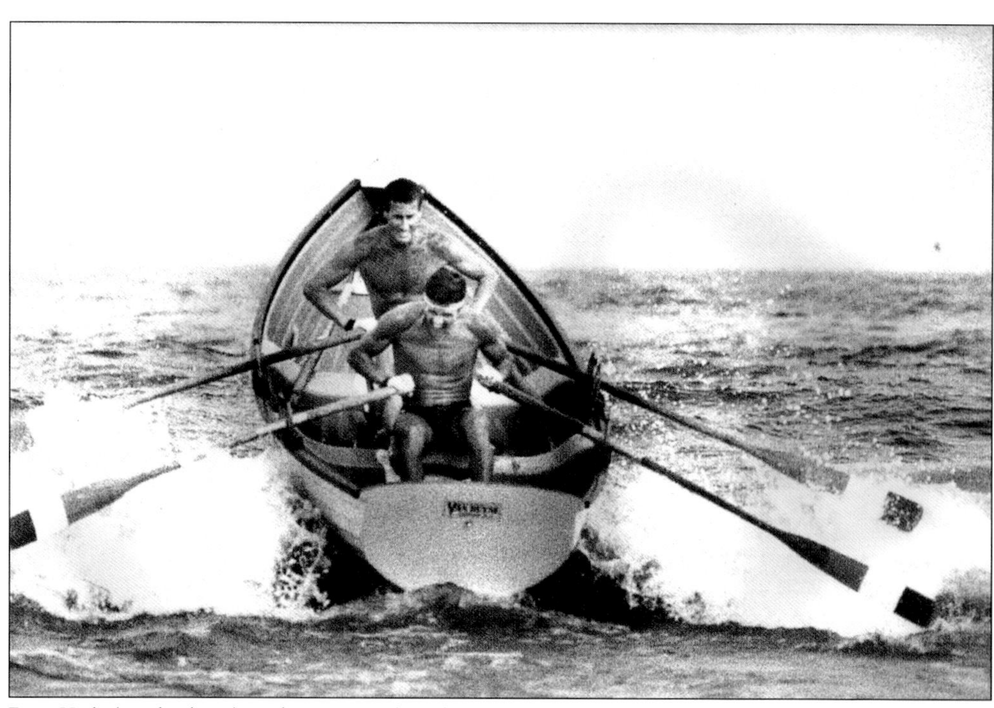

Ron Kirk (in the bow) and Tom Stephanik were the best doubles crew in South Jersey in 1984 and 1985. They won every beach patrol competition, including the South Jersey Lifeguard Championship, the Margate Memorial Championship, the Hoffman Memorial Championship, and the Cape May County Championship.

Pictured are the Ocean City Beach Patrol medics of 1984. From left to right are the following: (first row) Maureen Rafferty and Anne Costello; (second row) June Ashburn and Rea Butkus; (third row) Rosemarie Schambers and Ellen Hill. Hill holds the plaque presented to the 1984 medic squad by T. John Carey and Betty Carey in recognition of the more than 60 years of valuable contributions the Ocean City Beach Patrol medics have made serving the public.

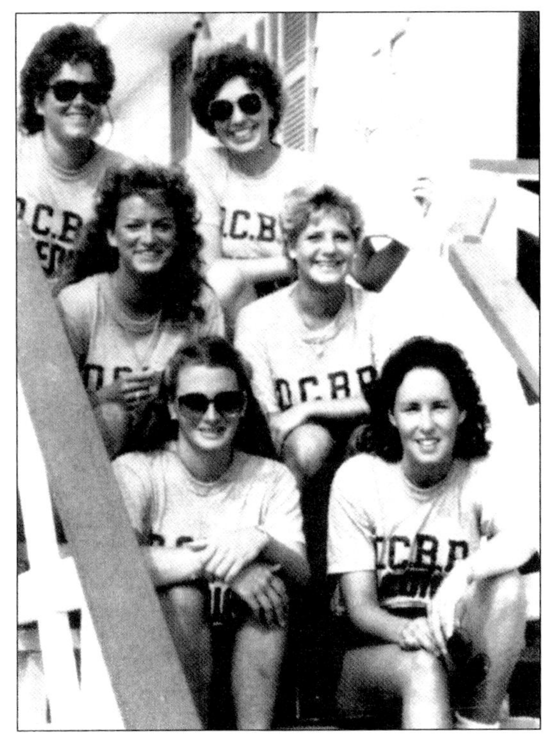

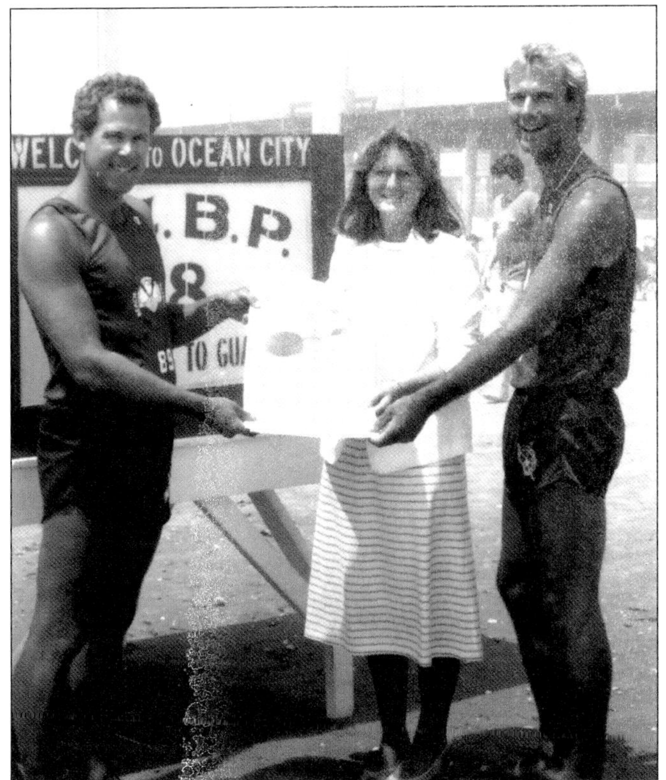

On August 2, 1984, Ocean City lifeguards Bob Stowe (left) and Bob Amsler and Red Cross representative Ann Gabriel hold a poster advertising the Ocean City Beach Patrol sponsored blood drive.

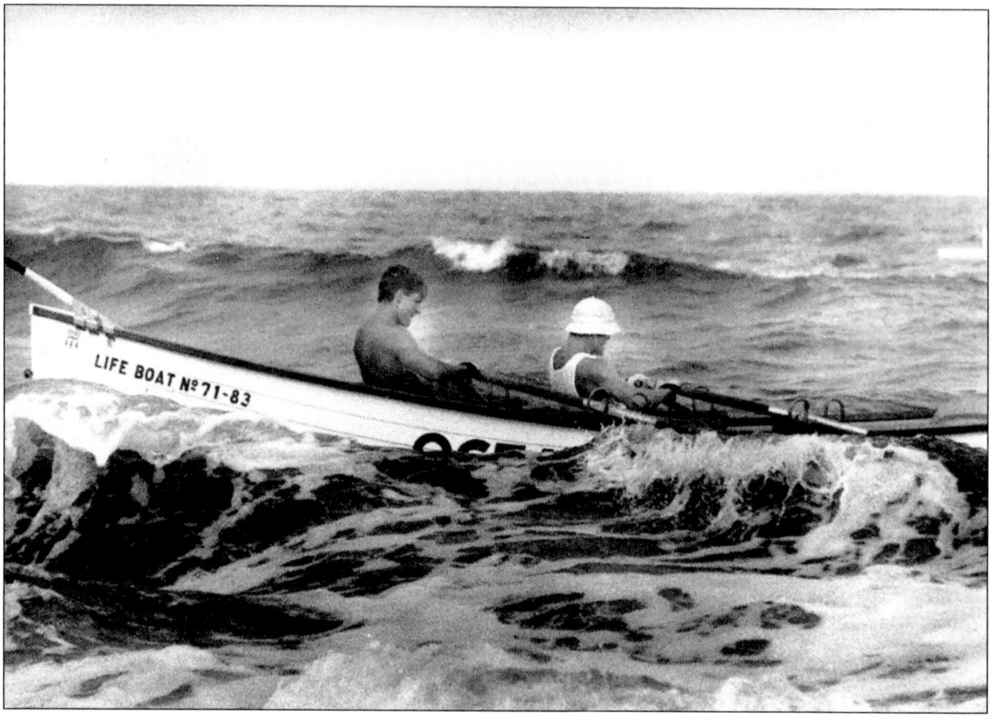

John Ridgway (left) and John Millar won every lifeguard doubles rowing race in 1986, including the South Jersey Lifeguard Championship, the Margate Memorial Championship, the Hoffman Memorial Championship, and the Cape May County Lifeguard Championship.

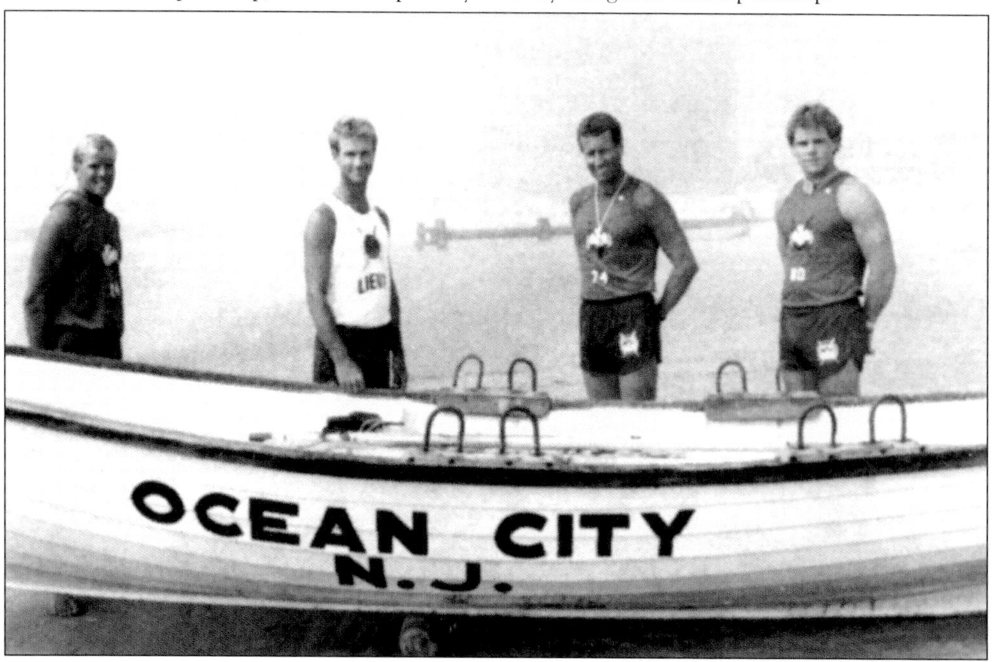

In 1988, Ted Evans, Bob Amsler, Ron Kirk, and Joe Sheffer teamed up to win the singles lifeboat relay race in the U.S. Lifesaving Association's National Lifeguard Championship, held in Cape May. They crossed the finish line two seconds ahead of the Los Angeles County boat.

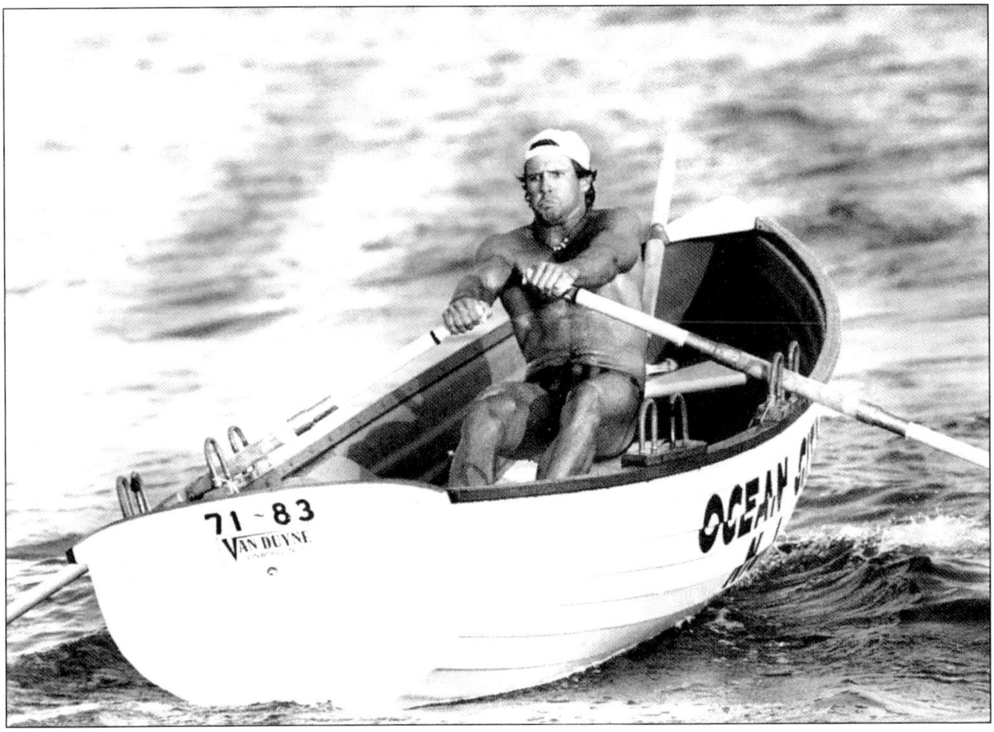

Ted Evans was the best singles rower in South Jersey in the late 1980s and the early 1990s. He won the singles rowing race in the South Jersey Lifeguard Championship in 1988, 1989, and 1990, becoming the only South Jersey lifeguard to win this event for three consecutive years.

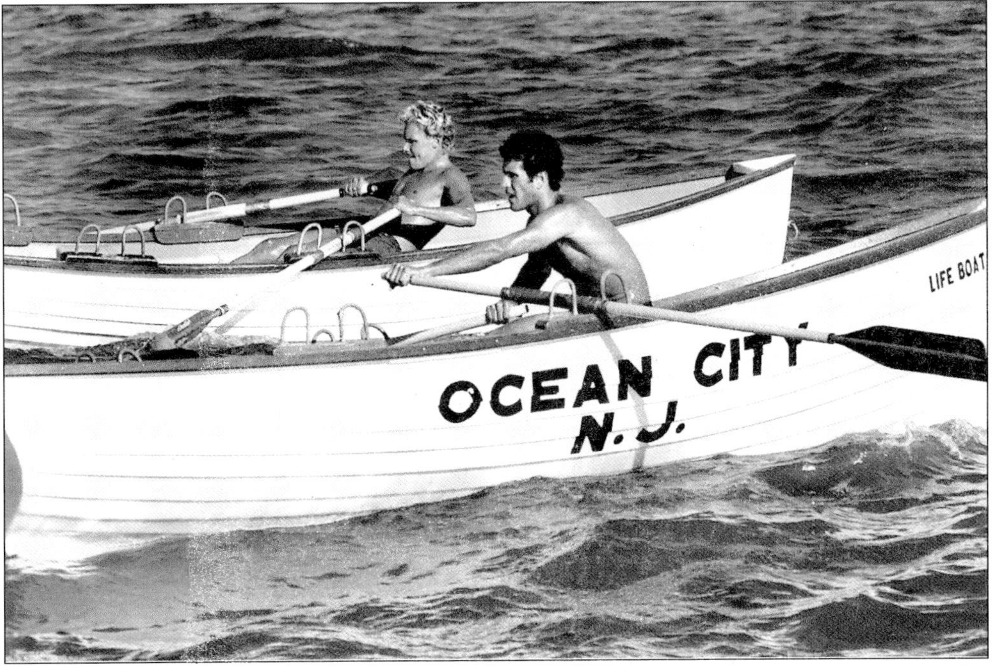

Ocean City's Rob Desipio passes last year's winner from Cape May on his way to victory in the 1990 Superathlon.

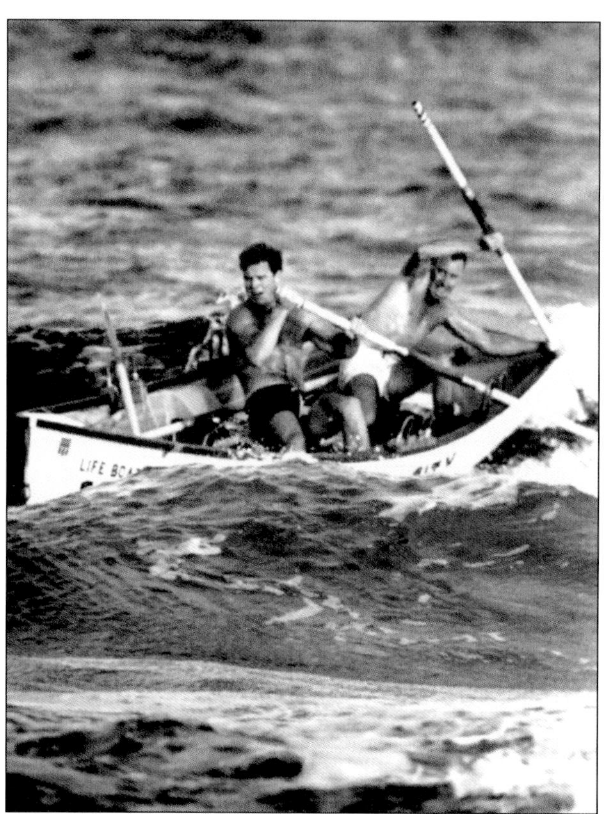

Ocean City lifeguards Joe Sheffer (left) and Chris Oves steer their lifeboat across the finish line to win the 1990 Hoffman Memorial title. They also won the Margate Memorial doubles race and the Cape May County doubles race that year.

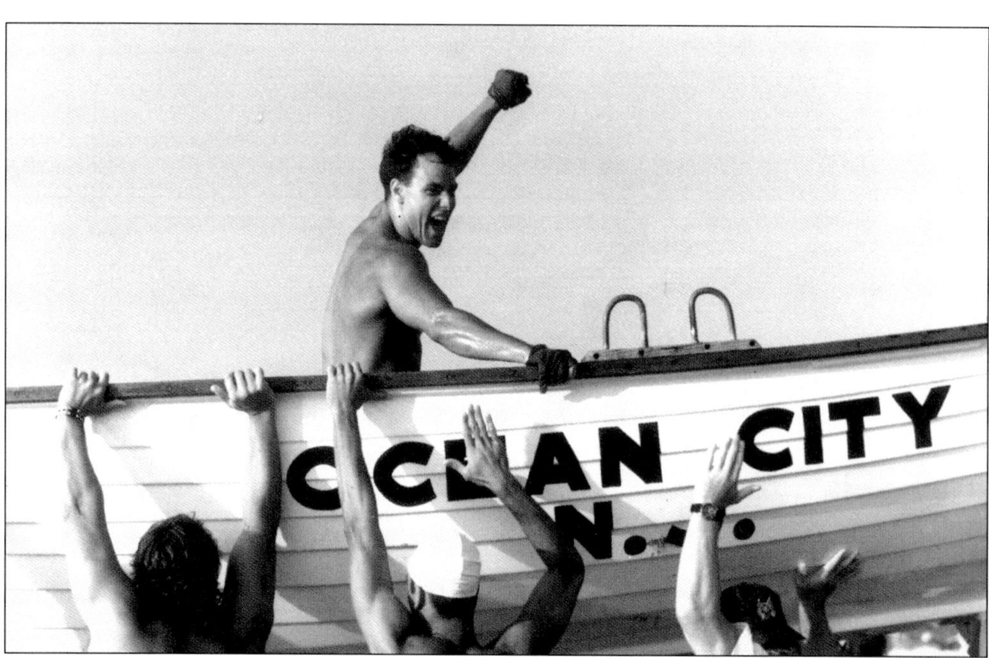

Ocean City Beach Patrol's Sonny Rutkowski celebrates his singles lifeboat win at the 1993 Cape May County Lifeguard Championship, as he gets the traditional victory ride off the Wildwood Crest beach.

The *American Lifeguard* magazine used a picture of Ocean City Beach Patrol's Ron Kirk on the cover of its autumn 1990 issue. Kirk won 30 intercity competitions during the 1980s, including a national championship and five South Jersey Lifeguard Championships.

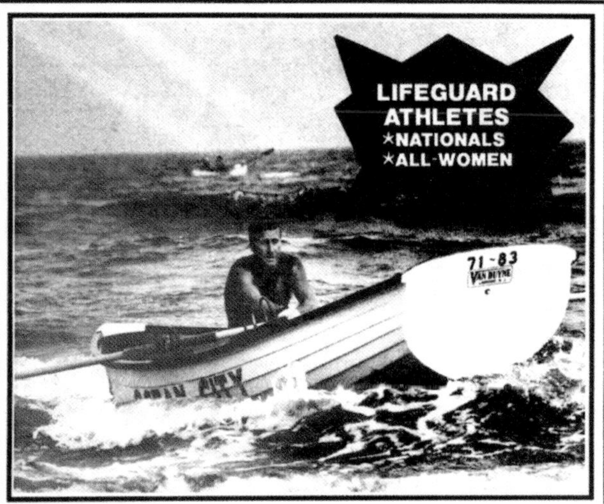

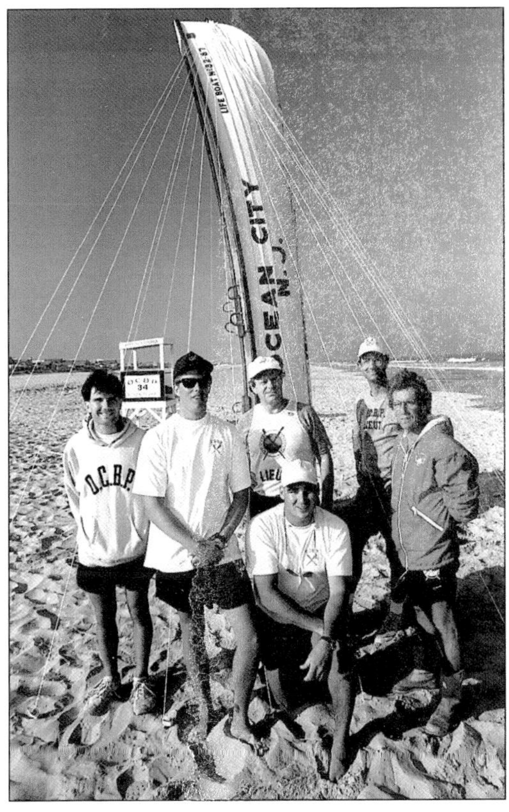

Look on any beach on the coast of New Jersey and chances are the lifeguards are using surfboats crafted by the Van Duyne family. This has been the case since 1951. The surfboat in this picture, a Van Duyne, was rigged up for a magazine article about John Van Duyne Sr. These Ocean City Beach Patrol lifeguards—from left to right, Doug Schmitt, Charlie Wigo, Lt. Fred Miller, Skip Reiff, Lt. Bob Amsler, and Jim Kirk—took advantage of the boat for this picture, which was featured on the cover of the patrol's 1993 yearbook, *Horizons*.

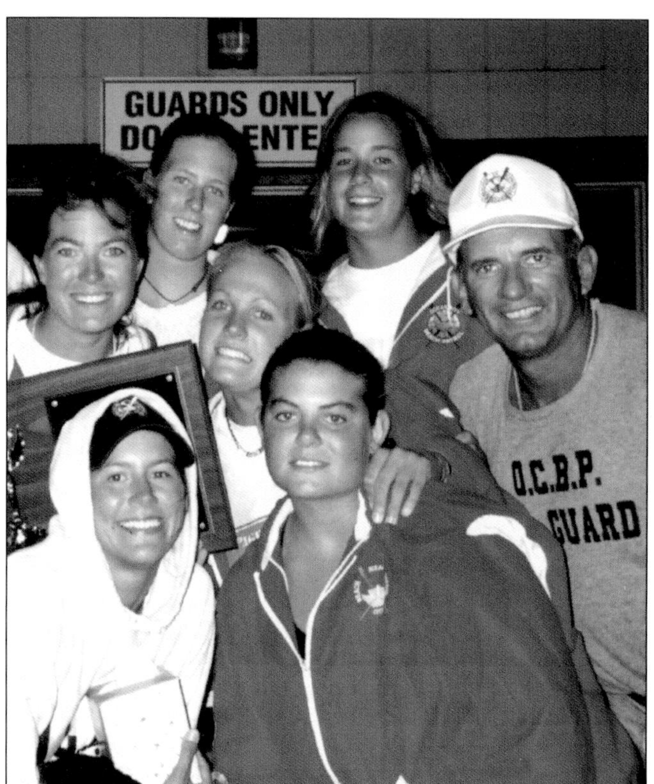

The Ocean City Beach Patrol won the Cape May County Women's Lifeguard Tournament in 1995. From left to right are the following: (first row) Meredieth Scully and Stephanie Wilson; (second row) Kristie Brown, Melissa Koch, and senior guard Mark Baum; (third row) Sara Griffith and Kelly Egan.

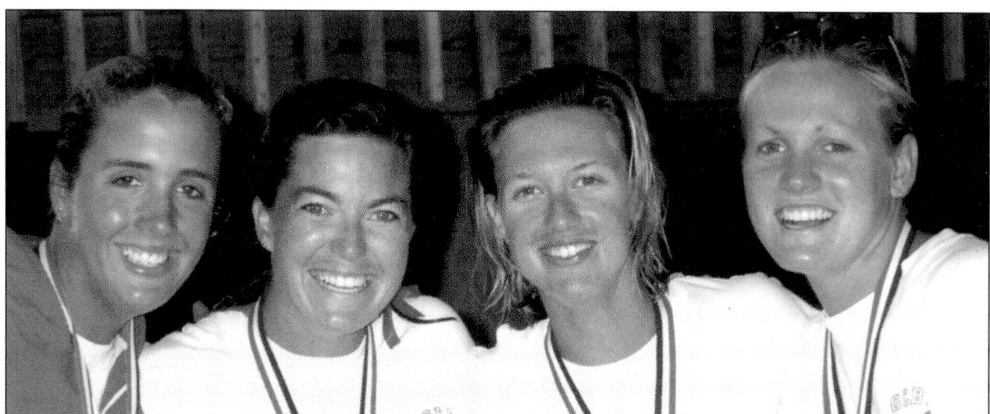

These Ocean City Beach Patrol members won the 1998 Longport Women's Lifeguard Invitational surf dash race. From left to right are Carolyn Stephanik, Kristie Brown, Ashlea Graham, and Melissa Koch.

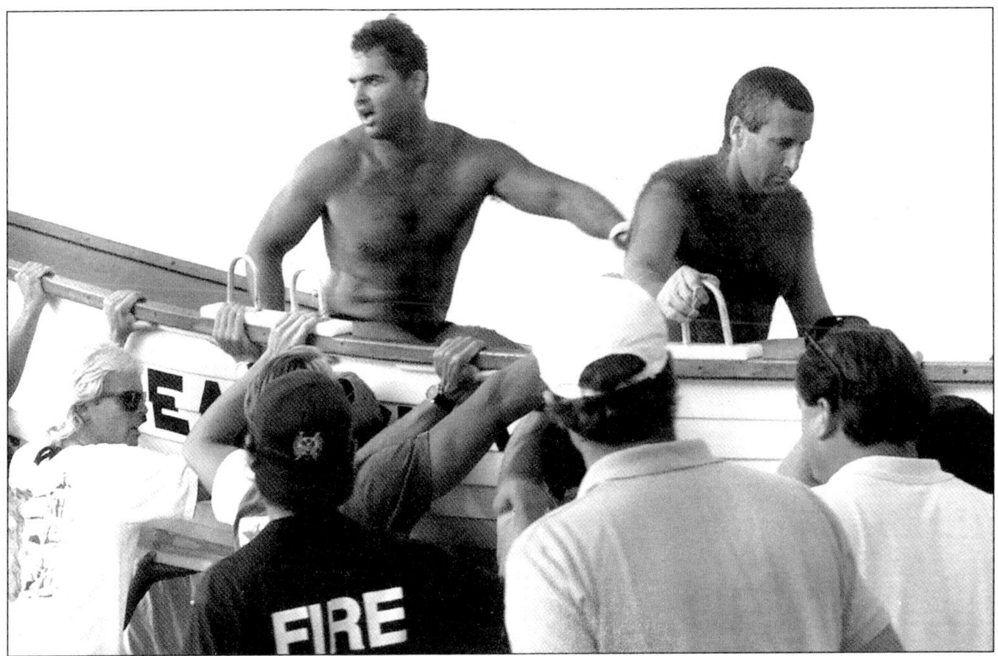

Bob Garbutt Jr. (left) and Ron Kirk get the traditional victory ride up the beach, carried by fellow lifeguards, after winning the South Jersey doubles lifeboat championship in 1994.

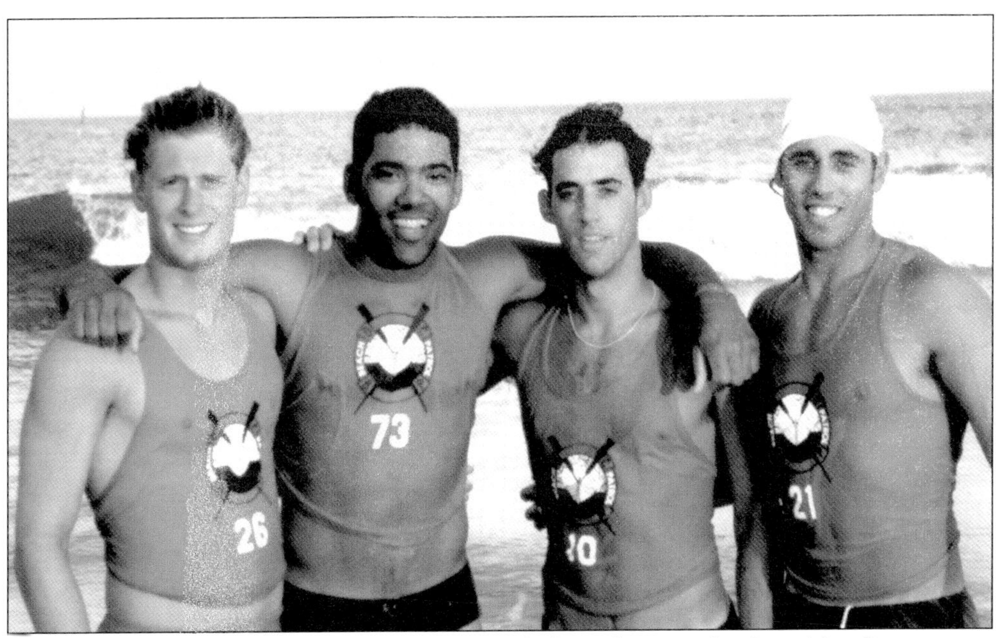

Ocean City's surf dash relay team won the second-place plaque at the Cape May County Tournament in 1998. From left to right are Zack Benson, Mike Langley, Bryan Theiss, and Shanin Theiss.

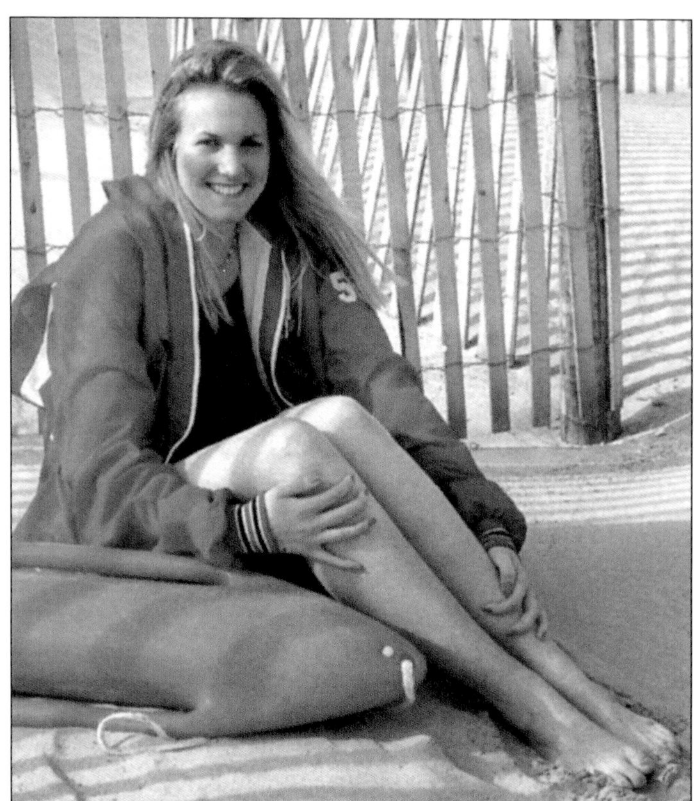

Ocean City Beach Patrol's Melissa Koch was featured in the May 6, 1996, *People* magazine. The article was entitled "Real-life Baywatch."

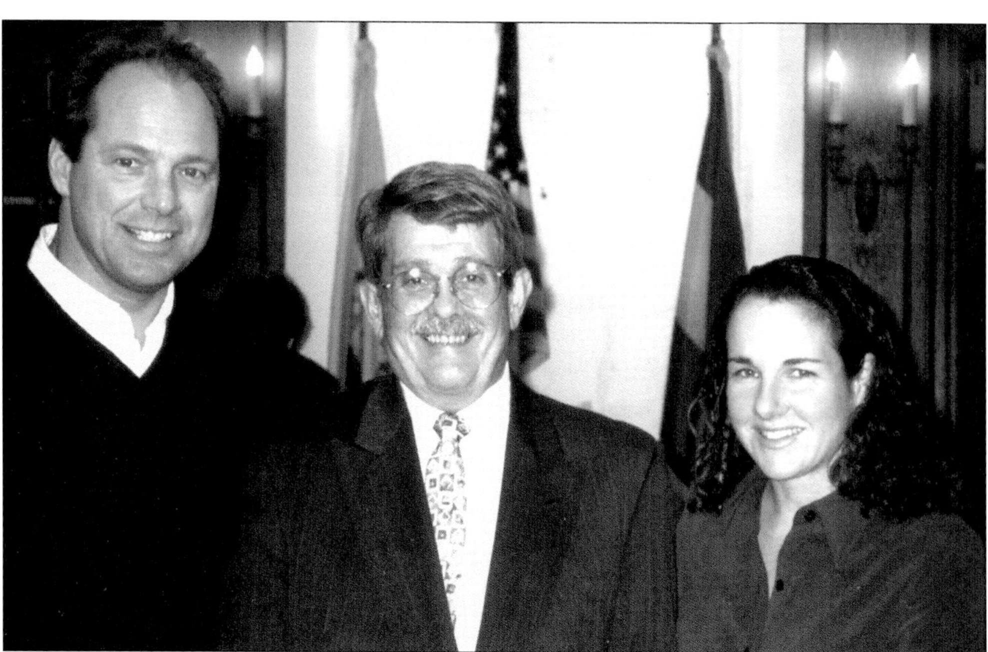

On January 13, 2000, Mayor Henry "Bud" Knight (center) honored Ocean City Beach Patrol lifeguards Tom Ashley and Kim McKay for an ocean rescue they made while off duty on September 6, 1999.

John McShane, a senior lieutenant, brings in his kayak after demonstrating how it can be used for ocean rescues.

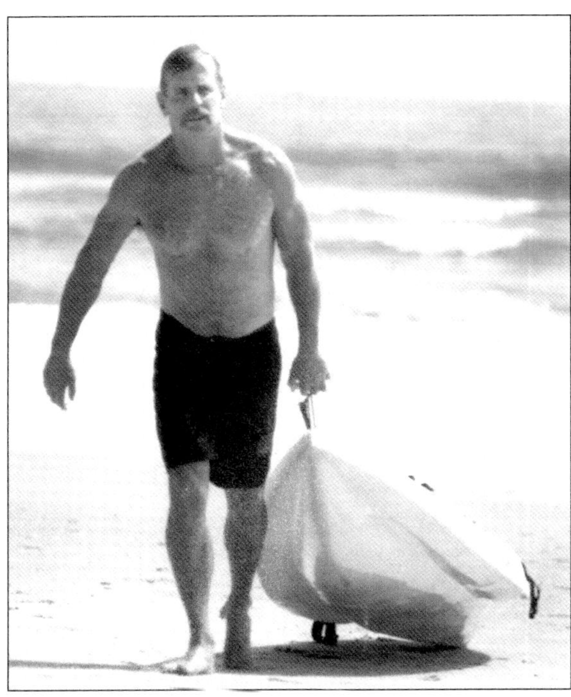

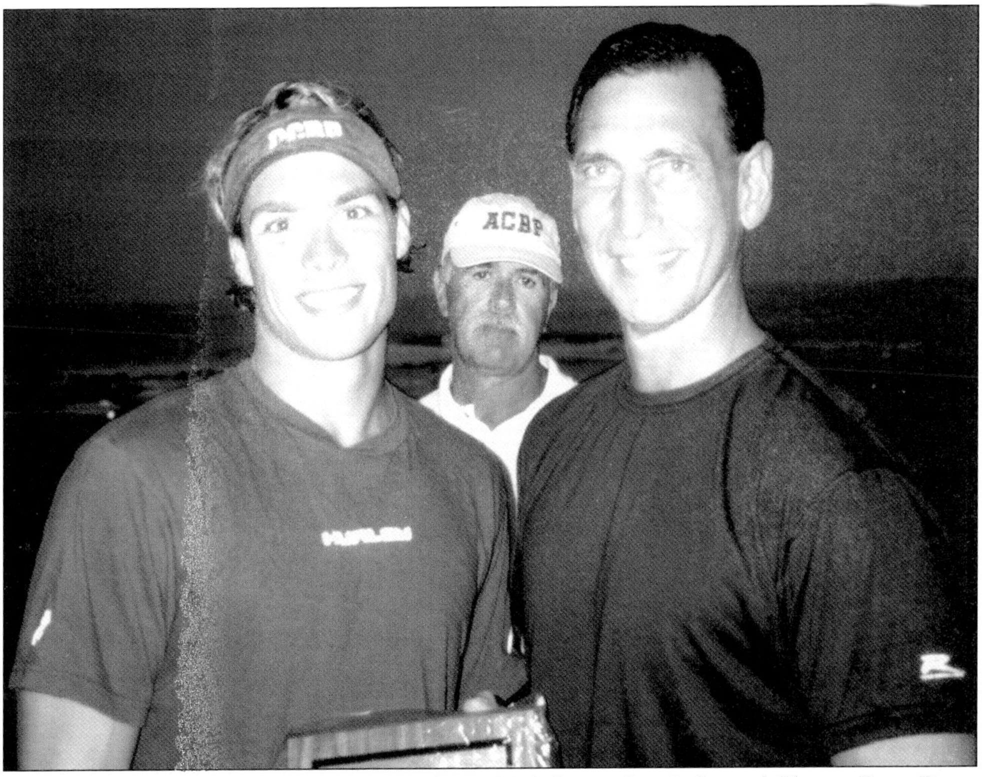

After winning the singles rowing race in the 2002 Atlantic City Lifeguard Classic, Ryan Dunn (left) is congratulated by Congressman Frank LoBiondo. Looking on is Bob Levy, Atlantic City Beach Patrol chief.

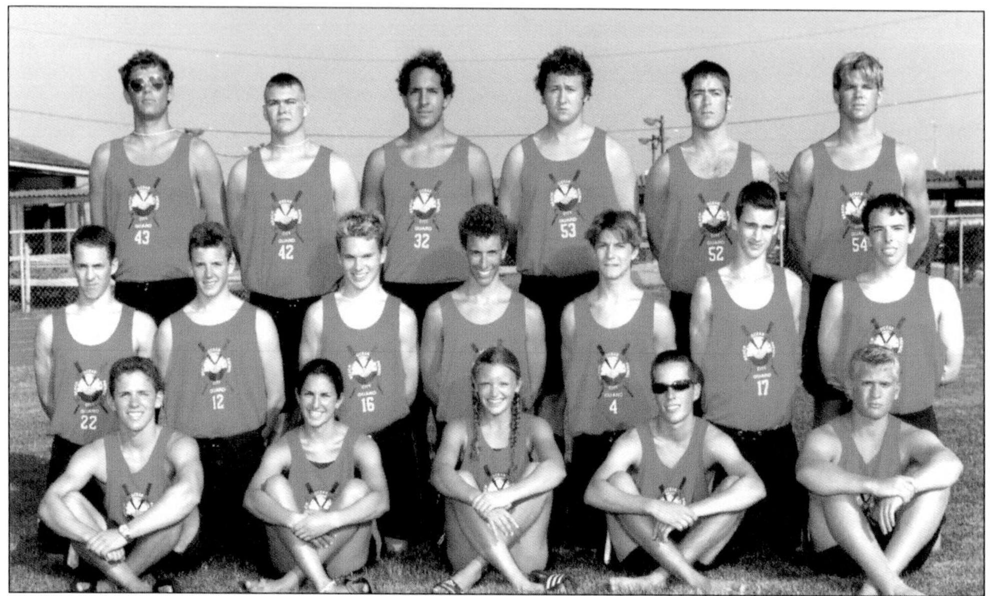

The 18 members of the 2002 Ocean City Beach Patrol rookie class proudly wear their uniforms for the first time.

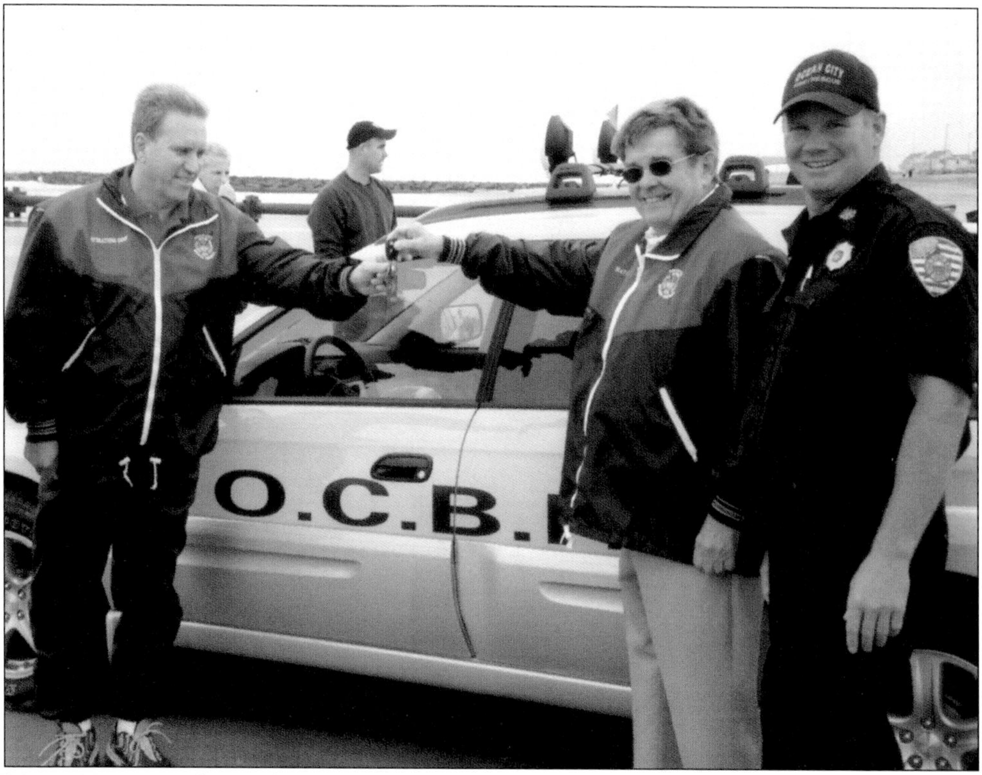

Mayor Henry "Bud" Knight (second from the right) hands over the keys to the beach patrol vehicle to Tom Mullineaux, Ocean City Beach Patrol chief of operations, while Charlie Bowman, deputy fire chief, looks on. Subaru loaned two of these vehicles to the city for use by the beach patrol in 2003.

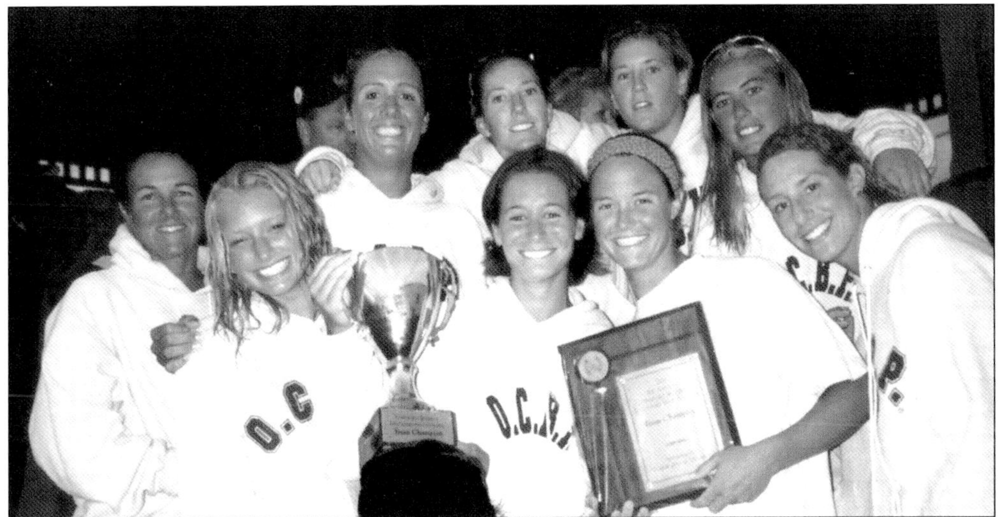

These Ocean City Beach Patrol members won all three women's lifeguard tournaments held during the summer of 2003. From left to right are the following: (first row) Taryn Townsend, Joanna Weber, Lesley Graham, and Wendy Wallace; (second row) Kim McKay, Carolyn Stephanik, Meredith Long, Maggie Long, and Sandy Wilson. This photograph was taken after their victory in the Longport Women's Lifeguard Championship.

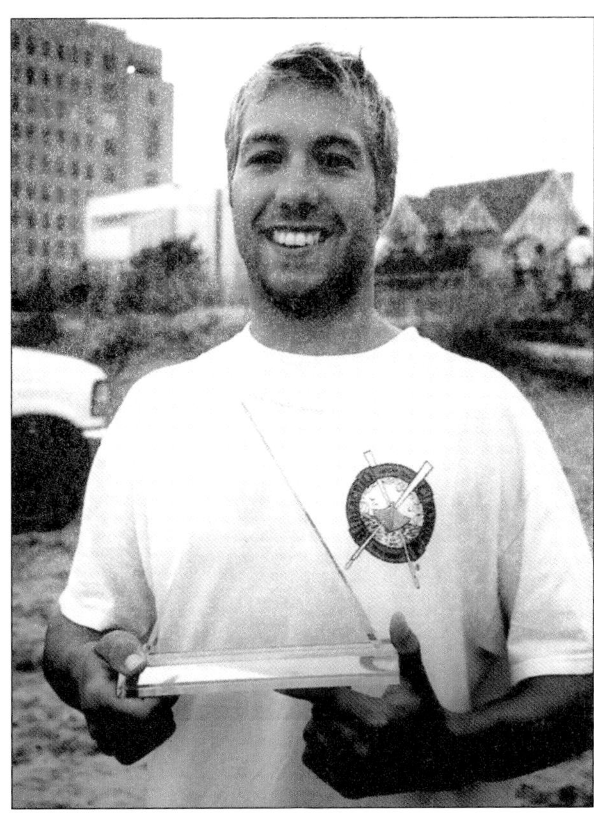

Ocean City Beach Patrol's Paul Mangen was the fastest swimmer in South Jersey in 2003. He won every swim event held during that summer.

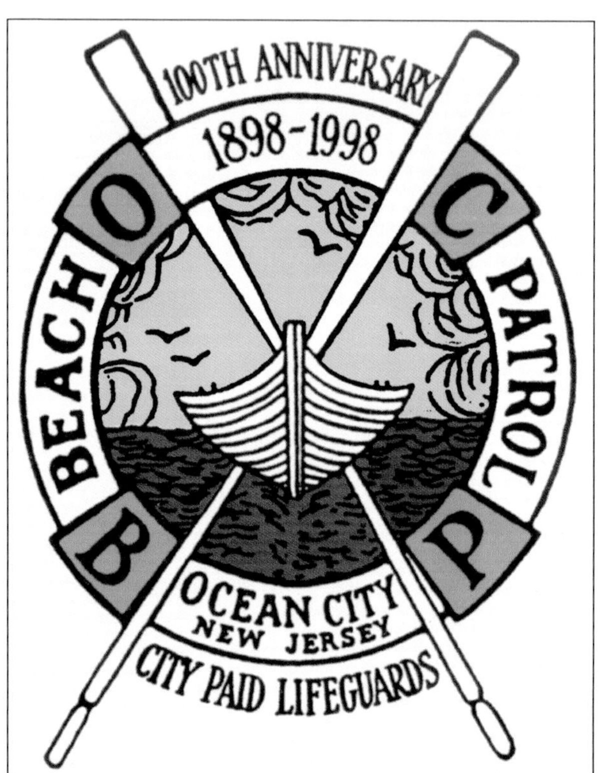

This logo was used by the Ocean City Beach Patrol in 1998 when it celebrated its 100th anniversary.

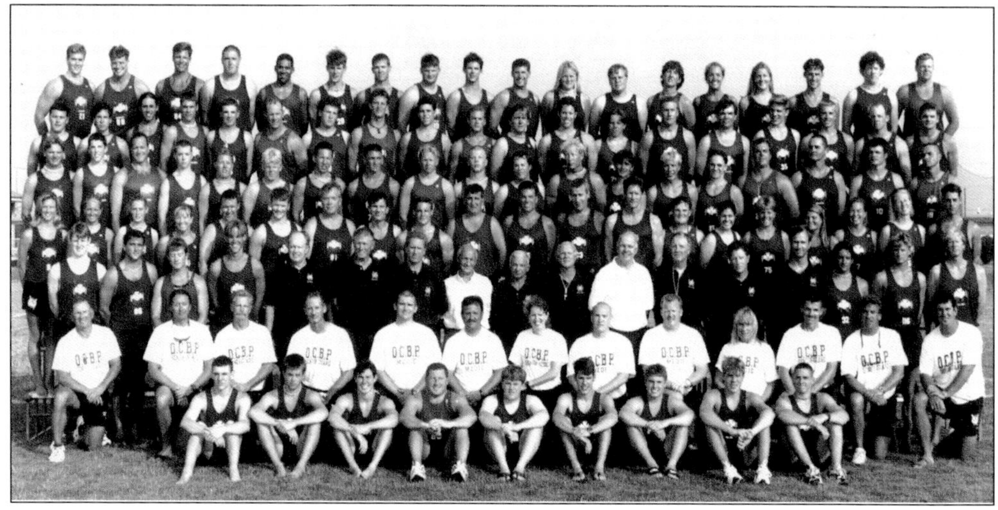

The Ocean City Beach Patrol, which started with just three men, had by its centennial year in 1998 grown to 150 men and women. Now guarding the full eight-mile coastline of Ocean City, the patrol continues to maintain its unparalleled record of bather protection.